JAMESTOWN EDUCATION

Literature

An Adapted Reader

Course 5

McGraw-Hill

New York, New York   Columbus, Ohio   Chicago, Illinois

JAMESTOWN ⚓ EDUCATION

Glencoe

ACKNOWLEDGMENTS
Grateful acknowledgment is given authors, publishers, photographers,
museums, and agents for permission to reprint the following copyrighted
material. Every effort has been made to determine copyright owners. In
case of any omissions, the Publisher will be pleased to make suitable
acknowledgments in future editions.
Acknowledgments continued on p. 302.

Send all inquiries to:
Glencoe/McGraw-Hill
8787 Orion Place
Columbus, OH 43240-4027

ISBN-13: 978-0-07-874317-7 (Student Edition)
ISBN-10: 0-07-874317-6 (Student Edition)

ISBN-13: 978-0-07-874330-6 (Annotated Teacher Edition)
ISBN-10: 0-07-874330-3 (Annotated Teacher Edition)

Printed in the United States of America
10 11 12 13 14 15 QVS 20 19 18 17 16

Contents

Why Use This Book?..vi

The What, Why, and How of Reading xiv

UNIT ① Short Story...............1

The False Gems .... Guy de Maupassant................ 2

The Boar Hunt .... José Vasconcelos 20

The Censors .... Luisa Valenzuela................. 36

Appetizer................... Robert H. Abel................. 48

Compare and Contrast 67

UNIT ② Short Story...............68

Catch the Moon............ Judith Ortiz Cofer 70

A Sound of Thunder......... Ray Bradbury....................88

Through the Tunnel......... Doris Lessing 114

Marigolds................... Eugenia W. Collier 136

Compare and Contrast 155

UNIT ③ Drama........................ 156

from **A Raisin in the Sun**...... Lorraine Hansberry 158

UNIT ④ Legend and Folktale 190

Where the Girl Rescued Her Brother .... Joseph Bruchac and Gayle Ross.... 192

Yuki-Onna .... Lafcadio Hearn 206

Compare and Contrast 219

UNIT ⑤ Nonfiction 220

The Angry Winter .... Loren Eiseley 222

from **An American Childhood** .... Annie Dillard 234

By Any Other Name .... Santha Rama Rau 250

from **Farewell to Manzanar** .... Jeanne Wakatsuki Houston........268
and James D. Houston

Compare and Contrast 289

Glossary 290

My Personal Dictionary 294

Acknowledgments 302

Why Use This Book?

Read a Variety of Texts

The notes and features of *Jamestown Literature* guide you through the process of reading and understanding each literature selection. As you use these notes and features, you practice the skills and strategies that good readers use whenever they read.

UNIT 1

Short Story

What's a Short Story?

Children start asking to hear stories as soon as they can speak. They want to hear tales of talking animals, princesses, and magical places. Even though people change their minds about the kinds of stories they like, their appetite for stories doesn't fade as they grow older.

A **short story** is a short piece of fiction that is filled with made-up characters and events. When you discuss a short story, you can talk about how all of its parts work together.

A **short story** has a setting that tells where the story takes place. It has characters who are the main actors. They can be people, animals, or whatever the author chooses. A good story has an interesting plot. And finally, it has a theme that tells you something about life.

What's your favorite kind of story?

I like _____ stories.

Why Read Short Stories?

Short stories give us an opportunity to see life through the eyes of others. Everyone's experiences are different. It's only by sharing stories that we gain a clear picture of the world around us. In the next section of this book, you will read four short stories. Each offers a unique view of life.

Your *reason* for reading might affect how you read a story.

• If you're reading simply for enjoyment, you might read quickly as you get involved with the characters and events.

• If you're reading for a class assignment, you might take your time, looking for specific details to discuss later.

How Do I Read Short Stories?

Focus on key **literary elements** and **reading skills** to get the most out of reading the four short stories in this unit. Here are two key literary elements and two key reading skills that you will practice in this unit.

Key Literary Elements

• **Theme**

A **theme** is the central message of a story that readers can apply to life. Common themes include insights into human nature and observations about life.

• Stated themes are directly presented in a story.

• Implied themes must be inferred, or assumed. That is, readers need to figure out the theme for themselves. Readers need to consider all the elements of a story and ask what message about life they convey.

• **Tone**

Tone is the writer's attitude toward the subject. The writer uses specific words and details to help create the tone. For example, the writer might describe a desert as "sunny, hot, filled with unexpected flowers" or as "scorching, extremely dry, dangerous." In the first description, the tone is cheerful and appreciative. In the second, the tone is fearful.

Key Reading Skills

• **Question**

Ask yourself **questions** as you read. Ask yourself *who, what, where, when, why,* and *how* questions to make sure you understand what you are reading. Ask yourself: What questions help me understand what the writer means and keep me on track? What information and ideas are important here?

• **Sequence**

The order in which events are presented is called the **sequence.** Many stories present the events in chronological order, or the order in which they happen. Words like *first, then, meanwhile, eventually,* and *later* can help you figure out when things happen. Each event can tell you more about a main character when one event leads to another.

What Is It? Why Read?

The genre, or type of writing, is defined for you at the beginning of the unit. Learn why a particular genre offers important and entertaining reading.

Literary Elements and Reading Skills

New literary elements and reading skills are introduced in each unit opener. Use these elements and skills to get the most out of your reading.

UNIT 2 Short Story

How Is a Short Story Organized?

Now that you have read a few short stories, let's stop to take a closer look at how a short story is put together. Understanding the parts of a story can help you be a bette

A short story always has a **beginning**, a **middle**, and an **end**

Most stories include a **conflict**. A conflict can be a struggl a character and his or her thoughts and feelings. Or a con a struggle between a character and another character, nat outside force.

What's the Plan?

Most plots develop in five stages.

Exposition introduces the story's characters and conflict.
Rising action develops the conflict with cc and twists.
Climax is the emotional high point of the turning point.
Falling action shows what happens after t
Resolution shows how the conflict is reso problem is solved.

As you read the next four stories, try to in each story. In the text, mark the plac occurs.

68

UNIT 3 Drama

What's Drama?

A drama is a story told ma characters. A drama, also on stage or screen for an au the lines of the script. These their lines and where they give details about the sett

The cast of characters is the cast list includes a b

Long plays are broken A new act or scene sho

UNIT 4 Legend and Folktale

What's a Legend? What's a Folktale?

Legends are set in particular times and places, and they focus on people who may have existed. Although these stories may contain exaggerated, magical, or supernatural elements, they are historically based. Robin Hood was a real person. King Arthur may have been a real man too, although no one knows for sure.

Originally, legends were passed on from generation to generation by word of mouth. Because legends were not written down and were retold by different storytellers, they changed with each retelling. This might explain why stories based on actual people and events end up containing very little information based on historical fact.

Folktales are also stories that have been passed down through generations by word of mouth. Unlike legends, which may be based on real people, folktale characters can be animals or people who have unusual powers or experiences. The characters can also be ordinary people who face unusual problems. Folk

folktales
from legends

good
e cultures
r values

UNIT 5 Nonfiction

What's Nonfiction?

Pick up a newspaper or magazine or check out many Web sites, and you will find writing that is nonfiction.

Nonfiction is the name for writing that is about real people and real events. Many types of nonfiction are meant to inform or to relate experiences. Nonfiction can tell facts and include the use of vivid descriptions. There are many kinds of nonfiction: biographies, autobiographies, memoirs, essays, letters, and feature articles.

A **biography** is the story of a person's life written by someone other than the subject. An **autobiography** is the story of a person's life written by that person. **Memoirs** are stories of the narrator's personal experience. An **essay** is a short piece of nonfiction about a single topic.

Nonfiction can deal with many topics. This list mentions some of them. **Check one subject below that you like to read about or write a subject of your own.**

- [ ] the experiences of a traveler
- [ ] the causes of violent weather
- [ ] how people live in a distant part of the world
- [ ] the history of a sport
- [ ] the life story of a famous person

Why Read Nonfiction?

Read nonfiction to learn about new places, new people, and new ideas. By reading nonfiction and learning new things, you can better understand the world around you. Nonfiction can even help you better understand yourself.

234

Explore Literature

Your book features several of the most popular types of writing. Find out what makes each genre unique. Discover new and exciting types of writing.

Get Set!

The first page of each lesson helps you get ready to read. It sets the stage for your reading. The more you know about the reading up front, the more meaning it will have for you.

Get Ready to Read!
Appetizer

Meet
Robert H. Abel

Fiction writers have a responsibility, says Robert H. Abel: "I feel the planet is threatened, that writing should attempt to define and respond to this emergency . . . with some vision of a workable, maybe even beautiful future." Abel was born in Painesville, Ohio, in 1941. In addition to writing fiction, Abel has worked as a reporter, a teacher, an editor, and a volunteer firefighter. He is also a fisherman. "Appetizer" was first published in 1991.

What You Know

Think about a surprising or frightening experience you've had with an animal. What were the circumstances? How did you react? What did the animal do?

Reason to Read

Read this story to find out what happens when the narrator encounters a bear while fishing in the Alaskan wilderness.

Background Info

Brown bears have long, shaggy coats that range in color from blond to black. They have stout bodies, massive heads, and long claws. Brown bears have a strong sense of smell, jaws that can snap small tree trunks, and the ability to sprint up to thirty-five miles an hour. Brown bears eat fish, mammals, nuts, berries, herbs, and grasses, but will feed exclusively on salmon when it is available. They sometimes eat more than a dozen fish in a few hours.

What You Know
Think about your own experience and share your knowledge and opinions. Then, build on what you know as you read the lesson.

Reason to Read
Set a purpose for reading. Having a reason to read helps you get involved in what you read.

Background Info
Get a deeper insight into the reading. Knowing some background information helps you gain a greater appreciation and understanding of what you read.

Meet the Author
Meet the authors to get to know where they come from, what or who inspires them, and why they write.

Build Vocabulary

Each lesson introduces you to words that help build your vocabulary. You'll find these words in the reading. Understanding these words before you read makes reading easier.

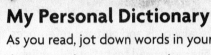

Word Power

In an after-reading activity, you practice the vocabulary words you learned in the lesson.

Word Power

Before you read, you learn key vocabulary words and their definitions. The definitions and sample sentences help you complete the questions that follow.

Word Power Footnotes

Look for pronunciations and definitions of vocabulary words at the bottom of pages throughout the reading. Vocabulary words appear in dark type in the text.

My Personal Dictionary

As you read, jot down words in your personal dictionary that you want to learn more about. Later, ask a classmate or your teacher what they mean, or look them up in a dictionary.

Read, Respond, Interact

Notes in "My Workspace" support and guide you through the reading process. Interact with and respond to the text by answering the questions or following the directions in the workspace notes.

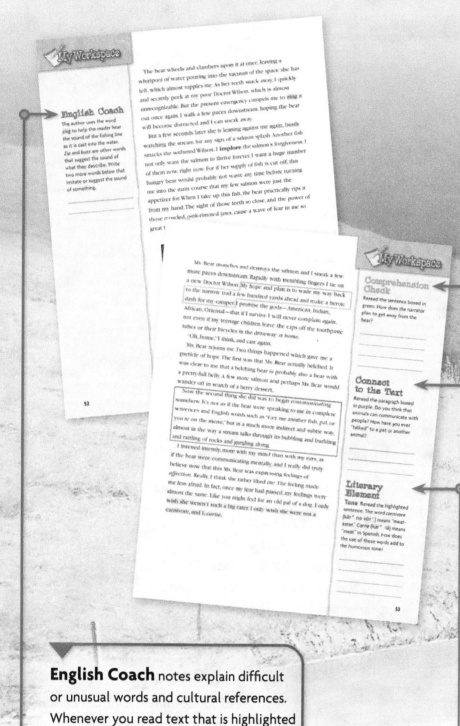

Comprehension Check notes help you understand what you're reading. Whenever you read text that is boxed in green, look for a Comprehension Check note in your workspace.

Connect to the Text notes help you connect what you're reading to something in your own life. Whenever you read text that is boxed in purple, look for a Connect to the Text note in your workspace.

Literary Element notes help you understand important features of literature. Whenever you read text that is highlighted in blue, look for a Literary Element note in your workspace.

English Coach notes explain difficult or unusual words and cultural references. Whenever you read text that is highlighted in red, look for an English Coach note in your workspace.

Background Info notes give information about a particular event, time, person, or place mentioned in the reading. Whenever you read text that is boxed in orange, look for a Background Info note in your workspace.

Reading Skill notes let you practice active reading strategies that help good readers think as they read. Whenever you read text that is highlighted in green, look for a Reading Skill note in your workspace.

The margin notes let you interact with what you're reading in several ways. Some notes ask you to write out your response. Other notes may ask you to draw a picture, underline answers in the text, or interact in some other way.

Use the **Did You Know?** feature to get a clear picture of something interesting in the text.

My Workspace

Background Info

A Chinook (shi nook´) is a type of salmon, often called the king salmon, which lives in the northern Pacific area of the United States. The Chinook is also the name of a group of Native Americans who live in the Pacific Northwest.

Reading Skill

Sequence Reread the highlighted sentence and the rest of the paragraph. Number the events in the order in which they happen to show how the narrator tries to get closer to the trail.

___ The salmon flips into a pool and the bear eats it.
___ The narrator catches a salmon.
___ The narrator puts on a new fly and goes downstream.

Now she nudges me with her nose.

"All right, all right," I say. "I'm doing the best I can."

Cast in the glide behind that big boulder, the bear communicates to me. *There are a couple of whoppers in* I do as I'm told and wham! the bear is right! Instantly I into a granddaddy Chinook, a really husky fellow. Even the is excited and begins shifting weight from paw to paw, motion for her that nevertheless has big consequences as her body slams against my hip, then slams again.

Partly because I don't want to lose the fish, but par because I want to use the fish as an excuse to move t getaway trail, I stumble downstream. This fish has m into an upside-down U and I'm hoping, my quick-tie also strong enough to take this salmon's lurching. When the salmon flips into a little side pool, the bear clambers over the rocks, pounces, stabs the salmon smartly behind the head and lumbers immediately to the bank. My leader snaps at once and while Ms. Bear attends to the destruction of the fish, I tie on another fly and make some awkward headway downstream. Yes, I worry about the hook still in the fish, but only because I do not want this bear to be irritated by anything. I want her to be full and to doze off in the sun. Mentally I try to tell her so. *Please, Bear, sleep.*

Inevitably, the fishing slows down, but Ms. Bear does not seem to mind. Again she belches. I am getting quite a headache and know that I am fighting exhaustion. I even find myself getting a little angry, and I marvel at the bear's persistence. And appetite. At supermarket prices, I calculate she has eaten about six hundred dollars worth of fish.

Word Power
inevitably (i nev´ ə tə ble) *adv.* certain to happen

54

I release a low moan, but my voice is lost in the throaty warning of Ms. Bear to the **trespasser.** The new arrival answers with a defiant cough. He is half again as large as my companion. His fur seems longer and coarser, the tips are black and this dark surface ripples over his massive frame. His nostrils are flared and he is staring with complete concentration at me.

Would it be better to catch another salmon or not? I surely cannot provide for two of these beasts and Mister Bear does not seem the type to be distracted by or made friendly by any pitifully small offering of salmon. His whole bearing—pardon the expression—tells me my intrusion into this bear world is a personal **affront** to his bear honor. Only Ms. Bear stands between us and whose side is she really on? By bear standards, I am sure a rather regal and handsome fellow has made his appearance. Why should the fur-covered heart of furry Ms. Bear go out to me? How much love can a few hundred dollars worth of salmon buy?

How disturbed I am is well illustrated by my next course of action. I cranked in my line and lay my rod across some rocks. Then I began the difficult process of pulling myself out of my waders while trying to balance myself on those awkward rocks in that fast water. I tipped and swayed as I tugged at my boots and pushed my waders down, the entire time with my arms in the foaming, frigid water... the waders filled, making it even more difficult to pull my feet free.

Did You Know?
Waders are waterproof trousers that have boots for legs.

Word Power
trespasser (tres´ pas ər) *n.* something or someone who goes somewhere he or she is not allowed to go
affront (ə frunt´) *n.* an insult; something that causes a person to feel offended

My Workspace

Literary Element

Tone Reread the highlighted sentence and the rest of the paragraph. Although the narrator is scared, he still describes the situation with humor. Underline the words and phrases that contribute to the humorous tone.

57

---

xi

Wrap It Up!

The Break Time, Respond to Literature, and Compare and Contrast pages help you focus your understanding of the text. You apply the skills and strategies you've practiced during reading.

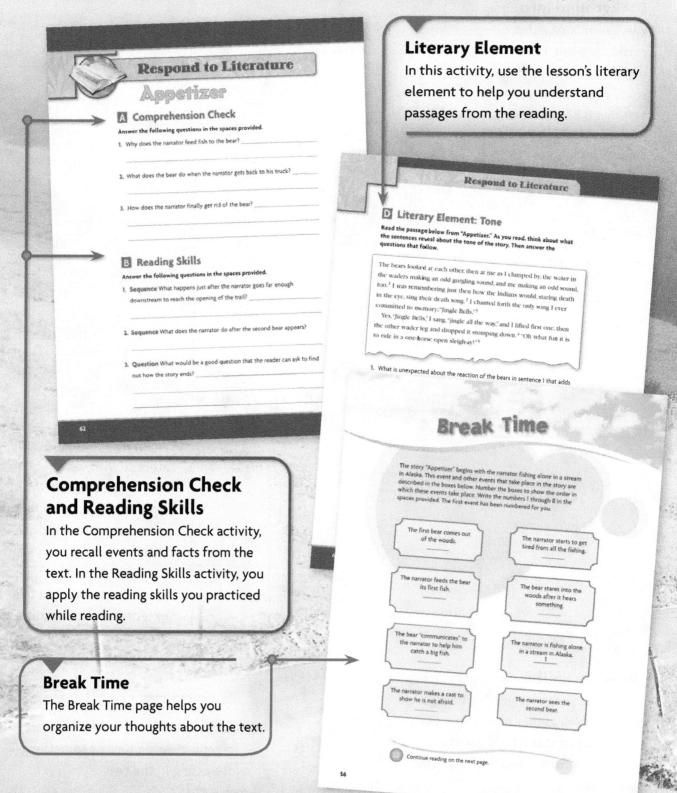

Respond to Literature

Appetizer

A Comprehension Check

Answer the following questions in the spaces provided.

1. Why does the narrator feed fish to the bear? _____

2. What does the bear do when the narrator gets back to his truck? _____

3. How does the narrator finally get rid of the bear? _____

B Reading Skills

Answer the following questions in the spaces provided.

1. **Sequence** What happens just after the narrator goes far enough downstream to reach the opening of the trail? _____

2. **Sequence** What does the narrator do after the second bear appears? _____

3. **Question** What would be a good question that the reader can ask to find out how the story ends? _____

Literary Element

In this activity, use the lesson's literary element to help you understand passages from the reading.

Respond to Literature

D Literary Element: Tone

Read the passage below from "Appetizer." As you read, think about what the sentences reveal about the tone of the story. Then answer the questions that follow.

The bears looked at each other, then at me as I clumped by, the water in the waders making an odd gurgling sound, and me making an odd sound, too.[1] I was remembering just then how the Indians would, staring death in the eye, sing their death song.[2] I chanted forth the only song I ever committed to memory:"Jingle Bells."[3]

Yes, "Jingle Bells," I sang. "jingle all the way," and I lifted first one, then the other wader leg and dropped it stomping down.[4] "Oh what fun it is to ride in a one-horse open sleigh-ay!"[5]

1. What is unexpected about the reaction of the bears in sentence 1 that adds

Break Time

The story "Appetizer" begins with the narrator fishing alone in a stream in Alaska. This event and other events that take place in the story are described in the boxes below. Number the boxes to show the order in which these events take place. Write the numbers 1 through 8 in the spaces provided. The first event has been numbered for you.

The first bear comes out of the woods.	The narrator starts to get tired from all the fishing.
The narrator feeds the bear its first fish.	The bear stares into the woods after it hears something
The bear "communicates" to the narrator to help him catch a big fish.	The narrator is fishing alone in a stream in Alaska. 1
The narrator makes a cast to show he is not afraid.	The narrator sees the second bear.

Continue reading on the next page.

56

Comprehension Check and Reading Skills

In the Comprehension Check activity, you recall events and facts from the text. In the Reading Skills activity, you apply the reading skills you practiced while reading.

Break Time

The Break Time page helps you organize your thoughts about the text.

E Personal Testament

Imagine that you are the narrator in the story. You are very pleased with how your waders helped you escape from the bears. Write a letter to the company that made the waders. In your letter, tell your story and explain how the waders saved your life.

Dear Sir or Madam,

I am writing about the waders made by your company.

I was fishing in Alaska when all of a sudden _____

The next thing I knew, _____

Things got even worse when another bear appeared.

So finally, I took off my wa_____
were a pair of legs. I _____

It worked like a charm! I _____
for the cannery, where _____

I hope that my story will _____
to see them as more than _____
the water.

Sincerely,

Writing Activity

Develop your writing skills by completing various types of activities. Here's your chance to be creative!

Assessment

Fill in the circle next to each correct answer.

1. What does the first bear "communicate" to the narrator?
   - ○ A. that another bear is nearby
   - ○ B. why she wants to help him
   - ○ C. that she wants him to leave the stream
   - ○ D. where to cast to catch a big fish

2. What does the narrator do after the second bear arrives?
   - ○ A. He takes off his waders.
   - ○ B. He runs downstream.
   - ○ C. He feeds it a fish.
   - ○ D. He catches another fish.

3. What is the **best** question to ask to understand how the narrator escapes from the bear at the end of the story?
   - ○ A. Why does the narrator drop his waders?
   - ○ B. Why is the narrator fishing all alone in the wilderness?
   - ○ C. Why does the narrator drive to the cannery?
   - ○ D. Why doesn't the narrator catch fish for the second bear?

4. Which word describes the overall tone of the story?
   - ○ A. humorous
   - ○ B. peaceful
   - ○ C. regretful
   - ○ D. serious

r of being reached easily"?

Assessment

The lesson assessment helps you evaluate what you learned in the lesson.

UNIT 1 **Wrap-up**

Compare and Contrast

Tone is an important literary element in "The Censors" and "Appetizer." The tone contributes to the humor in each story. In "The Censors," the tone is darkly humorous. The author uses the humorous tone to make a serious point. In "Appetizer," the humor is much more lighthearted to show how the narrator felt during a potentially dangerous situation. Think about how each author uses tone to make a point or tell about an experience.

Complete the chart below. In the left and right columns, explain what the tone is in each story. Explain how that tone shows the author's attitude toward the subject in each story. In the center column, explain the similarity in the tone in the stories.

"The Censors"	Similarity	"Appetizer"

Compare and Contrast

The Compare and Contrast activity helps you see how two texts are alike and different.

The What, Why, and How of Reading

LITERARY ELEMENTS

Each lesson focuses on one literary element. Before you begin a lesson, read carefully the explanations of the literary elements found at the beginning of the unit. You can refer to this chart for an overview. The more familiar you become with these important features, the more you will understand and appreciate each reading.

Unit 1	What Is It?	Example
	Theme A theme is the central message of a reading. Stated themes are directly presented in the text. Implied themes must be inferred or assumed.	One theme of "The False Gems," that money cannot buy happiness, is developed through the character of Monsieur Lantin and his attempt to live the rich life.
	Tone Tone is the writer's attitude toward the subject. The writer uses specific words and details to help create the tone.	In "Appetizer," the author uses humor to show his respect for grizzly bears. The humorous tone keeps the story light, but does not hide the possible danger.
Unit 2	**Plot** Plot is the story's basic framework. The exposition introduces the characters, the setting, and the conflict. The rising action sets the story in motion. The action builds to a climax. The falling action shows the results of the climax. The resolution is the story's end.	In "Catch the Moon," the rising action occurs when the character of Luis searches for a particular hubcap as a gift for Naomi, another character in the story.
	Climax The climax is the turning point of a story. It is the moment of greatest emotional intensity, interest, or suspense. Usually the climax is found at the point in a story where the conflict begins to be resolved.	In "Marigolds," the climax takes place when the character of Lizabeth destroys the one spot of beauty in someone's life: a garden of marigolds.

Unit 3	What Is It?	Example
	Character A character is an actor in a story. You can understand characters by looking at what they do and say, as well as what other characters say about them.	In *A Raisin in the Sun*, we get to know the characters of Ruth, Walter, and their family through the descriptions of them in the stage directions and through the conversations they have with each other.
Unit 4	**Setting** Setting is the time and place in which the events of a story occur. The description of a setting often helps create a particular atmosphere or mood. Revealing the values and beliefs of the time and place can be an important part of establishing the setting.	A battle is part of the setting in "Where the Girl Rescued Her Brother." The setting also tells us about the customs and culture of the people in the story.
	Dialogue Dialogue is the conversation between characters in a reading. From dialogue, you learn about what is happening and how the characters think and feel. Dialogue reveals the characters' personalities, gives you information, and moves the story forward.	The dialogue in "Yuki-Onna" gives us information about important events in the story. We also get to know the snow woman through her dialogue with the characters.
Unit 5	**Tone** Tone is the writer's attitude toward the subject. The writer uses specific words and details to help create the tone.	In "The Angry Winter," a part of the story's tone is menacing when the narrator attempts to take a bone away from his pet dog.
	Autobiography In an autobiography, a writer tells his or her life story from the first-person point of view and uses the pronouns *I, me, my,* or *mine*. Authors create autobiographies to share memories of events, people, and feelings that are important to them.	In *Farewell to Manzanar*, the author shares her personal reactions to the events in the story so we can learn about how she faced discrimination.

READING SKILLS

You will use reading skills to respond to questions in the lessons. Before you begin a lesson, read carefully the explanations of the reading skills found at the beginning of the unit. You can refer to this chart for an overview. The more you practice the skills in the chart, the more these active reading strategies will become a natural part of the way you read.

Unit 1	What Is It?	Why It's Important	How To Do It
	Question Questioning is asking yourself what information helps you get the most from the text.	As you answer your questions, you'll be making sure you understand the most important features of the text.	Ask yourself *who, what, where, when,* and *why* questions. Also ask yourself: How can I understand this better?
	Sequence Sequence is the order in which events occur in a story—first, next, and last.	Following the sequence of events helps you see how the reading is organized. It also helps you understand how events relate to each other.	As you read, look for clue words like *first, then, meanwhile, later,* and *finally.* These words can help you figure out the order in which things happen.
Unit 2	**Predict** Predicting is thinking ahead to guess how events in a story might turn out.	Predicting gives you a reason to read. It helps you get involved from the start of the reading.	Combine what you already know with clues from the reading to guess what will happen next.
	Evaluate Evaluating is making judgments about what you are reading and how it is presented.	When you make judgments about a reading, you can better understand its purpose and decide whether it is effective in accomplishing that purpose.	Think about your reaction to the writer's words. Evaluate by asking yourself questions: Does this make sense? Are the writer's thoughts and ideas clear?

Unit 3	What Is It?	Why It's Important	How To Do It
	Visualize Visualizing is picturing in your mind what you are reading.	Visualizing is one of the best ways to understand and remember ideas, characters, and other details in a reading.	Use details from the reading to help you create mental pictures. You will also draw on your own experiences to help you imagine the scene.
	Draw Conclusions You are drawing conclusions when you figure out what the author means.	Drawing conclusions can help you better understand the characters and the ways that other characters respond to them.	Notice details in the reading to gather evidence and make general statements about the characters and the events.
Unit 4	**Paraphrase** Paraphrasing is restating all or part of the text in your own words.	Paraphrasing helps you sort out and understand what you have read and what the author means.	To put text into your own words, replace large words with smaller ones and leave out unnecessary details.
	Infer Inferring is making an educated guess about information that is not directly stated in the text.	Inferring helps you look more deeply into the thoughts and motives of the characters and understand the theme or message of the reading.	Connect your own knowledge with details in the reading to figure out what the writer is hinting at.
Unit 5	**Problem & Solution** Characters in stories often come up against problems that they need to solve.	Identifying problems and solutions in a reading can help you understand why the characters act the way they do.	Identify the problem and who has it, find out what solutions the characters try, and discover what happens as a result.
	Respond Responding is considering your thoughts and feelings about something you've read.	When you react in a personal way to what you are reading, you enjoy a reading more and remember it better.	Notice how you feel about the reading as you read. Ask yourself: How would I act in this situation?

UNIT 1

Short Story

What's a Short Story?

Children start asking to hear stories as soon as they can speak. They want to hear tales of talking animals, princesses, and magical places. Even though people change their minds about the kinds of stories they like, their appetite for stories doesn't fade as they grow older.

A **short story** is a short piece of fiction that is filled with made-up characters and events. When you discuss a short story, you can talk about how all of its parts work together.

A **short story** has a setting that tells where the story takes place. It has characters who are the main actors. They can be people, animals, or whatever the author chooses. A good story has an interesting plot. And finally, it has a theme that tells you something about life.

What's your favorite kind of story?

I like _____ stories.

Why Read Short Stories?

Short stories give us an opportunity to see life through the eyes of others. Everyone's experiences are different. It's only by sharing stories that we gain a clear picture of the world around us. In the next section of this book, you will read four short stories. Each offers a unique view of life.

Your *reason* for reading might affect how you read a story.

• If you're reading simply for enjoyment, you might read quickly as you get involved with the characters and events.

• If you're reading for a class assignment, you might take your time, looking for specific details to discuss later.

How Do I Read Short Stories?

Focus on key **literary elements** and **reading skills** to get the most out of reading the four short stories in this unit. Here are two key literary elements and two key reading skills that you will practice in this unit.

Key Literary Elements

• Theme

A **theme** is the central message of a story that readers can apply to life. Common themes include insights into human nature and observations about life.

- **Stated themes** are directly presented in a story.

- **Implied themes** must be inferred, or assumed. That is, readers need to figure out the theme for themselves. Readers need to consider all the elements of a story and ask what message about life they convey.

• Tone

Tone is the writer's attitude toward the subject. The writer uses specific words and details to help create the tone. For example, the writer might describe a desert as "sunny, hot, filled with unexpected flowers" or as "scorching, extremely dry, dangerous." In the first description, the tone is cheerful and appreciative. In the second, the tone is fearful.

Key Reading Skills

• Question

Ask yourself **questions** as you read. Ask yourself *who, what, where, when, why,* and *how* questions to make sure you understand what you are reading. Ask yourself: What questions help me understand what the writer means and keep me on track? What information and ideas are important here?

• Sequence

The order in which events are presented is called the **sequence.** Many stories present the events in chronological order, or the order in which they happen. Words like *first, then, meanwhile, eventually,* and *later* can help you figure out when things happen. Each event can tell you more about a main character when one event leads to another.

Get Ready to Read!

The False Gems

Meet Guy de Maupassant

Although he died at the age of forty-two in 1893, few writers have achieved more than Guy de Maupassant (gē də mo´ pä sän´). Maupassant published more than three hundred short stories. Born in Paris in 1850, he lived there for many years where he worked as a government clerk as well as a writer. His stories paint a picture of life in France during the years 1850–1890. "The False Gems" was first published in 1883.

What You Know

Have you ever noticed that people and things are not always what they seem? Think about someone or something that turned out to be completely different from what you first thought. Perhaps you found out that an old painting in your living room was worth a lot of money. How did you feel when you found out the surprising information?

Reason to Read

Read to learn what happens to one man who discovers that things are not always as they seem.

Background Info

It is almost impossible to tell false gems from real gems. Some human-made gems can easily pass for diamonds. "The False Gems" takes place in Paris, France, sometime in the 1870s or early 1880s. Paris at that time was one of the most exciting European cities. Artists and writers captured the city's colorful lifestyle in their work. People in Paris from both the upper class and the growing middle class enjoyed going out to dance halls and cafés for entertainment.

Word Power

virtuous (vur´ chठठ əs) *adj.* having high morals; p. 4
The church committee hopes to find a *virtuous* person to teach Sunday School.

excessively (ik ses´ iv lē) *adv.* more than what is needed or wanted; p. 5
Hank talked *excessively* about baseball until we were all bored.

unconventional (un´ kən ven´ shən əl) *adj.* unusual, out of the ordinary; p. 6
Justin had an *unconventional* hobby: collecting old doorknobs.

widower (wid´ ō ər) *n.* a man whose wife has died; p. 8
The *widower* placed flowers on his wife's grave once a week.

hastily (hās´ ti lē) *adv.* doing or acting very quickly; p. 11
As she saw the school bus coming, Jill wrapped her sandwich *hastily*.

disdain (dis dān´) *n.* a feeling of disrespect for something thought to be inferior or unworthy; p. 13
Janelle looked at the cheap cloth with *disdain*.

aristocratic (ə ris´ tə krat´ ik) *adj.* belonging to upper-class society; p. 14
He tried to impress everyone with his *aristocratic* manner.

**Answer the following questions, using one of the new words above.
Write your answers in the spaces provided.**

1. Which word goes with "honest and good"? _____

2. Which word goes with "rich and upper-class tastes"? _____

3. Which word goes with "in a hurry"? _____

4. Which word goes with "strange"? _____

5. Which word goes with "husband"? _____

6. Which word goes with "feeling something is not good enough"? _____

7. Which word goes with "way too much"? _____

Adapted from
The False Gems

Guy de Maupassant

Monsieur Lantin had met the young girl at a party, and had fallen head over heels in love with her.

She was the daughter of a local tax collector, who had been dead several years. She and her mother had come to live in Paris. Her mother, who got to know some of the families in her neighborhood, hoped to find a husband for her daughter.

They did not have much money, and were honorable, gentle, and quiet.

The young girl was a perfect type of the **virtuous** woman in whose hands every sensible young man dreams of one day keeping safe his happiness. Her simple beauty had the charm of angelic modesty. The fine smile she had seemed to be the reflection of a pure and lovely soul.

Her praises were heard on every side. People never tired of repeating: "Happy the man who wins her love! He could not find a better wife."

_____

Word Power

virtuous (vurˊ choo̅ əs) *adj.* having high morals

4

Monsieur Lantin, then chief clerk in the Department of the Interior, enjoyed a comfortable little salary of three thousand five hundred francs. He proposed to this model young girl, and was accepted.

He was happy beyond words with her. She ran his household so efficiently that they seemed to live in luxury. She paid the most delicate attentions on her husband.

So great was her charm that six years after their marriage, Monsieur Lantin discovered that he loved his wife even more than during the first days of their honeymoon.

He found fault with only two of her tastes: Her love for the theater, and her taste for imitation jewelry. Her friends (the wives of some low-level officials) frequently obtained for her a seat at the theater, often for the first presentations of the new plays. Her husband was expected to accompany her, whether he wished it or not, to these entertainments, which bored him **excessively** after his day's work at the office.

After a time, Monsieur Lantin begged his wife to request one of the ladies she knew to accompany her, and to bring her home after the theater. She opposed this arrangement at first; but, after much persuasion, finally agreed, to the delight of her husband.

Now, with her love for the theater, came also the desire for decorations. Her dresses remained as before, simple, in good taste, and always modest. But she soon began to adorn her ears with huge rhinestones, which glittered and sparkled like real diamonds. Around her neck she wore strings of false pearls, on her arms bracelets of imitation gold, and combs with glass jewels.

Background Info

Francs were once the currency used in France. On January 1, 1999, France and ten other countries in Europe switched to the Euro. Three thousand five hundred francs are equal to around $642 (U.S. dollars). This amount was considered a nice sum of money to have in the time period when the story takes place.

Comprehension Check

Reread the boxed sentences. What are the two things that Monsieur Lantin doesn't like about his wife?

_____

_____

_____

_____

_____

_____

Word Power

excessively (ik ses´ iv lē) *adv.* more than what is needed or wanted

5

Connect to the Text

Reread the boxed sentence. Do you agree with Monsieur Lantin that if you cannot afford real diamonds, pearls, or gold, you should not wear any jewelry at all?

_____

_____

_____

_____

Reading Skill

Question Reread the highlighted text. What is the **best** question to ask to understand the wife's attitude toward her jewelry? Check the correct response.

☐ Where do Monsieur Lantin and his wife enjoy conversations?

☐ Why does Monsieur Lantin call the box of jewelry "trash"?

☐ What might be the "deep and secret joy" the wife gets from the jewelry?

Her husband frequently argued with her, saying:

> "My dear, as you cannot afford to buy real jewelry, you ought to appear adorned with your beauty and modesty alone, which are the rarest decorations of women."

But she would smile sweetly, and say:

"What can I do? I am so fond of jewelry. It is my only weakness. We cannot change our nature."

Then she would wind the pearl necklace round her fingers, make the facets of the crystal gems sparkle, and say:

"Look! Are they not lovely? One would swear they were real."

Monsieur Lantin would then answer, smilingly:

"You have **unconventional** tastes, my dear."

Did You Know?

Facets (fas′ its) are the small, flat surfaces of a diamond or other gem.

Sometimes, of an evening, when they were enjoying an intimate conversation by the fireside, she would place on the tea table the leather box containing the "trash," as Monsieur Lantin called it. She would examine the false gems with a passionate attention, as though they gave her some deep and secret joy. She often persisted in passing a necklace around her husband's neck. Laughing heartily, she would exclaim: "How funny you look!" Then she would throw herself into his arms, and kiss him affectionately.

One evening, in winter, she had been to the opera, and returned home chilled through and through. The next morning she was coughing, and eight days later she died.

Monsieur Lantin's despair was so great that his hair became white in one month. He constantly wept. His heart was broken as he remembered her smile, her voice, every charm of his dead wife.

Word Power

unconventional (un′ kən ven′ shən əl) *adj.* unusual; out of the ordinary

The Loge, c. 1882. Mary Cassatt. Courtesy National Gallery of Art, Washington.

Does this painting give an accurate description of what the theater experience may have been like for Madame Lantin? Why or why not?

Time did not lessen his grief. Often, during office hours, while his colleagues were discussing the topics of the day, his eyes would suddenly fill with tears, and he would express his grief in heartbreaking sobs. Everything in his wife's room remained as it was during her lifetime. All her furniture, even her clothing, was left as it was on the day of her death. Here he would be by himself daily and think of her who had been his treasure—the joy of his existence.

But life soon became a struggle. His income, which, in the hands of his wife, covered all household expenses, was now no longer sufficient for his own immediate wants. He wondered how she could have managed to buy such excellent wine and the rare delicacies which he could no longer afford with his modest income.

He acquired some debts, and was soon reduced to absolute poverty. One morning, finding himself without a cent in his pocket, he decided to sell something. Immediately the thought occurred to him of disposing of his wife's artificial jewels. He cherished in his heart a sort of hatred against these "deceptions," which had always irritated him in the past. The very sight of them spoiled, somewhat, the memory of his lost darling.

To the last days of her life she had continued to make purchases, bringing home new gems almost every evening. He turned them over some time before finally deciding to sell the heavy necklace, which she seemed to prefer, and which, he thought, ought to be worth about six or seven francs. It was of very fine workmanship, though only imitation.

He put it in his pocket, and started out in search of what seemed a reliable jeweler's shop. At length he found one, and went in, feeling a little ashamed to expose his misery, and also to offer such a worthless article for sale.

"Sir," said he to the merchant, "I would like to know what this is worth."

The man took the necklace, examined it, called his clerk, and quietly made some remarks. He then put the necklace back on the counter, and looked at it from a distance to judge the effect.

Monsieur Lantin, annoyed at all these ceremonies, was on the point of saying: "Oh! I know well enough it is not worth anything," when the jeweler said: "Sir, that necklace is worth from twelve to fifteen thousand francs; but I could not buy it, unless you can tell me exactly where it came from."

The **widower** opened his eyes wide and remained gaping, not comprehending the merchant's meaning. Finally he stammered: "You say—are you sure?" The other replied, without emotion: "You can try elsewhere, and see if anyone will offer you more. I consider it worth fifteen thousand at the most. Come back here, if you cannot do better."

 Stop here for **Break Time** on the next page.

Word Power
widower (wid ́ ō ər) *n.* a man whose wife has died

It is against the law for jewelers to buy and resell stolen items. The clerk needs to make sure that Monsieur Lantin is the rightful owner of the necklace to make sure he will not get into trouble with the law.

Reading Skill

Question Reread the highlighted sentences. Why do you think Monsieur Lantin is so surprised? Check the correct response.

- ☐ The necklace is worth much more than he had expected.
- ☐ He thinks the jeweler is lying to him.
- ☐ The necklace is worth much less than he expected.

Break Time

Sequence is the order in which events take place. "The False Gems" begins with Monsieur Lantin falling in love with a girl at a party. Some story events are shown in the boxes below. Number the boxes to show the order in which these events take place. Write the numbers 1–8 in the spaces provided. The first one has been done for you.

Monsieur Lantin's wife agrees to go to the theater with a friend.

_____

The jeweler tells Monsieur Lantin the necklace is worth a lot of money.

_____

Monsieur Lantin finds a jeweler's shop.

_____

Monsieur Lantin goes into debt.

_____

Monsieur Lantin's wife gets sick and dies.

_____

Monsieur Lantin decides to sell his wife's necklace.

_____

Monsieur Lantin falls in love with a girl at a party.

1
_____

Monsieur Lantin's wife begins to wear a lot of jewelry.

_____

 Turn the page to continue reading.

9

Reading Skill

Sequence Reread the highlighted sentence. How do we know when Monsieur Lantin enters another store to ask about the necklace? What clue words help you find out?

_____

_____

Background Info

In France in the 1200s, King Louis IX hated swear words, especially *pardieu* ("by God"). Luckily, King Louis had a pet dog named Bleu. People began saying *parbleu* instead of *pardieu* to avoid making the king angry.

Monsieur Lantin, beside himself with astonishment, took up the necklace and left the store. He wished time to think.

Once outside, he felt inclined to laugh, and said to himself: "The fool! Oh, the fool! Had I only taken him at his word! That jeweler cannot distinguish real diamonds from the imitation article."

A few minutes after, he entered another store, in the Rue de la Paix. As soon as the owner glanced at the necklace, he cried out:

"Ah, *parbleu!* I know it well; it was bought here."

Monsieur Lantin, greatly disturbed, asked:

"How much is it worth?"

"Well, I sold it for twenty thousand francs. I am willing to take it back for eighteen thousand, when you inform me, according to our legal custom, how it came to be in your possession."

This time, Monsieur Lantin was dumbfounded. He replied:

"But—but—examine it well. Until this moment I was under the impression that it was imitation."

The jeweler asked:

"What is your name, sir?"

"Lantin—I am in the employ of the Minister of the Interior. I live at number sixteen Rue des Martyrs."

The merchant looked through his books, found the entry, and said: "That necklace was sent to Madame Lantin's address, sixteen Rue des Martyrs, July 20, 1876."

The two men looked into each other's eyes—the widower speechless with astonishment; the jeweler suspecting a thief. The jeweler broke the silence.

"Will you leave this necklace here for twenty-four hours?" said he. "I will give you a receipt."

Monsieur Lantin answered **hastily:** "Yes, certainly." Then, putting the ticket in his pocket, he left the store.

He wandered aimlessly through the streets, his mind in a state of dreadful confusion. He tried to reason, to understand. His wife could not afford to purchase such a costly necklace. Certainly not. But, then, it must have been a present!—a present!—a present, from whom? Why was it given her?

He stopped, and remained standing in the middle of the street. A horrible doubt entered his mind—She? Then, all the other jewels must have been presents, too! The earth seemed to tremble beneath him—the tree before him to be falling. He threw up his arms, and fell to the ground, unconscious. He woke up in a pharmacy, into which the passers-by had carried him. He asked to be taken home, and, when he reached the house, he shut himself up in his room, and wept until nightfall. Finally, overcome with fatigue, he went to bed and fell into a heavy sleep.

The sun awoke him next morning. He began to dress slowly to go to the office. It was hard to work after such shocks. He sent a letter to his employer, requesting to be excused. Then he remembered that he had to return to the jeweler's. He did not like the idea; but he could not leave the necklace with that man. He dressed and went out.

It was a lovely day. A clear, blue sky smiled on the busy city below. Men of leisure were strolling about with their hands in their pockets.

Word Power

hastily (hās′ ti lē) *adv.* doing or acting very quickly

Literary Element

Theme Reread the sentence highlighted in blue. What does Monsieur Lantin's discovery about his wife tell you about the theme that things are not always as they appear to be?

_____

_____

_____

_____

_____

Reading Skill

Sequence Reread the sentence highlighted in green. What clue word tells you when Monsieur Lantin goes to bed?

_____

English Coach

Leisure means "free time." "Men of leisure" are so rich that they do not have to work. What do you do in your leisure time, when not in school?

_____

_____

_____

Connect to the Text

Reread the boxed paragraph. Do you agree that the rich are happy? Would a lot of money help you forget a sorrow? Explain.

_____

_____

_____

Reading Skill

Question Reread the highlighted sentence. What is the **best** question to ask yourself to understand Monsieur Lantin's problem with selling the necklace? Check the correct response.

☐ Why is Monsieur Lantin very hungry?

☐ Why is Monsieur Lantin ashamed to enter the store?

☐ Why is Monsieur Lantin very poor?

Monsieur Lantin, observing them, said to himself: "The rich, indeed, are happy. With money it is possible to forget even the deepest sorrow. One can go where one pleases, and in travel find that distraction which is the surest cure for grief. Oh! if I were only rich!"

He was hungry, but his pocket was empty. He again remembered the necklace. Eighteen thousand francs! Eighteen thousand francs! What a sum!

He soon arrived in the Rue de la Paix, opposite the jeweler's. Eighteen thousand francs! Twenty times he decided to go in, but shame kept him back. He was hungry, however—very hungry—and not a cent in his pocket. He decided quickly, ran across the street, in order not to have time to think, and rushed into the store.

The owner immediately came forward, and politely offered him a chair. The clerks glanced at him knowingly.

"I have made inquiries, Monsieur Lantin," said the jeweler, "and if you are still interested in disposing of the gems, I am ready to pay you the price I offered."

"Certainly, sir," stammered Monsieur Lantin.

Whereupon the owner took from a drawer eighteen large bills, counted, and handed them to Monsieur Lantin, who signed a receipt. With trembling hand, he put the money into his pocket.

As he was about to leave the store, he turned toward the merchant, who still wore the same knowing smile, and lowering his eyes, said:

"I have—I have other gems, which came from the same source. Will you buy them, also?"

The merchant bowed: "Certainly, sir."

Monsieur Lantin said gravely, "I will bring them to you." An hour later, he returned with the gems.

The large diamond earrings were worth twenty thousand francs; the bracelets, thirty-five thousand; the rings, sixteen

thousand; a set of emeralds and sapphires, fourteen thousand; a gold chain with a single gem, forty thousand—making the sum of one hundred and forty-three thousand francs.

The jeweler remarked, jokingly:

"There was a person who invested all her savings in precious stones."

Monsieur Lantin replied, seriously:

"It is only another way of investing one's money."

That day he lunched at Voisin's, and drank wine worth twenty francs a bottle. Then he hired a carriage and made a tour of the Bois. He gazed at the various carriages with a kind of **disdain,** and could hardly refrain from crying out to the occupants:

"I, too, am rich!—I am worth two hundred thousand francs."

Suddenly he thought of his employer. He drove up to the building, and entered merrily, saying:

"Sir, I have come to resign my position. I have just inherited three hundred thousand francs."

He shook hands with his former colleagues, and confided to them some of his projects for the future. He then went off to dine at the Café Anglais.

Word Power

disdain (dis dān´) *n.* a feeling of disrespect for something thought to be inferior or unworthy

Background Info

The *Bois* (bwä) refers to Bois de Bologne, a park area in Paris with many trees.

Connect to the Text

Reread the boxed text. Underline what Monsieur Lantin does after he sells his gems. What would you do if you suddenly became rich?

_____

_____

_____

Literary Element

Theme Reread the highlighted text. How do these sentences support the theme that money cannot buy happiness?

_____

_____

_____

_____

_____

_____

_____

Monsieur Lantin seated himself beside an **aristocratic** gentleman; and, during the meal, informed him secretly that he had just inherited a fortune of four hundred thousand francs.

For the first time in his life, he was not bored at the theater, and spent the remainder of the night in a happy state.

Six months afterward, he married again. His second wife was a very virtuous woman; but had a violent temper. She caused him much sorrow.

Portrait of Zacharie Astruc, 1863. Eduoard Manet. Oil on canvas, 35½ x 45¾ in. Kunsthalle, Bremen, Germany.

Which characteristics of Monsieur Lantin do you think are shown in this painting?

_____

Word Power

aristocratic (ə ris´ tə krat´ ik) *adj.* belonging to upper-class society

14

Respond to Literature

The False Gems

A Comprehension Check

Answer the following questions in the spaces provided.

1. What are the only two things that Monsieur Lantin does not like about his wife? _____

   _____

2. Why does Monsieur Lantin assume that the gems are false? _____

   _____

3. What does Monsieur Lantin find out after his wife dies? _____

   _____

   _____

B Reading Skills

Answer the following questions in the spaces provided.

1. **Question** How can asking yourself "Why did Madame Lantin pay so much attention to her jewelry?" help you understand the story?

   _____

   _____

2. **Sequence** Why does Monsieur Lantin sell the gems after his wife dies?

   _____

3. **Sequence** What does Monsieur Lantin do after he sells the gems?

   _____

C Word Power

Complete each sentence below, using one of the words in the box.

virtuous	aristocratic	disdain	hastily
excessively	unconventional	widower	

1. Ana felt shy around her rich aunt's _____ friends.

2. I packed my suitcase so _____ that I forgot my toothbrush.

3. Brandon picked up the cheap tennis racket and looked at it with _____.

4. If you watch TV _____, you may not get enough exercise.

5. Everyone liked the _____ young man for his honesty and goodness.

6. The _____ missed his wife very much after she died.

7. To be a circus clown is an _____ job.

D Literary Element: Theme

Read the passages below from "The False Gems." As you read, think about what the sentences reveal about the theme of the story, that money cannot buy happiness. Then answer the questions that follow.

> Monsieur Lantin, observing them, said to himself: "The rich, indeed, are happy.[1] With money it is possible to forget even the deepest sorrow.[2] One can go where one pleases, and in travel find that distraction which is the surest cure for grief.[3] Oh! if I were only rich!"[4]
>
> Six months afterward, he married again.[5] His second wife was a very virtuous woman; but had a violent temper.[6] She caused him much sorrow.[7]

1. In sentences 1–4, how does Monsieur Lantin believe that money will help him to be happier? _____

_____

_____

2. How do sentences 5–7 show that the money he received did not make him any happier? _____

_____

_____

_____

E A Personal Ad

Imagine that you are Monsieur Lantin. You have lost your wife and are looking for another. You have decided to place a personal ad in the paper to find your wife. Write an ad.

I am a widower. I am thirty-five years old, looking for a woman of about the same age for friendship and marriage. I am

_____

_____

_____

I enjoy _____

_____

I am looking for a wife who is _____

_____

_____

Please write to me.
M. Lantin

Assessment

Fill in the circle next to each correct answer.

1. At the beginning of the story, why did Monsieur Lantin dislike his wife's jewelry?
   - ○ A. He didn't think his wife needed it to look pretty.
   - ○ B. He wanted his wife to pay more attention to him instead of to the jewelry.
   - ○ C. He felt it was too expensive.
   - ○ D. He knew it was a present to his wife.

2. Which question must you answer to fully understand the story?
   - ○ A. Why did Monsieur Lantin marry his first wife?
   - ○ B. How did Monsieur Lantin's wife get the jewelry?
   - ○ C. Why did Monsieur Lantin marry a second wife?
   - ○ D. How did Monsieur Lantin spend the money from the jewelry?

3. When did Monsieur Lantin first realize his wife had been dishonest?
   - ○ A. when he took his wife's necklace to the first jeweler
   - ○ B. after he sold all the jewelry to the second jeweler
   - ○ C. when she agreed to go to the theater with a friend
   - ○ D. after he figured out all the jewelry had been presents to her

4. What does the theme of the story "The False Gems" reveal to us?
   - ○ A. Love is blind.
   - ○ B. Look before you leap.
   - ○ C. Money does not bring happiness.
   - ○ D. It is better to give than to receive.

5. Which of the following words means "having high morals"?
   - ○ A. virtuous
   - ○ B. unconventional
   - ○ C. aristocratic
   - ○ D. disdain

Get Ready to Read!

The Boar Hunt

Meet José Vasconcelos

José Vasconcelos (hō sā′ väs kōn sā′ lōs) was born in Oaxaca, Mexico, in 1882 and died in 1959. Vasconcelos was a writer, lawyer, philosopher, politician, and university president. He helped others to appreciate the dignity and nobility of their Mexican heritage and to feel a spirit of national pride. This translation of "The Boar Hunt" was first published in 1959.

What You Know

Have you ever had an experience that completely changed your attitude toward something? Perhaps you were injured while playing a sport, and you decided never to play that sport again.

Reason to Read

Read this short story to find out what changes one hunter's attitude toward hunting.

Background Info

"The Boar Hunt" takes place in an unexplored jungle in Peru, South America. Wild boars exist in this type of jungle. Wild boars are wild hogs with razor-sharp tusks, pointy ears, straight tails, and hard, thick hides. They weigh an average of 200 pounds, although some may weigh as much as 500 pounds. Wild boars are naturally aggressive toward other animals, including humans, and will attack when they feel threatened. People have hunted wild boars since ancient times, in spite of the danger—or maybe because of it.

Word Power

rejuvenate (ri jōō´ və nāt´) *v.* to make fresh or young again; p. 23
According to the TV commercial, this new face cream will *rejuvenate* your skin.

persistence (pər sis´ təns) *n.* the continued action of something in spite of problems or setbacks; p. 26
Danielle's *persistence* in playing the piano correctly was shown by four hours of daily practice.

proximity (prok sim´ ə tē) *n.* the closeness of one thing to another; p. 26
The firefighters worried about the *proximity* of the forest fire to the edge of town.

agile (aj´ əl) *adj.* able to move quickly and with great control; p. 26
The *agile* football player dodged the oncoming players and scored a touchdown.

anxiety (ang zī´ ə tē) *n.* a feeling of worry or nervousness; p. 28
Sam's hands shook, and he felt terrible *anxiety* as he waited to give his speech.

repentance (ri pent´ əns) *n.* a feeling of regret for doing something wrong; p. 29
Jennifer felt *repentance* and promised never to break the rules again.

vile (vīl) *adj.* very evil or disgusting; p. 30
Murder is an especially *vile* crime.

Answer the following questions, using one of the new words above. Write your answers in the spaces provided.

1. Which word goes with "being sorry"? _____

2. Which word goes with "being nearby"? _____

3. Which word goes with "bad and revolting"? _____

4. Which word goes with "not giving up"? _____

5. Which word goes with "making something like new again"? _____

6. Which word goes with "fearfulness"? _____

7. Which word goes with "fast and nimble"? _____

Adapted from

The Boar Hunt

José Vasconcelos

Background Info

Quito (kē′ tō) is the capital of the country Ecuador in South America.

Comprehension Check

Reread the boxed sentences. How do the men spend their time every night? Check the correct response.

- ☐ They get into fistfights.
- ☐ They play cards.
- ☐ They enjoy friendly arguments.

We were four companions, and we went by the names of our respective nationalities: the Colombian, the Peruvian, the Mexican. The fourth, a native of Ecuador, was called Quito for short. Chance had joined us together a few years ago on a large sugar plantation on the Peruvian coast.

We worked at different occupations during the day and met during the evening in our off time. Not being Englishmen, we did not play cards. Instead, our constant discussions led to disputes. These didn't stop us from wanting to see each other the next night, however, to continue the interrupted debates and support them with new arguments. Nor did the rough sentences of the preceding disagreements indicate a lessening of our affection. On Sundays we used to go on hunting parties. We roamed the fertile valleys, stalking, generally with poor results, the game of the warm region around the coast. Or we entertained ourselves killing birds that flew in the sunlight during the siesta hour.

We came to be tireless wanderers and excellent shots. Whenever we climbed a hill and gazed at the impressive range of mountains in the interior, its attractiveness stirred us and we wanted to climb it. What attracted us more was the trans-Andean region: fertile high, flat lands extending on the other side of the range in the direction of the Atlantic toward the immense land of Brazil. It was as if primitive nature drew us to her. The force of the fertile, untouched jungles promised to **rejuvenate** our minds. This same force rejuvenates the strength and the thickness of the trees each year. At times we devised crazy plans. As with all things that are given a lot of thought, these schemes generally materialized. Ultimately nature and events are largely what our imaginations make them out to be. And so we went ahead planning and acting. At the end of the year, with arranged vacations, accumulated money, good rifles, stone- and mud-proof boots, four hammocks, and a half dozen faithful Indians, our caravan descended the Andean slopes, leading to the endless green ocean.

Did You Know?

The Marañón (mä´ rä nyōn´) River runs through northeast Peru and flows into the Amazon River.

At last we came upon a village at the edge of the Marañón River. The region we were going to penetrate had no roads. It was unexplored underbrush into which we could enter only by going down the river in a canoe. In time we came to the area where we proposed to carry out the purpose of our journey, the hunting of wild boars.

English Coach

The prefix *trans-* can mean "across," "through," or "over." The adjective *Andean* describes the Andes, a mountain system in South America. *Trans-Andean* then means "across the Andes." What are other words you know that begin with *trans-*?

_____

_____

_____

Comprehension Check

Reread the boxed sentences. What are the men planning to do?

_____

_____

_____

_____

Selva, 1981. Luis Monje. Oil on Canvas, 51 ⅛ x 67 in. Private collection.

What parts of this painting show a sense of possible danger in the story?

We had been informed that boars travel in herds of several thousands, occupying a region, eating grass and staying together, organized just like an army. They are very easy to kill if one attacks them when they are scattered out satisfying their appetites—an army given over to the delights of victory. When they march about hungry, on the other hand, they are usually vicious. In our search we glided down river between vast, dense jungles with our supplies and the company of three faithful Indian paddlers.

One morning we stopped at some huts near the river. Thanks to the information gathered there, we decided to go ashore a little farther on in order to spend the night on land and continue the hunt for the boars the following day.

Sheltered in an inlet, we came ashore, and after a short exploration found a clearing in which to make camp. We unloaded the supplies and the rifles, and tied the boat securely. Then with the help of the Indians, we set up our camp about a third of a mile from the river bank. In marking the path to the canoe, we were careful not to lose ourselves in the brush. The Indians withdrew toward their huts, promising to return two days later. At dawn we would set out in search of the prey.

Though night had scarcely come and the heat was great, we gathered at the fire to see each other's faces, to look instinctively for protection. We talked a little, smoked, confessed to being tired, and decided to go to bed. Each hammock had been tied by one end to a single tree, firm though not very thick in the trunk. Stretching out from this axis in different directions, the hammocks were supported by the other end on other trunks. Each of us carried his rifle and some supplies which couldn't remain exposed on the ground. The sight of the weapons made us consider the place where we were, surrounded by the unknown. A slight feeling of terror made us laugh, cough, and talk. But fatigue overcame us, that heavy fatigue which makes the soldier scorn danger, put down his rifle, and fall asleep though the most persistent enemy pursues him. We scarcely noticed the supreme beauty of that distant tropical night.

I don't know whether it was the light of the magnificent dawn or the strange noises which awakened me. I sat up in my hammock and looked carefully at my surroundings. I saw nothing but the awakening of that life which at night falls into the drowsiness of the jungle. I called my sleeping companions and, alert and seated in our hanging beds, we dressed ourselves. We were preparing to jump to the ground when we clearly heard a somewhat distant, sudden sound of rustling branches. Since it did not continue, however, we descended confidently, washed our faces, and slowly prepared and enjoyed breakfast. By about 11:00 in the morning we were armed and bold and preparing to make our way through the jungle.

Background Info

An axis is a straight line or pole around which things can circle. Here, a single tree is an axis from which the men attach their hammocks.

Reading Skill

Sequence Reread the highlighted sentence and the rest of the paragraph. Which event happens first, the narrator hears strange noises, or the narrator jumps to the ground out of his hanging bed?

_____

_____

_____

But then the sound again. Its **persistence** and **proximity** in the brush made us change our minds. An instinct made us take refuge in our hammocks. We cautiously moved our rifles into them again. Without consulting each other we agreed on the idea of putting our supplies safely away. We passed them up into the hammocks, and we ourselves finally climbed in. Stretched out face down, comfortably suspended with rifles in hand, we did not have to wait long. Black, **agile** boars quickly appeared from all directions. We welcomed them with shouts of joy and well-aimed shots. Some fell immediately, giving comical snorts, but many more came out of the jungle. We shot again, spending all the bullets in our rifles. Then we stopped to reload. Finding ourselves safe in the height of our hammocks, we continued after a pause.

We counted dozens of them. At a glance we rapidly assessed the extent of the destruction. The boars continued to come out of the jungle in uncountable numbers. Instead of going on their way or fleeing, they seemed confused. All of them emerged from the jungle where it was easy for us to shoot them. Occasionally we had to stop firing because the frequent shooting heated the barrels of our rifles. While they were cooling we smoked and were able to joke, celebrating our good fortune. The ineffective anger of the boars amazed us. They raised their tusks in our direction, uselessly threatening us. We laughed at their snorts, quietly aimed at those who were near, and Bang! a dead boar. We carefully studied the angle of the shoulder blade so that the bullet would cross the heart. The slaughter lasted for hours.

Did You Know?
The tusks of wild boars are long, pointed teeth.
. . . .

Word Power

persistence (pər sis′ təns) *n.* the continued action of something in spite of problems or setbacks

proximity (prok sim′ ə tē) *n.* the closeness of one thing to another

agile (aj′ əl) *adj.* able to move quickly and with great control

At 4:00 P.M. we noticed an alarming shortage of our ammunition. We had been well supplied and had shot at will. Though the slaughter was gratifying, the boars must have numbered several thousands. They gathered directly beneath our hammocks in increasing groups. They slashed furiously at the trunk of the tree which held the four points of the hammocks. The marks of the tusks remained on the hard bark. Not without a certain fear we watched them gather compactly, persistently, in tight masses against the resisting trunk. We wondered what would happen to a man who fell within their reach. Our shots were now infrequent, well aimed, carefully managed. They did not drive away the aggressive beasts, but only increased their fury. One of us noted that from being the attackers we had gone on the defensive. We did not laugh very long at the joke. Now we hardly shot at all. We needed to save our ammunition.

The afternoon waned and evening came upon us. After consulting each other, we decided to eat in our hammocks. We applauded ourselves for taking the food up—meat, bread, and bottles of water. Stretching ourselves on our hammocks, we passed things to each other, sharing what we needed. The boars deafened us with their angry snorts.

After eating, we began to feel calm. We lit cigars. Surely the boars would go. Their numbers were great, but they would finally leave peacefully. As we said so, however, we looked with greedy eyes at the few unused cartridges of bullets that remained. Our enemies, like enormous angry ants, moved beneath us, encouraged by the ceasing of our fire. From time to time we carefully aimed and killed one or two of them. This drove off the huge group of uselessly angry boars at the base of the trunk which served as a prop for our hammocks.

Reading Skill

Sequence Reread the highlighted sentence and the rest of the paragraph. What events happen to make the men change from feeling like hunters to feeling like the hunted? Use the words *at first* and *after* in your response below.

_____

_____

_____

_____

_____

_____

Comprehension Check

Reread the boxed sentences. How confident are the hunters that the boars will go away?

_____

_____

_____

_____

_____

My Workspace

Literary Element

Theme Reread the highlighted sentences. Does the narrator still believe that hunting is a sport to admire? Why or why not?

_____

_____

_____

_____

_____

Connect to the Text

Reread the boxed sentences. When was the last time you had spent a long time waiting for something to happen? What did it feel like?

_____

_____

_____

_____

_____

Night enveloped us almost without our noticing. **Anxiety** also overtook us. When would the cursed boars leave? Already there were enough dead to serve as trophies to several dozen hunters. Our feat would be talked about. We had to show ourselves worthy of such fame. Since there was nothing else to do, it was necessary to sleep. Even if we had enough bullets it would have been impossible to continue the fight in the darkness. It occurred to us to start a fire to drive the herd off with flames. But apart from the fact that we couldn't leave the place in which we were suspended, there were no dry branches in the lush forest. Finally, we slept.

We woke up a little after midnight. The darkness was complete, but the well-known noise made us aware that our enemies were still there. We imagined they must be the last ones which were leaving, however. If a good army needs several hours to break camp and march off, what can be expected of a foul army of boars but disorder and delay? The following morning we would fire upon the stragglers, but this painful thought bothered us. They were in large and apparently active numbers. What were they up to? Why didn't they leave? We thus spent long hours of worry. Dawn finally came, splendid in the sky but noisy in the jungle still enveloped inwardly in shadows. We eagerly waited for the sun to break through in order to survey the field of battle of the day before.

What we finally saw made us gasp. It terrified us. The boars were continuing the work which they had been performing throughout the entire night. Guided by some extraordinary instinct, with their tusks they were digging out the ground underneath the tree from which our hammocks hung.

Word Power

anxiety (ang zī′ ə tē) *n.* a feeling of worry or nervousness

They gnawed the roots and continued to undermine them like large, hard-working rats. Before long the tree was bound to fall and we with it, among the beasts. From that moment we neither thought nor talked. In desperation we used up our last shots, killing more ferocious beasts. Still the rest renewed their activity. They seemed to have intelligence. However much we concentrated our fire against them, they did not stop their attack against the tree.

Soon our shots stopped. We emptied our pistols, and then silently listened to the tusks gnawing beneath the soft, wet, pleasant-smelling earth. From time to time the boars pressed against the tree, pushing it and making it creak, eager to smash it quickly. We looked on dazed by their devilish activity. It was impossible to flee because the black monsters covered every inch in sight. It seemed to us that, by a sudden inspiration, they were preparing to take revenge on us for the cruel nature of man, the unpunished destroyer of animals since the beginning of time. Our imagination, distorted by fear, showed us our fate that would make up for the unforgivable crimes hidden within the struggle of biological selection. Before my eyes passed the vision of sacred India, where the believer refuses to eat meat in order to prevent the killing of beasts and in order to make up for man's evil, bloody slaughter, such as ours, for mere vicious pleasure. I felt that the boars were raising their accusing voices against me. I now understood the evil reputation of the hunter. But what was **repentance** worth if I was going to die with my companions, hopelessly devoured by that horde of brutes with demonlike eyes?

Word Power

repentance (ri pent´ əns) *n.* a feeling of regret for doing something wrong

Reading Skill

Question Reread the highlighted sentence. What would be the **best** question you might ask yourself to understand what is happening to the men? Check the correct response.

☐ Why does the tree fall?

☐ Why are the men crying out?

☐ When does the terrifying sound occur?

Comprehension Check

Reread the boxed passage. How does the narrator finally escape?

_____

_____

_____

_____

_____

_____

Stirred by terror and without realizing what I was doing, I hung from the upper end of my hammock. Then I balanced myself in the air, I swung in a long leap, I grasped a branch of a tree facing the one on which the boars were digging. From there I leaped to other branches and to others, reviving in myself habits which the species had forgotten.

The next moment a terrifying sound and unforgettable cries told me of the fall of the tree and the end of my companions. I clung to a trunk, trembling and listening to the chattering of my jaws. Later, the desire to flee gave me back my strength. I looked for a path. I saw the boars in the distance, marching in tight groups and holding their proud snouts in the air. I knew that they were now withdrawing, and I got down from the tree. Horror overwhelmed me as I approached the site of our camp, but some idea of duty made me return there. Perhaps one of my friends had managed to save himself. I approached hesitantly. Each dead boar made me tremble with fear.

But what I saw next was so frightful that I could not fix it clearly in my mind. Remains of clothing—and footwear. There was no doubt. The boars had devoured them. Then I ran toward the river, following the tracks we had made two days before. I fled quickly, limbs stiff from panic.

Running with long strides, I came upon the boat. With a great effort, I managed to row to the huts. There I went to bed with a high fever which lasted many days.

I will participate in no more hunts. I will contribute, if I have to, to the destruction of harmful beasts. But I will not kill for pleasure. I will not amuse myself with the **vile** pleasure of the hunt.

Word Power

vile (vīl) *adj.* very evil or disgusting

Respond to Literature

The Boar Hunt

A Comprehension Check

Answer the following questions in the spaces provided.

1. What is the camp area the men set up like? _____
   _____

2. What does the narrator do to save his own life at the end of the story?
   _____
   _____

B Reading Skills

Answer the following questions in the spaces provided.

1. **Sequence** What does the narrator do **after** the hunters run out of
   ammunition? _____
   _____

2. **Sequence** What happens just **before** the narrator sees "the boars in the
   distance, marching in tight groups and holding their proud snouts in the
   air" as they leave the campsite? _____
   _____
   _____

3. **Question** What would be a good question to ask about the narrator's
   experience? What would be a possible answer? _____
   _____
   _____

C Word Power

Complete each sentence below, using one of the words in the box.

rejuvenate	persistence	proximity	agile
	anxiety	repentance	vile	

1. The _____ monkey leaped gracefully from branch to branch.

2. When people heard about the crime, they could not believe that anyone would commit such a _____ act.

3. Brandon loves his family's new apartment because of its _____ to the beach.

4. On a hot summer's day, there is nothing like a swim in a cool pool to _____ you.

5. Some students feel so much _____ before taking a test that they become physically ill.

6. The boys received a harsh punishment because they showed no _____ for breaking the neighbor's window with their baseball.

7. Miranda worked with great _____ until she solved the algebra problem.

D Literary Element: Theme

Read the passage below from "The Boar Hunt." As you read, think about what the sentences reveal about the story's theme that hunting or killing animals for pleasure may be wrong. Then answer the questions that follow.

It seemed to us that, by a sudden inspiration, they were preparing to take revenge on us for the cruel nature of man, the unpunished destroyer of animals since the beginning of time.[1] Our imagination, distorted by fear, showed us our fate that would make up for the unforgivable crimes hidden within the struggle of biological selection.[2] Before my eyes passed the vision of sacred India, where the believer refuses to eat meat in order to prevent the killing of beasts and in order to make up for man's evil, bloody slaughter, such as ours, for mere vicious pleasure.[3] I felt that the boars were raising their accusing voices against me.[4] I now understood the evil reputation of the hunter.[5]

1. How do sentences 1–2 show the hunter's opinion that hunting animals for pleasure is wrong? _____

_____

_____

2. How do sentences 3–5 support the idea that people's attitudes can be changed by experience? _____

_____

_____

_____

_____

_____

E News Photo

Imagine that the narrator has told his story to news reporters. A photographer takes a picture of the narrator. The photo caption tells about the narrator's ordeal. Draw the "photo" and complete the caption below.

This man is the sole survivor of _____

_____

His story is hard to believe, but three of his companions _____

_____

The men had not expected _____

_____

This man managed to avoid death by _____

_____

He says, _____

_____

Assessment

Fill in the circle next to each correct answer.

1. What is the main reason the men want to hunt wild boars?
   - ○ A. to have exciting fun
   - ○ B. to get respect
   - ○ C. to earn a lot of money
   - ○ D. to settle a dispute

2. What do the hunters do after they wake up to find the boars using their tusks to dig up the ground at the base of the tree?
   - ○ A. They make a fire to drive the boars away.
   - ○ B. They wait until the boars leave on their own.
   - ○ C. They use up all of their bullets trying to scare the boars away.
   - ○ D. They get away by climbing the branches from tree to tree.

3. Which is the **best** question to ask to fully understand the story?
   - ○ A. Which country is the narrator from?
   - ○ B. In what way does the narrator's attitude about hunting change?
   - ○ C. How do the men plan to bring back their trophies?
   - ○ D. Who helps the men set up their hunting camp in the jungle?

4. What is a possible message in the story "The Boar Hunt"?
   - ○ A. Every animal has an instinct to survive in jungles.
   - ○ B. Animals show more mercy than humans do.
   - ○ C. It is very difficult for people to change what they believe.
   - ○ D. People should not kill animals for pleasure.

5. Which of the following words means "the closeness of one thing to another"?
   - ○ A. anxiety
   - ○ B. proximity
   - ○ C. repentance
   - ○ D. persistence

THE CENSORS

Meet
Luisa Valenzuela

Luisa Valenzuela was born in 1938 in Buenos Aires, Argentina. She wrote her first short story, "City of the Unknown," when she was seventeen. Valenzuela writes about Argentinean politics and societies that have strict control over women. Many of her works combine reality and fantasy, a Latin American style of writing called "magical realism." "The Censors" was first published in 1976.

What You Know

Have you ever heard the expression "If you can't beat 'em, join 'em"? It refers to a strategy for dealing with strong opponents when other attempts at beating them have failed. Can you imagine a situation in which you might use this strategy?

Reason to Read

Read this short story to learn how a careful strategy backfires on the main character.

Background Info

The job of a censor is to limit the kinds of information people have access to. Censors examine print materials, television programs, or films, and either remove offensive parts or completely reject the material. For example, a censor might remove a book with crude language from a school library. A censor in the military might examine personal mail and delete information that would threaten national security. Some governments even control what kinds of news can be reported.

People disagree over the issue of censorship. Some think there should be no censorship at all. Others believe that it is a good idea to hold back information that might harm people. Still others use censorship as a form of power, to control people by controlling what they hear or read.

Word Power

confidential (kon´ fə den´ shəl) *adj.* told in secret; meant to be kept private; p. 38
Sarah didn't repeat the *confidential* information she had heard about her best friend.

censorship (sen´ sər ship´) *n.* the practice of removing anything thought unfit for people to see or read; p. 38
Librarians generally do not like the idea of *censorship* and believe that people should be able to read what they want to read.

intercept (in´ tər sept´) *v.* to stop or delay on the way; p. 39
Pedro tried to *intercept* the football before the other team could catch it.

promoted (prə mōt´ id) *v.* raised to a higher position or rank; p. 40
Laurie was *promoted* from assistant coach to head coach.

subversive (səb vur´ siv) *adj.* seeking to weaken, destroy, or overthrow; p. 41
When the president read the *subversive* newsletter criticizing the government, he ordered all copies to be destroyed.

distraction (dis trak´ shən) *n.* something that takes one's attention away from something else; p. 41
The neighbor's barking dog was a huge *distraction* for Elizabeth as she studied.

patriotic (pā´ trē ot´ ik) *adj.* showing great love for and support of one's own country; p. 41
On the Fourth of July, many *patriotic* citizens display U.S. flags.

Answer the following questions, using one of the new words above. Write your answers in the spaces provided.

1. Which word goes with "something that breaks your concentration"? _____

2. Which word goes with "given a better job"? _____

3. Which word goes with "removal of bad language"? _____

4. Which word goes with "proud of one's country"? _____

5. Which word goes with "stop a package from being delivered"? _____

6. Which word goes with "an activity to overthrow a ruler"? _____

7. Which word goes with "meant to be kept secret"? _____

Adapted from
THE CENSORS

Luisa Valenzuela

Poor Juan! One day they caught him unaware before he could even realize that what he thought was a stroke of luck was really one of fate's dirty tricks. These things happen the minute you're careless, as one often is. Juancito let happiness—a feeling you can't trust—get the better of him when he received from a **confidential** source Mariana's new address in Paris. He knew that she hadn't forgotten him. Without thinking twice, he sat down at his table and wrote her a letter. *The* letter that now keeps his mind off his job during the day and won't let him sleep at night (What had he written? What had he put on that sheet of paper he sent to Mariana?).

Juan knows there won't be a problem with the letter's contents, that it's blameless, harmless. But what about the rest? He knows that they examine, sniff, feel, and read between the lines of each and every letter. They check its tiniest comma and most accidental stain. He knows that all letters pass from hand to hand and go through all sorts of tests in the huge **censorship** offices. In the end, very few continue on their way. Usually it takes months, even years, if there aren't any snags.

Word Power

confidential (kon´ fə den´ shəl) *adj.* told in secret; meant to be kept private

censorship (sen´ sər ship´) *n.* the practice of removing anything thought unfit for people to see or read

All this time the freedom, maybe even the life, of both sender and receiver is in danger. And that's why Juan's so troubled. He thinks that something might happen to Mariana because of his letters. Of all people, Mariana, who must finally feel safe there where she always dreamt she'd live. But he knows that the *Censor's Secret Command* operates all over the world and benefits from the discount in air fares. There's nothing to stop them from going as far as that hidden Paris neighborhood, kidnapping Mariana, and returning to their cozy homes, certain of having fulfilled their noble mission.

Well, you've got to be quicker than them. Do what everyone tries to do: destroy the machinery, throw sand in its gears, get to the bottom of the problem so as to stop it.

This was Juan's solid plan when he, like many others, applied for a censor's job—not because of a strong desire for it or that he needed a job. No, he applied simply to **intercept** his own letter, a comforting although unoriginal idea. He was hired immediately. Each day more and more censors are needed and no one would bother to check on his past.

Hidden motives couldn't be overlooked by the *Censorship Division,* but they needn't be too strict with those who applied. They knew how hard it would be for the poor guys to find the letter they wanted. And even if they did, what's a letter or two when the new censor would seize so many others? That's how Juan managed to join the *Post Office's Censorship Division,* with a certain goal in mind.

Word Power

intercept (in´ tər sept´) *v.* to stop or delay on the way

My Workspace

Sequence Reread the highlighted sentence and the next paragraph. Then, number the events below from 1 to 4 in the order in which they happened.

_____ A worker's hand is blown off by a letter.

_____ A worker tries to organize a strike.

_____ Juan is sent to work in _Section K._

_____ Juan reports the organizer and gets promoted.

English Coach

Climbed a step on the ladder means "moved a step closer to a goal." If you "climbed a step on the ladder" in a job situation, did you get a promotion or get fired?

_____

_____

The building had a festive air on the outside that contrasted with its inner seriousness. Little by little, Juan was absorbed by his job. He felt at peace since he was doing everything he could to get his letter for Mariana. He didn't even worry when, in his first month, he was sent to _Section K_ where envelopes are very carefully screened for explosives.

It's true that on the third day, a fellow worker had his right hand blown off by a letter, but the division chief claimed it was pure carelessness on the victim's part. Juan and the other

employees were allowed to go back to their work, though feeling less secure. After work, one of them tried to organize a strike to demand higher pay for unhealthy work, but Juan didn't join in. After thinking it over, he reported the man to his superiors and thus got **promoted.**

You don't form a habit by doing something once, he told himself as he left his boss's office. And when he was transferred to _Section J,_ where letters are carefully checked for poison dust, he felt he had climbed a step on the ladder.

Did You Know?

A strike is when a group of workers refuse to perform a job until certain demands are met. Workers usually have strikes to demand higher pay or better working conditions.
. . . .

Based on this image, who do you think censorship affects the most in the story? Why do you think that?

_____

Word Power

promoted (prə mōt´ id) _v._ raised to a higher position or rank

By working hard, he quickly reached *Section E* where the job became more interesting. He could now read and analyze the letters' contents. Here he could even hope to get hold of his letter. Judging by the time that had passed, the letter had gone through the other sections and was probably floating around in this one.

Soon his work became so absorbing that his noble mission blurred in his mind. Day after day he crossed out whole paragraphs in red ink without a care, throwing away many letters into the censored basket. These were horrible days when he was shocked by the clever ways used by people to pass on **subversive** messages. His instincts were so sharp that he found behind a simple "the weather's unsettled" or "prices continue to soar" the restless hand of someone secretly planning to overthrow the Government.

His enthusiasm brought him swift promotion. We don't know if this made him happy. Very few letters reached him in *Section B*— only a handful passed the other hurdles. He read them over and over again, passed them under a magnifying glass, searched for fine print with an electronic microscope, and tuned his sense of smell so that he was beat by the time he made it home. He'd barely manage to warm up his soup, eat some fruit, and fall into bed, satisfied with having done his duty. Only his darling mother worried, but she couldn't get him back on the right track. She'd say, though it wasn't always true: Lola called, she's at the bar with the girls, they miss you, they're waiting for you. Or else she'd leave a bottle of red wine on the table. But Juan wouldn't overdo it. Any **distraction** could make him lose his edge. The perfect censor had to be alert, attentive, and sharp to catch cheats. He had a truly **patriotic** task, both self-denying and uplifting.

Word Power

subversive (səb vur´ siv) *adj.* seeking to weaken, destroy, or overthrow

distraction (dis trak´ shən) *n.* something that takes one's attention away from something else

patriotic (pā´ trē ot´ ik) *adj.* showing great love for and support of one's own country

Reading Skill

Question Reread the highlighted sentences. What is the **best** question to ask to understand Juan's attitude toward his work? Check the correct response.

☐ Exactly how many letters are in Juan's "censored basket"?

☐ Why does Juan use red ink to cross out whole paragraphs?

☐ Why does Juan get caught up in his job so that he almost forgets about the letter?

English Coach

The prefix *over-* in *overdo* means "too much." To *overdo* means "to do too much" of something. What are two other words that have the prefix *over-* with the meaning of "too much"?

_____

_____

_____

41

How would you feel if you received a letter that was censored like the one shown in the photo?

_____

Literary Element

Tone Reread the highlighted sentences. Juan "censors" his own life when the government executes him. What tone is expressed in this passage? Check the correct response.

- ☐ darkly humorous
- ☐ extremely happy
- ☐ very angry

His basket for censored letters became the best fed as well as the most clever basket in the whole *Censorship Division*. He was about to congratulate himself for having finally discovered his true mission, when his letter to Mariana reached his hands. Naturally, he censored it without regret. And just as naturally, he couldn't stop them from executing him the following morning. Another victim of his devotion to his work.

Respond to Literature

THE CENSORS

A Comprehension Check

Answer the following questions in the spaces provided.

1. Why does Juan want to get a job at the censorship office?

   _____

   _____

2. What is Juan's daily life like when he is promoted to *Section B*?

   _____

   _____

B Reading Skills

Answer the following questions in the spaces provided.

1. **Question** What question can you ask yourself to help you understand why Juan becomes a censor and tries to intercept the letter?

   _____

   _____

2. **Sequence** What happens to Juan after he censors his own letter?

   _____

   _____

C Word Power

Complete each sentence below, using one of the words in the box.

confidential	censorship	intercept
promoted	subversive	distraction	patriotic

1. Mrs. Kim felt it was her _____ duty to write letters to the soldiers fighting the war overseas.

2. Mr. Ruiz tried to _____ the note that Brian passed to Madison.

3. The thief was caught looking through the files to find _____ information about people's bank accounts.

4. The dictator accused the newspaper reporters of writing _____ articles to overthrow his government.

5. The noise from the traffic was a big _____ to the students who were taking the test.

6. The parents decided to support the _____ of the movie because some scenes were too upsetting for children.

7. Leo was _____ to head cashier after working for only a short time at the store.

D Literary Element: Tone

Read the passage below from "The Censors." As you read, think about what the sentences reveal about the tone of the story. Think about how the author feels about censorship. Then answer the questions that follow.

His basket for censored letters became the best fed as well as the most clever basket in the whole *Censorship Division.*[1] He was about to congratulate himself for having finally discovered his true mission, when his letter to Mariana reached his hands.[2] Naturally, he censored it without regret.[3] And just as naturally, he couldn't stop them from executing him the following morning.[4] Another victim of his devotion to his work.[5]

1. In sentence 1, what details contribute to the humorous tone? Does the author think that it is a good thing or a bad thing that Juan's letter basket is so full? _____

_____

_____

_____

2. Sentences 3–5 describe an unexpected ending. How does the humorous tone show that the author is making fun of censorship?

_____

_____

_____

_____

E The Application

Imagine that you are the supervisor in *Section E*. Write a note recommending that Juan be promoted to *Section B*. Explain what Juan has done to deserve this promotion and tell why you think he is worthy of being promoted.

Date _____

I am recommending another promotion for Juan. When he began in Section K, he wasn't afraid to _____

_____

When a worker had his hand blown off by a letter, _____

_____

_____

In Section E, Juan has proved himself many times. He _____

_____

_____

He has even found subversive messages behind simple phrases, such as

_____

_____

I am sure that Juan will continue to be an excellent worker. I therefore recommend that he _____

_____

Name _____

Respond to Literature

Assessment

Fill in the circle next to each correct answer.

1. How does Juan earn his first promotion?
   - ○ A. He turns in Mariana.
   - ○ B. He turns in a coworker.
   - ○ C. He censors his own letter.
   - ○ D. He writes a letter to his boss.

2. Which question should you ask yourself to **best** help you understand the ending of the story?
   - ○ A. Why doesn't Juan try to save his own life?
   - ○ B. Why does Juan get promoted?
   - ○ C. Why does Juan stop seeing his friends?
   - ○ D. Why doesn't Juan cross out paragraphs in blue ink?

3. When does Juan's job first become interesting to him?
   - ○ A. when he begins reading and analyzing letters
   - ○ B. when he starts looking for the letter he wrote
   - ○ C. when he begins striking for better work conditions
   - ○ D. when he starts turning in his coworkers to his bosses

4. Which sentence has a humorous tone?
   - ○ A. This was Juan's solid plan when he, like many others, applied for a censor's job.
   - ○ B. The building had a festive air on the outside that contrasted with its inner seriousness.
   - ○ C. By working hard, he quickly reached *Section E* where the job became more interesting.
   - ○ D. His basket for censored letters became the best fed as well as the most clever basket in the whole *Censorship Division.*

5. Which of the following words means "to stop or delay on the way"?
   - ○ A. promoted
   - ○ B. distraction
   - ○ C. intercept
   - ○ D. confidential

Get Ready to Read!

Appetizer

Meet Robert H. Abel

Fiction writers have a responsibility, says Robert H. Abel: "I feel the planet is threatened, that writing should attempt to define and respond to this emergency . . . with some vision of a workable, maybe even beautiful future." Abel was born in Painesville, Ohio, in 1941. In addition to writing fiction, Abel has worked as a reporter, a teacher, an editor, and a volunteer firefighter. He is also a fisherman. "Appetizer" was first published in 1991.

What You Know

Think about a surprising or frightening experience you've had with an animal. What were the circumstances? How did you react? What did the animal do?

Reason to Read

Read this story to find out what happens when the narrator encounters a bear while fishing in the Alaskan wilderness.

Background Info

Brown bears have long, shaggy coats that range in color from blond to black. They have stout bodies, massive heads, and long claws. Brown bears have a strong sense of smell, jaws that can snap small tree trunks, and the ability to sprint up to thirty-five miles an hour. Brown bears eat fish, mammals, nuts, berries, herbs, and grasses, but will feed exclusively on salmon when it is available. They sometimes eat more than a dozen fish in a few hours.

Word Power

intimidated (in tim´ ə dāt´ id) *adj.* feeling frightened by something more powerful or superior; p. 50
At the rodeo, the young cowboy was too *intimidated* by the bull to try to ride it.

nimbleness (nim´ bəl nes) *n.* the ability to move quickly and with controlled movements; p. 51
The young sailor walked with *nimbleness* on the boat's slippery deck.

implore (im plôr´) *v.* to ask urgently; p. 52
The principal said, "I *implore* you to follow the rules during the fire drill."

inevitably (i nev´ ə tə blē) *adv.* certain to happen; p. 54
Spring *inevitably* brings warmer and milder weather to the region.

trespasser (tres´ pəs ər) *n.* something or someone who goes somewhere he or she is not allowed to go; p. 57
The *trespasser* was not allowed to drive his truck on the farmer's land.

affront (ə frunt´) *n.* an insult; something that causes a person to feel offended; p. 57
It was an *affront* to the tribe when tourists took pictures of their sacred ceremony.

superfluous (soo pur´ floo əs) *adj.* beyond what is necessary; p. 58
The rescuer's cry of "Hang on!" seemed *superfluous* as Joe dangled from the cliff.

accessible (ak ses´ ə bəl) *adj.* capable of being reached easily; p. 59
Household cleaners should not be kept where they are *accessible* to young children.

**Answer the following questions, using one of the new words above.
Write your answers in the spaces provided.**

1. Which word goes with "more than what is needed"? _____

2. Which word goes with "scared"? _____

3. Which word goes with "not welcome"? _____

4. Which word goes with "speed and gracefulness"? _____

5. Which word goes with "going to happen no matter what"? _____

6. Which word goes with "beg"? _____

7. Which word goes with "close at hand"? _____

8. Which word goes with "insulting someone"? _____

Fly Fishing. Rosemary Lowndes. Oil on Canvas.
Private collection.

Adapted from

Appetizer

Robert H. Abel

I'm fishing this beautiful stream in Alaska, catching salmon, char and steelhead, when this bear lumbers out of the woods and down to the stream bank. He fixes me with this half-amused, half-curious look which says: You are meat.

The bear's eyes are brown and his shiny golden fur is standing up in spikes, which shows me he has been fishing, too. He's not making any sound I can hear over the rumble of the water in the softball-sized rocks, but his presence is very loud.

I say "his" presence because temporarily I am not interested in or able to determine the creature's sex. I am looking at a head that is bigger around than my steering wheel, a pair of paws awash in river bubbles that could cover half my windshield. I am glad that I am wearing polarized fishing glasses so the bear cannot see the little teardrops of fear that have crept into the corner of my eyes. To assure him/her I am not the least bit **intimidated,** I make another cast.

Word Power

intimidated (in tim´ ə dāt´ id) *adj.* feeling frightened by something more powerful or superior

50

Immediately I tie into a fat Chinook. The splashing of the fish in the stream engages the bear's attention. I play the fish smartly and when it comes gliding in, I pluck it out of the water and I do exactly what you would do in the same situation—throw it to the bear.

The bear's eyes widen and she—for I can see now that she is a she—turns and pounces on the fish with such speed and **nimbleness** that I am numbed. While she is occupied devouring the fish, I do what you or anyone else would do and cast again.

I am blessed with the strike of another fat salmon. Ms. Bear has just licked her whiskers clean and has now moved knee-deep into the water and leans against me rather like a large and friendly dog. Her ears are at the level of my shoulder and her back is broader than that of any horse I have ever seen. Her head twists and twitches as the fish circles, darts, takes line away, shakes head, rolls over, leaps.

With a bear at your side, it is not the simplest thing to play a fish properly, but the presence of this huge animal, and especially her long snout, thick as my thigh, wonderfully concentrates the mind. Now I debate whether I should just drift the salmon in under the bear's nose and let her take it that way, but I'm afraid she will break off my fly and leader. Right now that fly—a Doctor Wilson number eight—is saving my life. So I bring the fish in on the side away from the bear, quickly unhook it, and toss the fish behind me to the bank.

Did You Know?

In fly-fishing, a fly is an artificial lure, or bait, that is tied to a hook and made to look like an insect. The fly is tied to the fishing line by the leader, a length of nylon.

. . . .

Word Power

nimbleness (nimʹ bəl nis) *n.* the ability to move quickly and with controlled movements

The bear wheels and clambers upon it at once, leaving a whirlpool of water pouring into the vacuum of the space she has left, which almost topples me. As her teeth snack away, I quickly and secretly peek at my poor Doctor Wilson, which is almost unrecognizable. But the present emergency compels me to zing it out once again. I walk a few paces downstream, hoping the bear will become distracted and I can sneak away.

But a few seconds later she is leaning against me again, busily watching the stream for any sign of a salmon splash. Another fish smacks the withered Wilson. I **implore** the salmon's forgiveness. I not only want the salmon to thrive forever, I want a huge number of them now, right now. For if her supply of fish is cut off, this hungry bear would probably not waste any time before turning me into the main course that my few salmon were just the appetizer for. When I take up this fish, the bear practically rips it from my hand. The sight of those teeth so close, and the power of those muscled, pink-rimmed jaws, cause a wave of fear in me so great that I nearly faint.

How would you feel if a large bear came to the shore where you were fishing? Could you identify with the feelings of the author of the story? Explain.

Word Power
implore (im plôr´) *v.* to ask urgently

Ms. Bear munches and destroys the salmon and I sneak a few more paces downstream. Rapidly with trembling fingers I tie on a new Doctor Wilson. My hope and plan is to wade my way back to the narrow trail a few hundred yards ahead and make a heroic dash for my camper. I promise the gods—American, Indian, African, Oriental—that if I survive I will never complain again, not even if my teenage children leave the caps off the toothpaste tubes or their bicycles in the driveway at home.

"Oh, home," I think, and cast again.

Ms. Bear rejoins me. Two things happened which gave me a particle of hope. The first was that Ms. Bear actually belched. It was clear to me that a belching bear is probably also a bear with a pretty-full belly. A few more salmon and perhaps Ms. Bear would wander off in search of a berry dessert.

Now the second thing she did was to begin *communicating* somehow. It's not as if the bear were speaking to me in complete sentences and English words such as "Get me another fish, pal, or you're on the menu," but in a much more indirect and subtle way, almost in the way a stream talks through its bubbling and burbling and rattling of rocks and gurgling along.

I listened intently, more with my mind than with my ears, as if the bear were communicating mentally, and I really did truly believe now that this Ms. Bear was expressing feelings of *affection*. Really, I think she rather liked me. The feeling made me less afraid. In fact, once my fear had passed, my feelings were almost the same. Like you might feel for an old pal of a dog. I only wish she weren't such a big eater. I only wish she were not a carnivore, and I, *carne*.

Comprehension Check

Reread the sentence boxed in green. How does the narrator plan to get away from the bear?

_____

_____

_____

_____

Connect to the Text

Reread the paragraph boxed in purple. Do you think that animals can communicate with people? How have you ever "talked" to a pet or another animal?

_____

_____

_____

Literary Element

Tone Reread the highlighted sentence. The word *carnivore* (kär´ nə vôr´) means "meat-eater." *Carne* (kär´ nā) means "meat" in Spanish. How does the use of these words add to the humorous tone?

_____

_____

_____

_____

Background Info

A Chinook (shi nook´) is a type of salmon, often called the king salmon, which lives in the northern Pacific area of the United States. The Chinook is also the name of a group of Native Americans who live in the Pacific Northwest.

Reading Skill

Sequence Reread the highlighted sentence and the rest of the paragraph. Number the events in the order in which they happen to show how the narrator tries to get closer to the trail.

___ The salmon flips into a pool and the bear eats it.

___ The narrator catches a salmon.

___ The narrator puts on a new fly and goes downstream.

Now she nudges me with her nose.

"All right, all right," I say. "I'm doing the best I can."

Cast in the glide behind that big boulder, the bear communicates to me. *There are a couple of whoppers in there.*

I do as I'm told and wham! the bear is right! Instantly I'm tied into a granddaddy Chinook, a really husky fellow. Even the bear is excited and begins shifting weight from paw to paw, a little motion for her that nevertheless has big consequences for me as her body slams against my hip, then slams again.

Partly because I don't want to lose the fish, but partly also because I want to use the fish as an excuse to move closer to my getaway trail, I stumble downstream. This fish has my fly rod bent into an upside-down *U* and I'm hoping my quick-tied knots are also strong enough to take this salmon's lurching. When the salmon flips into a little side pool, the bear clambers over the rocks, pounces, nabs the salmon smartly behind the head and lumbers immediately to the bank. My leader snaps at once and while Ms. Bear attends to the destruction of the fish, I tie on another fly and make some awkward headway downstream. Yes, I worry about the hook still in the fish, but only because I do not want this bear to be irritated by anything. I want her to be full and to doze off in the sun. Mentally I try to tell her so. *Please, Bear, sleep.*

Inevitably, the fishing slows down, but Ms. Bear does not seem to mind. Again she belches. I am getting quite a headache and know that I am fighting exhaustion. I even find myself getting a little angry, and I marvel at the bear's persistence. And appetite. At supermarket prices, I calculate she has eaten about six hundred dollars worth of fish.

Word Power

inevitably (i nev´ ə tə blē) *adv.* certain to happen

54

At last I am immediately across from the opening to the trail which twines back through the woods to where my camper rests. Still, five hundred yards separate me from this imagined haven. Perhaps someone else will come along and frighten the bear away, but I have already spent many days here without seeing another soul. I have told myself for many years that I really do love nature, love being among the animals, am restored by wilderness adventure. This seems to be a sentiment in need of some revision.

Now the bear turns beside me, her rump pushing me into water deeper than I want to be in, where my footing is shaky. She stares into the woods, ears forward. She has heard something I cannot hear, or smelled something I cannot smell. I hope some backpackers or some bear-poaching Indians are about to appear and send Ms. Bear a-galloping away. I continue casting, but I also cannot help glancing over my shoulder in hopes of seeing what Ms. Bear sees. And in a moment I do.

It is another bear.

Fly Fishing. Herman Herzog. Oil on canvas.

How does the scene in this painting relate to the story thus far?

_____

Reading Skill

Question Reread the highlighted sentences. What would be the **best** question to ask to understand what the narrator means here? Check the correct response.

☐ Does the narrator still love bears?

☐ Does the narrator still love nature and the outdoors?

☐ Does the narrator still love to eat fish?

STOP Stop here for **Break Time** on the next page.

Break Time

The story "Appetizer" begins with the narrator fishing alone in a stream in Alaska. This event and other events that take place in the story are described in the boxes below. Number the boxes to show the order in which these events take place. Write the numbers 1 through 8 in the spaces provided. The first event has been numbered for you.

The first bear comes out
of the woods.
_____

The narrator starts to get
tired from all the fishing.
_____

The narrator feeds the bear
its first fish.
_____

The bear stares into the
woods after it hears
something.
_____

The bear "communicates" to
the narrator to help him
catch a big fish.
_____

The narrator is fishing alone
in a stream in Alaska.
1

The narrator makes a cast to
show he is not afraid.
_____

The narrator sees the
second bear.
_____

GO Continue reading on the next page.

I release a low moan, but my voice is lost in the throaty warning of Ms. Bear to the **trespasser.** The new arrival answers with a defiant cough. He is half again as large as my companion. His fur seems longer and coarser, the tips are black and this dark surface ripples over his massive frame. His nostrils are flared and he is staring with complete concentration at me.

Would it be better to catch another salmon or not? I surely cannot provide for two of these beasts and Mister Bear does not seem the type to be distracted by or made friendly by any pitifully small offering of salmon. His whole bearing—pardon the expression—tells me my intrusion into this bear world is a personal **affront** to his bear honor. Only Ms. Bear stands between us and whose side is she really on? By bear standards, I am sure a rather regal and handsome fellow has made his appearance. Why should the fur-covered heart of furry Ms. Bear go out to me? How much love can a few hundred dollars worth of salmon buy?

Did You Know?
Waders are waterproof trousers that have boots for legs.

How disturbed I am is well illustrated by my next course of action. I cranked in my line and lay my rod across some rocks. Then I began the difficult process of pulling myself out of my waders while trying to balance myself on those awkward rocks in that fast water. I tipped and swayed as I tugged at my boots and pushed my waders down, the entire time with my arms in the foaming, frigid water. Then the waders filled, making it even more difficult to pull my feet free.

Word Power

trespasser (tres´ pəs ər) *n.* something or someone who goes somewhere he or she is not allowed to go

affront (ə frunt´) *n.* an insult; something that causes a person to feel offended

Background Info

A nymph is the larval, or beginning, stage of many insects. Some nymphs form a cocoon like that of a butterfly. As an adult, they emerge from the cocoon to continue their life cycle.

Comprehension Check

Reread the boxed paragraph. What does the narrator do with his waders? Why?

_____

_____

_____

_____

_____

Literary Element

Tone Reread the highlighted sentences. How does comparing "Jingle Bells" to an Indian death song add to the lighthearted tone?

_____

_____

_____

_____

_____

_____

_____

I emerged like a nymph from a cocoon, wet and trembling. The bears regarded me with clear astonishment, as if one of them had casually stepped out of his or her fur.

I drained what water I could from the waders, then dropped my fly rod into them, and held them before me. I marched toward the trail opening, lifting and dropping first one, then the other leg of my waders. I was half thinking that if the big one attacks, maybe he'll be fooled into chomping the waders first and I'll at least be able to run. Would you have done differently?

I tried to make myself look as much as possible like some extreme and inedible form of four-footedness as I plodded along the trail. The bears looked at each other, then at me as I clomped by, the water in the waders making an odd gurgling sound, and me making an odd sound, too. I was remembering just then how the Indians would, staring death in the eye, sing their death song. I chanted forth the only song I ever committed to memory: "Jingle Bells."

Yes, "Jingle Bells," I sang, "jingle all the way," and I lifted first one, then the other wader leg and dropped it stomping down. "Oh what fun it is to ride in a one-horse open sleigh-ay!"

The male reared up, blotting out the sun, bellowed, then twisted on his haunches and crashed off into the woods. The female, head cocked in curiosity, followed at a slight distance, within what still might be called striking distance. The **superfluous** thought struck me: suppose someone sees me now, plumping along like this, singing "Jingle Bells," a bear in attendance? Vanity, obviously, never sleeps.

Word Power

superfluous (soo pur´ floo əs) *adj.* beyond what is necessary

When I came within about one hundred feet of my camper, I dropped the waders and sped for the cab. The bear broke into a trot, too. I could hear those big feet slapping the ground behind me in a heavy rhythm that sang to me of my own frailty, fragile bones and tender flesh.

I plunged on like a madman, grabbed the camper door and hurled myself in. I lay on the seat panting, shuddered when the bear slammed against the pickup's side. The bear pressed her nose to the window, then licked the glass with her tongue. She could have shattered the glass with a single blow, and I tried to imagine what I should do if indeed she resorted to this. I had nothing in the cab of the truck to defend myself with except a tire iron, and that was not readily **accessible** behind the seat. My best defense was to start the pickup and drive away.

Just as I inserted the key, however, Ms. Bear slammed her big paws onto the hood and hoisted herself aboard. The pickup shuddered with the weight of her, and suddenly the windshield was full of her golden fur. I beeped the horn loud and long, but this only caused her to shake her huge head, which vibrated the truck terribly. She stomped around on the hood and then lay down, back against the windshield, which now appeared to have been covered by a huge shag rug.

My truck was being smothered in bear. Ms. Bear had decided the camper hood was the perfect place for a nap, and she was snoring profoundly, her body twitching like a cat's. I was trapped. Blinded by bear body!

Reading Skill

Sequence Reread the highlighted sentence. What clue words in the sentence tell you exactly when the bear climbs onto the hood of the truck?

_____

_____

Comprehension Check

Reread the boxed paragraph. What does the bear do? What problem does this cause for the narrator?

_____

_____

_____

_____

Word Power
accessible (ak ses′ ə bəl) *adj.* capable of being reached easily

59

Background Info

A cannery is a factory where fish are brought to be processed, where they are cleaned, packaged, and sent to stores.

Comprehension Check

Reread the boxed sentence. Why does the narrator speed up on the highway? Check the correct response.

☐ He wants to make the bear fall off and get hurt.

☐ He wants to get to the cannery quickly.

☐ He doesn't want to be hit by a logging truck.

My exhaustion had been doubled by my sprint for the camper, and now I felt the cold of the water that had soaked my clothes and I began to tremble. Perhaps Mister Bear was still in the vicinity, and if Ms. Bear was not smart enough, or cruel enough, to smash my window to get at me, he just might be.

Therefore, I started the engine and rolled down the window enough to stick my head out and see down the rocky, limb-strewn trail. I figured a few jolts in those ruts and Ms. Bear would be off like a shot.

Ms. Bear did indeed awaken and rouse herself to a sitting position, a bit like an overgrown hood ornament, but quickly grew quite expert at balancing herself against the lurching and jolting of my truck. I tried some quick braking and sharp turn maneuvers I thought might send her tumbling off, but her bulk was so massive, her paws so artfully spread, that she was just too stable. She wanted a ride and there was nothing I could do about it.

When I came out of the woods to the gravel road known locally as the Dawson Artery, I didn't drive so fast that if Ms. Bear decided to clamber down she would be hurt, but I did head for the main road which led to the Buckville Cannery. Ms. Bear swayed happily along the whole ten miles and seemed not to bat an eye when first one big logging truck, then another plummeted downhill. I pulled out onto the highway, and for the safety of both of us—those logging trucks have questionable brakes and their drivers get paid by the trip—I had to speed up considerably.

I couldn't see much of Ms. Bear except her back and rump as I had to concentrate on the road, some of which is pretty curvy. But from her posture, I'd say she was having a whale, or should I say a salmon of a time. I saw a few cars and pickups veering out of the oncoming lane onto the shoulder as we swept by, but I didn't have time to appreciate the astonishment of their drivers. I drove to the Buckville Cannery and turned into the long driveway.

Ms. Bear rose on all fours now and stuck her nose straight out like a bird dog on a pheasant. As soon as I came out of the trees into the parking area, she went over the front of the camper like someone plunging into a pool.

Don't tell me you would have done any differently. I stopped right there and watched Ms. Bear march down between the rows of cars and right up the truck ramp into the cannery itself. She was not the least bit intimidated by all the noise of the machines in there, or the shouting of the workers.

Now the Buckville Cannery isn't that big—about two dozen people work there on any given day. Since it is so remote, it has no hurricane fence around it, and no security guard. The main building is up on a little hill and conveyors run down from there to the docks where the salmon boats pull in and unload their catch.

In about three minutes after Ms. Bear walked into the cannery, twenty of the twenty-four workers were climbing out down the conveyors, dropping from open windows, or charging out the doors. The other four just hadn't got wind of the event yet, but in a little while they came bounding out, too, one fellow pulling up his trousers as he ran.

I did not want to be held liable for the disturbance at the Buckville Cannery, and so I made a U-turn and drove on into Buckville where I took a room above the Buckville Tavern and had a hot shower and a really nice nap. That night I got to hear many an excited story about the she-bear who freeloaded at the cannery for a couple of hours before she was driven off by blowing, ironically enough, the lunch whistle loud and long. I for once kept my mouth shut. You don't like trouble any more than I do, and I'm sure you would have done about the same.

Respond to Literature

Appetizer

A Comprehension Check

Answer the following questions in the spaces provided.

1. Why does the narrator feed fish to the bear? _____

   _____

2. What does the bear do when the narrator gets back to his truck? _____

   _____

3. How does the narrator finally get rid of the bear? _____

   _____

   _____

B Reading Skills

Answer the following questions in the spaces provided.

1. **Sequence** What happens just after the narrator goes far enough

   downstream to reach the opening of the trail? _____

   _____

2. **Sequence** What does the narrator do after the second bear appears?

   _____

3. **Question** What would be a good question that the reader can ask to find

   out how the story ends? _____

   _____

   _____

C Word Power

Complete each sentence below, using one of the words in the box.

intimidated	nimbleness	implore	inevitably
trespasser	affront	superfluous	accessible

1. The graffiti on the fence was an _____ to everyone in the neighborhood.

2. Whenever Tasha washes her car, it _____ rains.

3. The dance instructor was surprised by Ryan's _____ on the dance floor.

4. Justin's babysitter placed the cookie jar on a high shelf where it would be less _____ to the child.

5. The mayor told the gathered crowd, "I _____ you to help raise money for the new library."

6. The Falcons were _____ by the Bobcats, who had not lost a single game all year.

7. The _____ had entered the property through a hole in the fence.

8. As he trudged five miles to the gas station, the _____ thought came to Ross that he should have filled his tank before the trip.

D Literary Element: Tone

Read the passage below from "Appetizer." As you read, think about what the sentences reveal about the tone of the story. Then answer the questions that follow.

> The bears looked at each other, then at me as I clumped by, the water in the waders making an odd gurgling sound, and me making an odd sound, too.[1] I was remembering just then how the Indians would, staring death in the eye, sing their death song.[2] I chanted forth the only song I ever committed to memory: "Jingle Bells."[3]
>
> Yes, "Jingle Bells," I sang, "jingle all the way," and I lifted first one, then the other wader leg and dropped it stomping down.[4] "Oh what fun it is to ride in a one-horse open sleigh-ay!"[5]

1. What is unexpected about the reaction of the bears in sentence 1 that adds to the humorous tone of this passage?

   _____

   _____

2. How does the narrator's choice of song in sentences 3–5 add to the humorous tone of the passage?

   _____

   _____

   _____

E Personal Testament

Imagine that you are the narrator in the story. You are very pleased with how your waders helped you escape from the bears. Write a letter to the company that made the waders. In your letter, tell your story and explain how the waders saved your life.

Dear Sir or Madam,

I am writing about the waders made by your company.

I was fishing in Alaska when all of a sudden _____

_____

The next thing I knew, _____

_____

Things got even worse when another bear appeared.

So finally, I took off my waders and pretended that they were a pair of legs. I _____

_____

It worked like a charm! I managed to start my truck and head for the cannery, where _____

I hope that my story will inspire other people who use waders to see them as more than just a way to stay warm and dry in the water.

Sincerely,

_____

Assessment

Fill in the circle next to each correct answer.

1. What does the first bear "communicate" to the narrator?
   - ○ A. that another bear is nearby
   - ○ B. why she wants to help him
   - ○ C. that she wants him to leave the stream
   - ○ D. where to cast to catch a big fish

2. What does the narrator do after the second bear arrives?
   - ○ A. He takes off his waders.
   - ○ B. He runs downstream.
   - ○ C. He feeds it a fish.
   - ○ D. He catches another fish.

3. What is the **best** question to ask to understand how the narrator escapes from the bear at the end of the story?
   - ○ A. Why does the narrator drop his waders?
   - ○ B. Why is the narrator fishing all alone in the wilderness?
   - ○ C. Why does the narrator drive to the cannery?
   - ○ D. Why doesn't the narrator catch fish for the second bear?

4. Which word describes the overall tone of the story?
   - ○ A. humorous
   - ○ B. peaceful
   - ○ C. regretful
   - ○ D. serious

5. Which of the following words means "capable of being reached easily"?
   - ○ A. inevitably
   - ○ B. accessible
   - ○ C. nimbleness
   - ○ D. superfluous

Wrap-up

Compare and Contrast

Tone is an important literary element in "The Censors" and "Appetizer." The tone contributes to the humor in each story. In "The Censors," the tone is darkly humorous. The author uses the humorous tone to make a serious point. In "Appetizer," the humor is much more lighthearted to show how the narrator felt during a potentially dangerous situation. Think about how each author uses tone to make a point or tell about an experience.

Complete the chart below. In the left and right columns, explain what the tone is in each story. Explain how that tone shows the author's attitude toward the subject in each story. In the center column, explain the similarity in the tone in the stories.

"The Censors"	Similarity	"Appetizer"

UNIT 2

Short Story

How Is a Short Story Organized?

Now that you have read a few short stories, let's stop for a moment to take a closer look at how a short story is put together. Understanding the parts of a story can help you be a better reader.

A short story always has a **beginning,** a **middle,** and an **end.**

Most stories include a **conflict.** A conflict can be a struggle between a character and his or her thoughts and feelings. Or a conflict can be a struggle between a character and another character, nature, or an outside force.

What's the Plan?

Most plots develop in five stages.

Exposition introduces the story's characters, setting, and conflict.
Rising action develops the conflict with complications and twists.
Climax is the emotional high point of the story. It is the turning point.
Falling action shows what happens after the climax.
Resolution shows how the conflict is resolved or how the problem is solved.

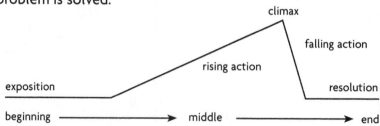

As you read the next four stories, try to find the five stages in each story. In the text, mark the places where each stage occurs.

68

How Do I Read Short Stories?

Focus on key **literary elements** and **reading skills** to get the most out of reading the four short stories in this unit. Here are two key literary elements and two key reading skills that you will practice in this unit.

Key Literary Elements

• Plot

Plot is the sequence of events in a story. It is the story's basic framework. If you tell someone what a story is about and what happens, you are telling the plot. A plot begins with the **exposition,** which introduces the characters, the setting, and the problem or conflict that the characters have. The story is set in motion in the **rising action.** The action builds to a **climax.** The **falling action** often shows the results of the climax. The **resolution** is the story's end. It presents a conclusion to the story.

• Climax

The **climax** is the turning point of a story. It is the moment of greatest emotional intensity, interest, or suspense. Usually the climax is found at the point in a story where the conflict begins to be resolved. For instance, in a story about a race, the climax would probably occur as the main character approaches the finish line.

Key Reading Skills

• Predict

When you **predict,** you make an educated guess about what will happen next. Make predictions and check them as you read to add to your involvement in the story. As you're making predictions, notice the clues and details. Even small details can signal big events or deeper meaning. As you gather more information, you may find that you want to change your predictions as you read.

• Evaluate

Form opinions and make judgments about the story while you are reading. A writer may not always be right. **Evaluate** what you read by asking yourself questions: Does this turn of events make sense? How would I judge this character's thoughts and actions? You can also evaluate the writing. Is the story interesting? Does it hold your attention?

Get Ready to Read!

Catch the Moon

Meet Judith Ortiz Cofer

Judith Ortiz Cofer was born in Puerto Rico in 1952. When she was a child, her family moved from Puerto Rico to Paterson, New Jersey. They visited Puerto Rico often, so the writer has always felt close to her cultural roots. Vivid memories of her childhood in both places and her passion for reading led Ortiz Cofer to become a writer of poetry and fiction. "Catch the Moon" was originally published in 1995.

What You Know

Have you ever given someone a special gift or done something really nice for another person? How did that person react?

Reason to Read

Read to find out how a teenager's gift-giving brings rewards to him in return.

Background Info

This story takes place toward the end of the 1990s in the *barrio* of a city in the northern United States. In Spanish, *barrio* means "neighborhood" or "area of a town." A *barrio* is usually an urban neighborhood in which most of the people are of Hispanic heritage. People in a *barrio* may have been born in the United States or come from Spanish-speaking countries, such as Mexico, the Dominican Republic, and Cuba.

Word Power

acre (āʹ kər) *n.* an area of land equal to 43,560 square feet; p. 72
The home was on an *acre* of land close to the river.

botched (bocht) *adj.* failed; poorly done; p. 73
Mr. Jones was angry when he saw the *botched* paint job on his car.

correspondence (kōrʹ ə sponʹ dəns) *n.* a communication exchange through the mail; p. 74
Through her *correspondence* with a pen pal in Ireland, Maggie learned a lot about country life.

vintage (vinʹ tij) *adj.* old, but highly valued because of quality or importance; p. 74
People cheered as the parade of *vintage* Model T cars drove by.

decapitate (di kapʹ ə tātʹ) *v.* to cut off the head of someone or something; p. 77
The farmer used an ax to *decapitate* the chicken.

sarcastic (sär kasʹ tik) *adj.* a way of saying the opposite of what one means to make fun of someone or something; p. 78
Chris was being *sarcastic* when he said that his sister was one of the best drivers.

relics (relʹ iks) *n.* objects used a long time ago that still survive today; p. 79
Grandma Jenny decorated her kitchen with *relics* such as an old washboard and a butter churn.

**Answer the following questions that contain the new words above.
Write your answers in the spaces provided.**

1. When people are *sarcastic*, are they being nice or mean? _____

2. Would a student who never likes to write be likely or unlikely to have

   correspondence with people? _____

3. Would a customer at a beauty salon be happy or angry about a *botched* haircut?

   _____

4. Are *relics* modern or old-fashioned objects? _____

5. Does the word *acre* describe the size or the price of a piece of land? _____

6. When something is *decapitated*, does it lose its hand or its head? _____

7. Would you be more likely to find *vintage* clocks at department stores or antique

   stores? _____

Adapted from

Catch the Moon

Judith Ortiz Cofer

Reading Skill

Predict Reread the title and the highlighted sentences. What do you know about Luis? What do you predict will happen to Luis in the story?

_____

_____

_____

_____

Comprehension Check

Reread the boxed sentence. What is Luis doing by saying "Someday, son, all this will be yours"? Check the correct response.

☐ He is bragging.
☐ He is celebrating.
☐ He is making a joke.

Luis Cintrón sits on top of a six-foot pile of hubcaps and watches his father walk away into the steel jungle of his car junkyard. Released into his old man's custody after six months in juvenile hall—for breaking and entering—and he didn't even take anything. He did it on a dare.

But the old lady with the million cats was a light sleeper, and good with her aluminum cane. He has a scar on his head to prove it.

Jorge Cintrón of Jorge Cintrón & Son, Auto Parts and Salvage, has decided that Luis should wash and polish every hubcap in the yard. Luis grunts and stands up on top of his silver mountain. He yells at no one, "Someday, son, all this will be yours," and sweeps his arms like the Pope blessing a crowd over the piles of car sandwiches and mounds of metal parts that cover this **acre** of land outside the city. He is the "Son" of Jorge Cintrón & Son, and so far his father has had more than one reason to wish it was plain Jorge Cintrón on the sign.

Luis has been getting in trouble since he started high school two years ago, mainly because of the "social group" he organized.

Word Power
acre (ā´ kər) *n.* an area of land equal to 43,560 square feet

Their thing was taking something to the limit on a dare or doing something dangerous, like breaking into a house, not to steal, just to prove that they could do it. That was Luis's specialty, coming up with very complicated plans and assigning the "jobs" to guys who wanted to join the Tiburones.

Tiburón means "shark." Luis had gotten the name from watching an old movie about a Puerto Rican gang called the Sharks with his father. Luis thought it was one of the dumbest films he had ever seen. But he liked their name, the Sharks, so he made it Spanish and had it air-painted on his black T-shirt with a killer shark under it. The jaws were open wide and dripping with blood.

Luis outsmarted everybody by calling his organization a social club and registering it at Central High. That meant they were legal, even let out of last-period class on Fridays for their "club" meetings. It was just this year, after a couple of **botched** jobs, that the teachers had started getting suspicious. The first one to go wrong was when he sent Kenny Matoa to *borrow* some "souvenirs" out of Anita Robles's locker. He got caught. It seems that Matoa had been reading Anita's diary and didn't hear her coming down the hall. You could hear her screams all the way to Market Street.

She told the principal all she knew about the Tiburones. Luis had to talk fast to convince old Mr. Williams that the club did put on cultural activities such as the Save the Animals talent show. What Mr. Williams didn't know was that the animal that was being "saved" with the ticket sales was Luis's pet boa. They kept E.S. (which stood for "Endangered Species") in Luis's room, but she belonged to the club. It was the members' responsibility to raise the money to feed their mascot. So last year they had sponsored their first annual Save the Animals talent show.

Word Power

botched (bocht) *adj.* failed; poorly done

73

Reading Skill

Evaluate Reread the paragraph highlighted in green. What do you think of the Tiburones? Are they good or bad? Does putting on a good show excuse some of the things they have done?

_____

_____

_____

Literary Element

Plot Reread the sentence highlighted in blue. Where does the exposition end? How do you know the exposition has ended?

_____

_____

_____

_____

_____

_____

The Tiburones had come dressed as Latino Elvises and did a grand finale to "All Shook Up" that made the audience go wild. Mr. Williams had smiled while Luis talked, maybe remembering how the math teacher, Mrs. Laguna, had dragged him out in the aisle to rock-and-roll with her. Luis had gotten out of that one, but barely.

His father objected to the T-shirt logo, calling it disgusting and vulgar. Mr. Cintrón prided himself on his own neat, elegant style of dressing after work, and on his manners and large vocabulary, which he picked up by taking **correspondence** courses. Luis thought that it was just his way of staying busy since Luis's mother had died, almost three years ago, of cancer.

All this was going through Luis's head as he slid down the hill of hubcaps. The tub full of soapy water, the can of polish, and the bag of rags had been neatly placed in front of a makeshift table made from two car seats and a piece of plywood. Luis heard a car drive up and someone honk their horn. Luis watched as the most beautiful girl he had ever seen climbed out of a **vintage** white Volkswagen Bug. She stood in the sunlight in her white sundress waiting for his father, while Luis stared. Her skin was mahogany, almost black. Her arms and legs were long and thin, but curved in places so that she did not look bony and hard. And her ebony hair was braided close to her head. Luis let his breath out, feeling a little dizzy. Both the girl and his father heard him. Mr. Cintrón waved him over.

Did You Know?
The Volkswagen Beetle was a small, inexpensive car and was often called a "VW" or "Bug." The Bug was popular in the 1960s and early 1970s. It also made a recent comeback with the New Beetle model.

· ·

Word Power

correspondence (kôr´ ə spon´ dəns) *n.* a communication exchange through the mail

vintage (vin´ tij) *adj.* old, but highly valued because of quality or importance

"Luis, the *señorita* here has lost a wheel cover. Her car is twenty-five years old, so it will not be an easy match. Come look on this side."

Luis tossed a wrench he'd been holding into a toolbox like he was annoyed, just to make a point about slave labor. Then he followed his father, who knelt on the gravel and began to point out every detail of the hubcap. Luis watched the girl take a piece of paper from her handbag.

"*Señor Cintrón*, I have drawn the hubcap for you. My home address and telephone number are here, and also my parents' office number." She handed the paper to Mr. Cintrón, who nodded.

"*Sí, señorita*, very good. This will help my son look for it. Perhaps there is one in that stack there. Of course, I do not know if it's near the top or the bottom. You will give us a few days, yes?"

Luis just stared at his father like he was crazy. But he didn't say anything because the girl was smiling at him with a funny expression on her face.

"Please call me Naomi, *Señor Cintrón*. You know my mother. She is the director of the funeral home. . . ." Mr. Cintrón seemed surprised at first; then his friendly expression changed to one of sadness as he recalled the day of his wife's burial. Naomi reached over and placed her hand on Mr. Cintrón's arm for a moment. Then she said "*Adiós*" softly, and got in her shiny white car. She waved to them as she left, and her gold bracelets flashing in the sun nearly blinded Luis.

Mr. Cintrón shook his head. "How about that," he said as if to himself. "They are the Dominican owners of Ramírez Funeral Home. She seems like such a nice young woman. Reminds me of your mother when she was her age."

 Stop here for **Break Time** on the next page.

Reading Skill

Predict Reread the highlighted sentences. The young girl needs a hubcap. Do you think that Luis will find one for her? What do you think will happen between Luis and the girl?

_____

_____

_____

_____

Comprehension Check

Reread the boxed sentence. What does Naomi do when Mr. Cintrón thinks about his wife's burial? Check the correct response.

☐ She tells him to stop thinking about her.

☐ She doesn't pay any attention to him.

☐ She places her hand on his arm.

Background Info

Mr. Ramírez means that Naomi and her family are from the Dominican Republic, a small, Spanish-speaking country on an island in the Caribbean Sea. Many Dominicans came to the United States in the 1960s to escape poverty in their home country.

Break Time

Now that you have read the first half of "Catch the Moon," complete the chart below by answering the questions. Write your answers in the spaces provided.

1. What are the names of the three main characters of the story?
_____
_____

2. Where does the story take place?
_____
_____

3. Why does Naomi come to the junkyard?
_____
_____

4. Do you think Luis and Naomi will become friends? Why or why not?
_____
_____

GO Continue reading on the next page.

Luis remembered too. The day his mother died, he had been in her room at the hospital while his father had gone for coffee. The alarm had gone off on her monitor and nurses had come running in, pushing him outside. After that, all he recalled was the anger that had made him punch a hole in his bedroom wall. And afterward he had refused to talk to anyone at the funeral. Strange, he did see a black girl there who didn't try like the others to talk to him, but actually ignored him as she escorted family members to the viewing room and brought flowers in. Could it be that the skinny girl in a frilly white dress had been Naomi? She didn't act like she had recognized him today, though. Or maybe she thought that he was a jerk.

Luis grabbed the drawing from his father. Luis was in no mood to listen to the old stories about his falling in love on a tropical island. No beaches and palm trees here. Only junk as far as he could see. He climbed back up his hill and studied Naomi's sketch. It had obviously been done very carefully. It was signed "Naomi Ramírez" in the lower right-hand corner. He memorized the telephone number.

Luis washed hubcaps all day until his hands were red and raw, but he did not come across the small silver bowl that would fit the VW. After work he took a few practice Frisbee shots across the yard before showing his father what he had accomplished: rows and rows of shiny rings drying in the sun. His father showed him the bump on his temple where one of Luis's flying saucers had gotten him.

"Practice makes perfect, you know. Next time you'll probably **decapitate** me." Luis heard him struggle with the word *decapitate*, which Mr. Cintrón pronounced in syllables. Showing off his big vocabulary again, Luis thought. He looked closely at the bump, though. He felt bad about it.

Word Power

decapitate (di kap′ ə tāt′) *v.* to cut off the head of someone or something

Reading Skill

Evaluate Reread the highlighted sentences. Do you think how Luis reacts when his mother dies is how many people react when bad things happen? Why?

_____

_____

_____

_____

_____

Connect to the Text

Reread the boxed sentences. Luis throws some hubcaps, and one hits his father. Have you ever made someone angry by accident? How did this person feel?

_____

_____

_____

_____

My Workspace

Background Info

The word hijo (ĕ′ hō) means "son" in Spanish and is often used as a term of affection.

Reading Skill

Predict Look back at the prediction you wrote at the beginning of the story about what would happen to Luis. Did the story match your prediction? Use clues you have learned about Luis to revise your prediction.

_____

_____

_____

_____

_____

English Coach

The word "mint" in *"mint condition"* does not refer to a breath mint or the plant. The phrase comes from a coin's perfect condition when it has just been created, or "minted." What are other words you know that mean the same as "mint condition"?

_____

_____

_____

"They look good, hijo." Mr. Cintrón made a sweeping gesture with his arms over the yard. "My dream is to have all the parts divided by year, make of car, and condition. Maybe now that you are here to help me, this will happen."

"Pop . . ." Luis put his hand on his father's shoulder. They were the same height and build, about five foot six and muscular. "The judge said six months of free labor for you, not life, okay?" Mr. Cintrón nodded. It was then that Luis suddenly noticed how gray his hair had turned—it used to be shiny black like his own—and that there were deep lines in his face. His father had turned into an old man and he hadn't even noticed.

"Son, you must follow the judge's instructions. Next time you get in trouble, she's going to treat you like an adult, and I think you know what that means. Hard time, no breaks."

"Yeah, yeah. That's what I'm doing, right? Working my hands to the bone instead of enjoying my summer. But listen, she didn't put me under house arrest, right? I'm going out tonight."

"Home by ten. She did say something about a curfew, Luis." Mr. Cintrón was looking upset. It had always been hard for them to talk more than a minute or two before his father got offended at something Luis said, or at his **sarcastic** tone.

Luis threw the rag down on the table and went to sit in his father's ancient Buick, which was in mint condition. They drove home in silence.

After sitting down at the kitchen table with his father to eat a pizza they had picked up on the way home, Luis asked to borrow the car. He didn't get an answer then, just a look that meant "Don't bother me right now."

Word Power

sarcastic (sär kas′ tik) *adj.* a way of saying the opposite of what one means to make fun of someone or something

Before bringing up the subject again, Luis put some ice cubes in a plastic bag and handed it to Mr. Cintrón, who had made the little bump on his head worse by rubbing it. It had GUILTY written on it, Luis thought.

"*Gracias, hijo.*" His father placed the bag on the bump and made a face as the ice touched his skin.

They ate in silence for a few minutes more; then Luis decided to ask about the car again.

"I really need some fresh air, Pop. Can I borrow the car for a couple of hours?"

"You don't get enough fresh air at the yard? We're lucky that we don't have to sit in a smelly old factory all day."

"Yeah, Pop. We're real lucky." Luis always felt irritated that his father was so grateful to own a junkyard, but he held his anger back and just waited to see if he'd get the keys without having to get in an argument.

"Where are you going?"

"Not going anywhere. Just out for a while. Is that okay?"

His father didn't answer, just handed him a set of keys, as shiny as the day they were manufactured. His father polished everything that could be polished: doorknobs, coins, keys, spoons, knives, and forks. Luis thought his father must be really lonely to polish utensils only he used anymore. They were like **relics.** Now the dishes, forks, and spoons were not used to eat the yellow rice and red beans, the fried chicken, or the mouth-watering sweet plantains that his mother had cooked for them.

Did You Know?
A *plantain* (plant´ ən) is a tropical fruit like a banana. It must be cooked before eating.
. . . .

Reading Skill

Evaluate Reread the highlighted passage. What do you think of Luis's behavior toward his father?

_____

_____

_____

_____

_____

_____

Word Power

relics (rel´ iks) *n.* objects used a long time ago that still survive today

Comprehension Check

Reread the boxed sentence. *Barrio* (bär′ ē ō′) is Spanish for "neighborhood." Why does Luis want to visit his old neighborhood?

_____

_____

_____

_____

Literary Element

Plot Reread the highlighted paragraph. Sometimes an author interrupts the sequence of events to include a flashback, or a scene from the past. What do we learn about Luis's earlier life?

_____

_____

_____

_____

They were just kept in the cabinets that his father had turned into a museum for her. Mr. Cintrón could cook as well as his wife, but he didn't have the heart to do it anymore. Luis thought that maybe if they ate together once in a while things might get better between them, but he always had something to do around dinnertime and ended up at a hamburger joint. Tonight was the first time in months they had sat down at the table together.

Luis took the keys. "Thanks," he said. His father kept looking at him with those sad, patient eyes. "Okay. I'll be back by ten, and keep the ice on that egg," Luis said without looking back.

He had just meant to ride around his old *barrio*, see if any of the Tiburones were hanging out in the building where most of them lived. It wasn't far from the single-family home his father had bought when the business started paying off: a house that his mother lived in for three months before she took up residence at St. Joseph's Hospital. These days Luis wished he still lived in that tiny apartment where there was always something to do, somebody to talk to.

Instead Luis found himself parked in front of the last place his mother had gone to: Ramírez Funeral Home. In the front yard was a huge oak tree that Luis remembered having climbed during the funeral to get away from people. The tree looked different now, not like a skeleton, as it had then, but green with leaves. The branches reached to the second floor of the house, where the family lived.

Luis sat in the car allowing the memories to flood back into his brain. He remembered his mother before the illness changed her. She had not been beautiful, as his father told everyone. She had been a sweet lady, not pretty but not ugly. To him, she had been the person who always told him that she was proud of him and loved him. As a joke he would sometimes ask her, "Proud of what? I haven't done anything." And she'd always say, "I'm just proud that you are my son."

September 16, c. 1955. René Magritte. Oil on canvas, 14 x 10 7/8 in. The Minneapolis Institute of Arts.

In what way does this painting express the title of the story?

She wasn't perfect. She had bad days when nothing he did could make her smile, especially after she got sick. But he never heard her say anything negative about anyone. She always blamed *el destino*, fate, for what went wrong. He missed her so much. Suddenly a flood of tears that had been building up for almost three years started pouring from his eyes. Luis sat in his father's car, with his head on the steering wheel, and cried, "Mami, I miss you."

When he finally looked up, he saw that he was being watched. Sitting at a large window with a pad and a pencil on her lap was Naomi. At first Luis felt angry and embarrassed, but she wasn't laughing at him. Then she told him with her dark eyes that it was okay to come closer. He walked to the window. She held up the sketch pad on which she had drawn him sitting on top of a mountain of silver disks, holding one up over his head. He had to smile.

The plate-glass window was locked. It had a security bolt on it. An alarm system, he figured, so nobody would steal the princess. He asked her if he could come in. It was soundproof too. He mouthed the words slowly for her to read his lips. She wrote on the pad, "I can't let you in. My mother is not home tonight." So they looked at each other and talked through the window for a little while. Then Luis got an idea. He signed to her that he'd be back, and drove to the junkyard.

Literary Element

Plot Reread the highlighted sentence. What is the climax, or high point, of the story?

_____

_____

_____

_____

Reading Skill

Predict Refer back to your original prediction. Did your prediction match what happened in the story? What details from the story helped you make your prediction?

_____

_____

_____

_____

Luis climbed up on his mountain of hubcaps. For hours he sorted the wheel covers by make, size, and condition, stopping only to call his father and tell him where he was and what he was doing. By lamppost light, Luis worked and worked, beginning to understand a little why his father kept busy all the time. Doing something that had a beginning, a middle, and an end did something to your head. It was like the satisfaction Luis got out of planning "adventures" for his Tiburones, but there was another element involved here that had nothing to do with showing off for others. This was a treasure hunt. And he knew what he was looking for.

Finally, when it seemed that it was a hopeless search, when it was almost midnight, he found it. It was the perfect match for Naomi's drawing, the moon-shaped wheel cover for her car, Cinderella's shoe. Luis jumped off the small mound of disks left under him and shouted, "Yes!" He looked around and saw neat stacks of hubcaps that he would wash the next day. He would build a display wall for his father. People would be able to come into the yard and point to whatever they wanted.

Luis washed the VW hubcap and polished it until he could see himself in it. He used it as a mirror as he washed his face and combed his hair. Then he drove to the Ramírez Funeral Home. It was almost pitch-black, since it was a moonless night. Luis put some gravel in his pocket and climbed the oak tree to the second floor. He knew he was in front of Naomi's window—he could see her shadow through the curtains. She was at a table, apparently writing or drawing, maybe waiting for him. Luis hung the silver disk carefully on a branch near the window, then threw the gravel at the glass. Naomi ran to the window and drew the curtains aside while Luis held on to the thick branch and waited to give her the first good thing he had given anyone in a long time.

Respond to Literature

Catch the Moon

A Comprehension Check

Answer the following questions in the spaces provided.

1. Why does Luis work at his father's junkyard? _____

_____

2. Why does Naomi come to the junkyard? _____

_____

3. What does Luis leave in the tree for Naomi? _____

B Reading Skills

Answer the following questions in the spaces provided.

1. **Predict** Do you predict that Naomi will be pleased when she sees the hubcap in the tree? Do you think that Luis and Naomi will become good friends? Explain. _____

_____

2. **Evaluate** Why do you think Luis works so hard to find the hubcap?

_____

_____

3. **Evaluate** Do you think "Catch the Moon" is a good title for the story? Why or why not? _____

_____

_____

C Word Power

Complete each sentence below, using one of the words in the box.

acre	botched	correspondence	vintage
	decapitate	sarcastic	relics

1. Professor Gladstone placed the ancient _____ back in the mummy's tomb.

2. Jeremy learned a lot about Paris through his _____ with his French pen pal.

3. Amber's _____ comments sometimes hurt her friends' feelings.

4. At the park, we watched a bug called a praying mantis _____ another praying mantis and then eat it!

5. Thomas received a bad grade for his _____ science project.

6. The _____ clock was beautiful, but it no longer kept the time accurately.

7. Mr. Stevens grew flowers on an _____ of land behind his house.

D Literary Element: Plot

Read the passages below from "Catch the Moon." As you read, think about what the sentences reveal about the plot of the story. Then answer the questions that follow.

> He is the "Son" of Jorge Cintrón & Son, and so far his father has had more than one reason to wish it was plain Jorge Cintrón on the sign.[1]
>
> Luis climbed up on his mountain of hubcaps.[2] For hours he sorted the wheel covers by make, size, and condition, stopping only to call his father and tell him where he was and what he was doing.[3]
>
> Finally, when it seemed that it was a hopeless search, when it was almost midnight, he found it.[4] It was the perfect match for Naomi's drawing, the moon-shaped wheel cover for her car, Cinderella's shoe.[5]

1. Why does sentence 1 belong to the exposition of the story?

   _____

   _____

   _____

2. Which sentences belong to the rising action and which belong to the climax? Explain why.

   _____

   _____

   _____

E A Letter

Imagine that you are Luis. You are about to graduate from high school and are writing a letter to your father. You want to thank him for all that he has done for you.

Dear Pop,

Now that I am about to graduate from high school, I want to thank you for being such a good father.

I know that I did some things that I should not have done while in high school. I regret that _____

_____

_____

I spent six months in juvenile hall. But when I came out, I worked with you at the junkyard and this has taught me

_____

_____

When I gave the hubcap to Naomi, I felt _____

_____

Today, I am proud that I will be _____

_____

Love,
Luis

Assessment

Fill in the circle next to each correct answer.

1. Why does Naomi go to the junkyard?
   - ○ A. to buy a car
   - ○ B. to meet Luis
   - ○ C. to find a hubcap
   - ○ D. to help Mr. Cintrón

2. Which event from the story helps you predict Luis will find the hubcap?
   - ○ A. when Luis's father lets him borrow the car
   - ○ B. when Luis breaks down and cries for his mother
   - ○ C. when Luis learns that Naomi is from the funeral home
   - ○ D. when Naomi draws a picture of him holding the hubcap

3. Who is most responsible for the change in Luis?
   - ○ A. Naomi
   - ○ B. the Tiburones
   - ○ C. Luis's father
   - ○ D. Mr. Williams

4. Which event belongs to the falling action of the story?
   - ○ A. Luis hangs the hubcap outside Naomi's window.
   - ○ B. Luis remembers his mother's death.
   - ○ C. Luis meets Naomi.
   - ○ D. Luis looks for a hubcap for Naomi at the junkyard.

5. Which of the following words means "an exchange of communication through the mail"?
   - ○ A. acre
   - ○ B. correspondence
   - ○ C. botched
   - ○ D. relics

Get Ready to Read!

A Sound of Thunder

Meet Ray Bradbury

Bradbury was born in Waukegan, Illinois in 1920. An early love of reading led to a love of writing. At the age of twelve, using a toy typewriter, he wrote a story about Martians. A master of science fiction, Bradbury has published more than five hundred works since his first book was published in 1947. "A Sound of Thunder" was first published in 1952.

What You Know

What happens if you line up a set of dominoes on end, one in front of the other, and knock down the first one?

Reason to Read

Read to find out how one small action causes a complex chain of events.

Background Info

Science fiction deals with amazing events that authors imagine might happen in the future. Although the term *science fiction* was not used until the early twentieth century, science fiction stories have been told since before the invention of writing. One of the earliest science fiction writers was Lucian of Samosata. Around A.D. 100, Lucian wrote a story about a journey to the moon. Modern science fiction began to take shape in the 1800s. Landmarks of this period include Mary Shelley's *Frankenstein* (1818) and H.G. Wells's *The Time Machine* (1895).

Word Power

dictatorship (dik´tā´tər ship´) *n.* a government in which one person has complete power; p. 91
People who live under a *dictatorship* usually cannot speak out against their leader.

annihilate (ə nī´ə lāt´) *v.* to destroy completely; p. 94
Certain harmful chemicals were once used to *annihilate* insects that damaged crops.

expendable (iks pen´də bəl) *adj.* not necessary; able to be sacrificed without being missed; p. 95
Lauren decided that cheerleading was the most *expendable* activity in her schedule.

resilient (ri zil´yənt) *adj.* capable of springing back to shape after being bent, stretched, or smashed; p. 100
Willow trees have soft, *resilient* branches that bend in the wind instead of breaking.

malfunctioning (mal´fungk´shən ing) *adj.* not working properly; p. 103
The maintenance man put a sign up to warn people of the *malfunctioning* elevator.

primeval (pri mē´vəl) *adj.* having to do with the first or earliest age of the world; primitive; p. 105
The sailors netted a strange, *primeval* fish that looked like a dinosaur with fins.

exquisite (iks kwiz´it) *adj.* beautiful and delicate; p. 108
Jenna felt nervous drinking from the *exquisite* teacup.

Complete the following sentences that contain the new words above. Write your answers in the spaces provided.

1. A necklace is *exquisite* when it is _____.

2. A *malfunctioning* washing machine does not _____.

3. If you want to *annihilate* bugs in your home, then you want them _____
_____.

4. A type of government that is a *dictatorship* has _____.

5. An untamed jungle can seem *primeval* because it seems _____.

6. Some trees are *resilient* and are _____.

7. Newspapers are *expendable* and can be recycled because they are _____
_____.

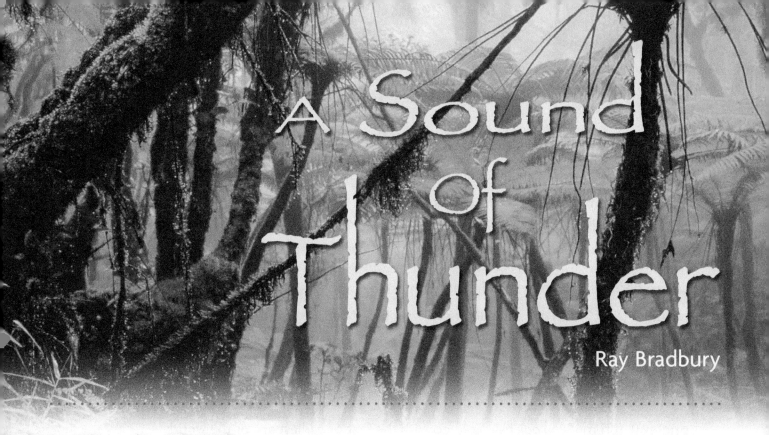

A Sound of Thunder

Ray Bradbury

Reading Skill

Predict Reread the highlighted text on this page. What kind of animal do you predict Eckels will hunt on his safari? How do you think he feels about the trip? Based on his feelings, how do you think the trip will go?

_____

_____

_____

_____

_____

_____

The sign on the wall seemed to quaver under a film of sliding warm water. Eckels felt his eyelids blink over his stare, and the sign burned in this momentary darkness:

TIME SAFARI, INC.
SAFARIS TO ANY YEAR IN THE PAST.
YOU NAME THE ANIMAL.
WE TAKE YOU THERE.
YOU SHOOT IT.

A warm phlegm gathered in Eckels' throat; he swallowed and pushed it down. The muscles around his mouth formed a smile as he put his hand slowly out upon the air, and in that hand waved a check for ten thousand dollars to the man behind the desk.

"Does this safari guarantee I come back alive?"

"We guarantee nothing," said the official, "except the dinosaurs." He turned. "This is Mr. Travis, your Safari Guide in the Past. He'll tell you what and where to shoot. If he says no shooting, no shooting. If you disobey instructions, there's a stiff penalty of another ten thousand dollars, plus possible government action, on your return."

Eckels glanced across the vast office at a mass and tangle, a snaking and humming of wires and steel boxes, at an aurora that flickered now orange, now silver, now blue. There was a sound like a gigantic bonfire burning all of Time, all the years and all the parchment calendars, all the hours piled high and set aflame.

A touch of the hand and this burning would, on the instant, beautifully reverse itself. Eckels remembered the wording in the advertisements to the letter. Out of chars and ashes, out of dust and coals, like golden salamanders, the old years, the green years, might leap; roses sweeten the air, white hair turn Irish-black, wrinkles vanish; all, everything fly back to seed, flee death, rush down to their beginnings, suns rise in western skies and set in glorious easts, moons eat themselves opposite to the custom, all and everything cupping one in another like Chinese boxes, rabbits into hats, all and everything returning to the fresh death, the seed death, the green death, to the time before the beginning. A touch of a hand might do it, the merest touch of a hand.

"Unbelievable." Eckels breathed, the light of the Machine on his thin face. "A real Time Machine." He shook his head. "Makes you think. If the election had gone badly yesterday, I might be here now running away from the results. Thank God Keith won. He'll make a fine President of the United States."

"Yes," said the man behind the desk. "We're lucky. If Deutscher had gotten in, we'd have the worst kind of **dictatorship.** There's an anti-everything man for you, a militarist, anti-Christ, anti-human, anti-intellectual. People called us up, you know, joking but not joking. Said if Deutscher became President they wanted to go live in 1492. Of course it's not our business to conduct Escapes, but to form Safaris. Anyway, Keith's President now. All you got to worry about is—"

Comprehension Check

Reread the boxed paragraph. What is the author describing? Check the correct response.

- [ ] the end of the earth
- [ ] the start of a new planet
- [ ] traveling back in time
- [ ] traveling into the future

Word Power

dictatorship (dik´tā´tər ship´) *n.* a government in which one person has complete power

Reading Skill

Predict What kind of animal did you predict Eckels would hunt? Does the prediction you made match the animal that Eckels plans to hunt? (Don't worry if your predictions don't match! You can change your predictions as you get new information from the story!)

_____

_____

_____

_____

Literary Element

Plot Reread the highlighted sentence. Where does the exposition end? Where does the action of the story begin? How do you know?

_____

_____

_____

_____

_____

_____

_____

_____

_____

If it were possible, would you travel back in time to hunt dinosaurs? Why or why not?

_____

"Shooting my dinosaur," Eckels finished it for him.

"A _Tyrannosaurus rex._ The Tyrant Lizard, the most incredible monster in history. Sign this release. Anything happens to you, we're not responsible. Those dinosaurs are hungry."

Eckels flushed angrily. "Trying to scare me!"

"Frankly, yes. We don't want anyone going who'll panic at the first shot. Six Safari leaders were killed last year, and a dozen hunters. We're here to give you the severest thrill a _real_ hunter ever asked for. Traveling you back sixty million years to bag the biggest game in all of Time. Your personal check's still there. Tear it up."

Mr. Eckels looked at the check for a long time. His fingers twitched.

"Good luck," said the man behind the desk. "Mr. Travis, he's all yours."

They moved silently across the room, taking their guns with them, toward the Machine, toward the silver metal and the roaring light. First a day and then a night and then a day and then a night, then it was day-night-day-night-day. A week, a month, a year, a decade! A.D. 2055. A.D. 2019. 1999! 1957! Gone! The Machine roared.

They put on their oxygen helmets and tested the intercoms.

Eckels swayed on the padded seat, his face pale, his jaw stiff. He felt the trembling in his arms and he looked down and found his hands tight on the new rifle. There were four other men in the Machine. Travis, the Safari Leader, his assistant, Lesperance, and two other hunters, Billings and Kramer. They sat looking at each other, and the years blazed around them.

"Can these guns get a dinosaur cold?" Eckels felt his mouth saying.

"If you hit them right," said Travis on the helmet radio. "Some dinosaurs have two brains, one in the head, another far down the spinal column. We stay away from those. That's stretching luck. Put your first two shots into the eyes, if you can, blind them, and go back into the brain."

The Machine howled. Time was a film run backward. Suns fled and ten million moons fled after them. "Think," said Eckels. "Every hunter that ever lived would envy us today. This makes Africa seem like Illinois."

The Machine slowed; its scream fell to a murmur. The Machine stopped.

The sun stopped in the sky.

> The fog that had enveloped the Machine blew away and they were in an old time, a very old time indeed, three hunters and two Safari Heads with their blue metal guns across their knees.

"Christ isn't born yet," said Travis. "Moses has not gone to the mountain to talk with God. The Pyramids are still in the earth, waiting to be cut out and put up. Remember that. Alexander, Caesar, Napoleon, Hitler—none of them exists."

English Coach

By "get a dinosaur *cold*," Eckels wants to know if the guns are powerful enough to kill a dinosaur right away. The word "cold" is used in a negative way here. If someone gave you the "cold" shoulder, would he or she be friendly or unfriendly to you?

_____

Comprehension Check

Reread the boxed sentence. Number the events in the order in which they occur.
- ☐ The Time Machine goes back 60 million years.
- ☐ Eckels pays $10,000 to go on the safari.
- ☐ Eckels reads a sign about Time Safari, Inc.

The men nodded.

"That"—Mr. Travis pointed—"is the jungle of sixty million two thousand and fifty-five years before President Keith."

He indicated a metal path that struck off into green wilderness, over steaming swamp, among giant ferns and palms.

"And that," he said, "is the Path, laid by Time Safari for your use. It floats six inches above the earth. Doesn't touch so much as one grass blade, flower, or tree. It's an anti-gravity metal. Its purpose is to keep you from touching this world of the past in any way. Stay on the Path. Don't go off it. I repeat. *Don't go off*. For any reason! If you fall off, there's a penalty. And don't shoot any animal we don't okay."

"Why?" asked Eckels.

They sat in the ancient wilderness. Far birds' cries blew on a wind, and the smell of tar and an old salt sea, moist grasses, and flowers the color of blood.

"We don't want to change the Future. We don't belong here in the Past. The government doesn't *like* us here. We have to pay big graft to keep our franchise. A Time Machine is finicky business. Not knowing it, we might kill an important animal, a small bird, a roach, a flower even, thus destroying an important link in a growing species."

"That's not clear," said Eckels.

"All right," Travis continued, "say we accidentally kill one mouse here. That means all the future families of this one particular mouse are destroyed, right?"

"Right."

"And all the families of the families of the families of that one mouse! With a stamp of your foot, you **annihilate** first one, then a dozen, then a thousand, a million, a *billion* possible mice!"

Word Power

annihilate (ə ni′ə lāt′) *v.* to destroy completely

94

"So they're dead," said Eckels. "So what?"

"So what?" Travis snorted quietly. "Well, what about the foxes that'll need those mice to survive? For want of ten mice, a fox dies. For want of ten foxes, a lion starves. For want of a lion, all manner of insects, vultures, infinite billions of life forms are thrown into chaos and destruction. Eventually it all boils down to this: fifty-nine million years later, a cave man, one of a dozen on the *entire* world, goes hunting wild boar or saber-tooth tiger for food. But you, friend, have stepped on all the tigers in that region. By stepping on one single mouse. So the cave man starves. And the cave man, please note, is not just any **expendable** man, no! He is an *entire future nation.* From his loins would have sprung ten sons. From their loins one hundred sons, and thus onward to a civilization. Destroy this one man, and you destroy a race, a people, an entire history of life. It is comparable to slaying some of Adam's grandchildren. The stomp of your foot, on one mouse, could start an earthquake, the effects of which could shake our earth and destinies down through Time, to their very foundations.

Word Power

expendable (iks pen´də bəl) *adj.* not necessary; able to be sacrificed without being missed

Background Info

Travis mentions "Adam's grandchildren." Here he is referring to the descendants of Adam and Eve from the Bible.

95

Reading Skill

Predict Reread the highlighted sentence. Travis stresses how important it is to stay on the Path. Do you think someone will step off it? What might happen?

_____

_____

_____

Background Info

This story was first published in 1952. By "a change in social temperament," Bradbury may be talking about the fears many people in the United States during the 1950s had of countries turning communist. This conflict between the United States and the U.S.S.R. was called the "Cold War" because it was a war of ideas rather than of weapons.

Comprehension Check

Reread the boxed sentences. Why is it important that they wear oxygen helmets?

_____

_____

_____

_____

With the death of that one cave man, a billion others yet unborn are throttled in the womb. Perhaps Rome never rises on its seven hills. Perhaps Europe is forever a dark forest, and only Asia waxes healthy and teeming. Step on a mouse and you crush the Pyramids. Step on a mouse and you leave your print, like a Grand Canyon, across Eternity. Queen Elizabeth might never be born. Washington might not cross the Delaware, there might never be a United States at all. So be careful. Stay on the Path. _Never_ step off!"

"I see," said Eckels. "Then it wouldn't pay for us even to touch the _grass_?"

"Correct. Crushing certain plants could add up infinitesimally. A little error here would multiply in sixty million years, all out of proportion. Of course maybe our theory is wrong. Maybe Time can't be changed by us. Or maybe it can be changed only in little subtle ways. A dead mouse here makes an insect imbalance there, a population disproportion later, a bad harvest further on, a depression, mass starvation, and, finally, a change in social temperament in far-flung countries. Something much more subtle, like that. Perhaps only a soft breath, a whisper, a hair, pollen on the air, such a slight, slight change that unless you looked close you wouldn't see it. Who knows? Who really can say he knows? We don't know. We're guessing. But until we do know for certain whether our messing around in Time can make a big roar or a little rustle in history, we're being careful. This Machine, this Path, your clothing and bodies, were sterilized, as you know, before the journey. We wear these oxygen helmets so we can't introduce our bacteria into an ancient atmosphere."

"How do we know which animals to shoot?"

"They're marked with red paint," said Travis. "Today, before our journey, we sent Lesperance here back with the Machine. He came to this particular era and followed certain animals."

"Studying them?"

"Right," said Lesperance. "I track them through their entire existence, noting which of them lives longest. Very few. How many times they mate. Not often. Life's short. When I find one that's going to die when a tree falls on him, or one that drowns in a tar pit, I note the exact hour, minute, and second. I shoot a paint bomb. It leaves a red patch on his hide. We can't miss it. Then I correlate our arrival in the Past so that we meet the Monster not more than two minutes before he would have died anyway. This way, we kill only animals with no future, that are never going to mate again. You see how *careful* we are?"

"But if you came back this morning in Time," said Eckels eagerly, "you must've bumped into us, our Safari! How did it turn out? Was it successful? Did all of us get through—alive?"

Travis and Lesperance gave each other a look.

"That'd be a *paradox,*" said the latter. "Time doesn't permit that sort of mess—a man meeting himself. When such occasions threaten, Time steps aside. Like an airplane hitting an air pocket. You felt the Machine jump just before we stopped? That was us passing ourselves on the way back to the Future. We saw nothing. There's no way of telling *if* this expedition was a success, *if* we got our monster, or whether all of us—meaning *you,* Mr. Eckels— got out alive."

Eckels smiled palely.

"Cut that," said Travis sharply. "Everyone on his feet!"

They were ready to leave the Machine. The jungle was high and the jungle was broad and the jungle was the entire world forever and forever. Sounds like music and sounds like flying tents filled the sky, and those were pterodactyls soaring with cavernous gray wings, gigantic bats of delirium and night fever. Eckels, balanced on the narrow Path, aimed his rifle playfully.

Background Info

In the La Brea tar pits in Los Angeles, California, well-preserved skeletons of prehistoric Ice Age saber-toothed tigers, bears, llamas, camels, wolves, sloths, and other animals have been found.

English Coach

The word *paradox* means "something that doesn't make sense; or when two facts appear to be in conflict with each other." Which of the following sentences is a paradox? Check the correct response.

☐ You can buy the car in any color, as long as it's black.

☐ You can buy the car in any color you choose.

Did You Know?
Pterodactyls (ter ´ ə dak ´ tilz) are extinct flying reptiles with wingspans of up to forty feet.

Reading Skill

Evaluate Reread the highlighted paragraph. Eckels is still thinking about the election, even though he is about to face a *Tyrannosaurus rex*. Why do you think the author wants to remind you about the election? Why might the election be so important?

_____

_____

_____

_____

"Stop that!" said Travis. "Don't even aim for fun, blast you! If your gun should go off—"

Eckels flushed. "Where's our *Tyrannosaurus*?"

Lesperance checked his wristwatch. "Up ahead. We'll bisect his trail in sixty seconds. Look for the red paint! Don't shoot till we give the word. Stay on the Path. *Stay on the Path!*"

They moved forward in the wind of morning.

"Strange," murmured Eckels. "Up ahead, sixty million years, Election Day over. Keith made President. Everyone celebrating. And here we are, a million years lost, and they don't exist. The things we worried about for months, a lifetime, not even born or thought about yet."

"Safety catches off, everyone!" ordered Travis. "You, first shot, Eckels. Second, Billings. Third, Kramer."

"I've hunted tiger, wild boar, buffalo, elephant, but now, this is *it*," said Eckels. "I'm shaking like a kid."

"Ah," said Travis.

Everyone stopped.

Travis raised his hand. "Ahead," he whispered. "In the mist. There he is. There's His Royal Majesty now."

The jungle was wide and full of twitterings, rustlings, murmurs, and sighs.

Suddenly it all ceased, as if someone had shut a door.

Silence.

A sound of thunder.

STOP Stop here for **Break Time** on the next page.

Break Time

Complete the story map with details about what you have read so far. In the exposition, tell who the characters are. Explain the setting and the main problem that the characters face.

   Then complete the rising action by finishing the sentences in the order in which they occurred. Finally, write your prediction about what you think will happen next.

Exposition:

Characters _____

Setting _____

Problem _____

_____

Rising Action:

1. Eckels pays $10,000 to _____

2. They go into the Machine and _____

3. Travis warns everyone to _____

4. In the forest they eventually see _____

What do you think will happen next? Write your prediction.

_____

_____

GO   Turn the page to continue reading.

Out of the mist, one hundred yards away, came *Tyrannosaurus rex*.

"It," whispered Eckels. "It . . ."

"Sh!"

It came on great oiled, **resilient,** striding legs. It towered thirty feet above half of the trees, a great evil god, folding its delicate watchmaker's claws close to its oily reptilian chest. Each lower leg was a piston, a thousand pounds of white bone, sunk in thick

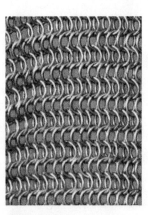

ropes of muscle, sheathed over in a gleam of pebbled skin like the mail of a terrible warrior. Each thigh was a ton of meat, ivory, and steel mesh. And from the great breathing cage of the upper body those two delicate arms dangled out front, arms with hands which might pick up and examine men like toys, while the snake neck coiled. And the head itself, a ton of sculptured stone, lifted easily upon the sky. Its mouth gaped, exposing a fence of teeth like daggers. Its eyes rolled, ostrich eggs, empty of all expression save hunger. It closed its mouth in a death grin. It ran, its pelvic bones crushing aside trees and bushes, its taloned feet clawing damp earth, leaving prints six inches deep wherever it settled its weight. It ran with a gliding ballet step, far too poised and balanced for its ten tons. It moved into a sunlit arena warily, its beautifully reptilian hands feeling the air.

"Why, why," Eckels twitched his mouth. "It could reach up and grab the moon."

"Sh!" Travis jerked angrily. "He hasn't seen us yet."

Reading Skill

Evaluate Reread the highlighted sentences. Underline the descriptive details of the dinosaur in the highlighted sentences. How effectively do the details help you picture how the dinosaur looked or acted?

_____

_____

_____

_____

Word Power

resilient (ri zil´yənt) *adj.* capable of springing back to shape after being bent, stretched, or smashed

100

"It can't be killed." Eckels pronounced this verdict quietly, as if there could be no argument. He had weighed the evidence and this was his considered opinion. The rifle in his hands seemed a cap gun. "We were fools to come. This is impossible."

"Shut up!" hissed Travis.

"Nightmare."

"Turn around," commanded Travis. "Walk quietly to the Machine. We'll remit one half your fee."

"I didn't realize it would be this *big*," said Eckels. "I miscalculated, that's all. And now I want out."

"It *sees* us!"

"There's the red paint on its chest!"

The Tyrant Lizard raised itself. Its armored flesh glittered like a thousand green coins. The coins, crusted with slime, steamed. In the slime, tiny insects wriggled, so that the entire body seemed to twitch and undulate, even while the monster itself did not move. It exhaled. The stink of raw flesh blew down the wilderness.

"Get me out of here," said Eckels. "It was never like this before. I was always sure I'd come through alive. I had good guides, good safaris, and safety. This time, I figured wrong. I've met my match and admit it. This is too much for me to get hold of."

"Don't run," said Lesperance. "Turn around. Hide in the Machine."

"Yes." Eckels seemed to be numb. He looked at his feet as if trying to make them move. He gave a grunt of helplessness.

"Eckels!"

He took a few steps, blinking, shuffling.

"Not *that* way!"

The Monster, at the first motion, lunged forward with a terrible scream. It covered one hundred yards in four seconds. The rifles jerked up and blazed fire. A windstorm from the beast's mouth engulfed them in the stench of slime and old blood. The Monster roared, teeth glittering with sun.

Literary Element

Plot Reread the highlighted sentences. Which part of the story's plot do these sentences belong to? Check the correct response.

- [ ] exposition
- [ ] rising action
- [ ] resolution
- [ ] falling action

Reading Skill

Predict How did you predict the trip would turn out for Eckels? Do you need to revise your prediction now about what will happen to Eckels? What details support your original prediction?

_____

_____

_____

_____

Reading Skill

Predict Travis had warned everyone to stay on the Path. What did you predict would happen? Does your prediction match what really happens? Revise your prediction below as needed.

_____

_____

_____

_____

_____

Eckels, not looking back, walked blindly to the edge of the Path, his gun limp in his arms, stepped off the Path, and walked, not knowing it, in the jungle. His feet sank into green moss. His legs moved him, and he felt alone and remote from the events behind.

The rifles cracked again. Their sound was lost in shriek and lizard thunder. The great lever of the reptile's tail swung up, lashed sideways. Trees exploded in clouds of leaf and branch. The Monster twitched its jeweler's hands down to fondle at the men, to twist them in half, to crush them like berries, to cram them into its teeth and its screaming throat. Its boulder-stone eyes leveled with the men. They saw themselves mirrored. They fired at the metallic eyelids and the blazing black iris.

Like a stone idol, like a mountain avalanche, *Tyrannosaurus* fell. Thundering, it clutched trees, pulled them with it. It wrenched and tore the metal Path. The men flung themselves back and away. The body hit, ten tons of cold flesh and stone. The guns fired. The Monster lashed its armored tail, twitched its snake jaws, and lay still. A fount of blood spurted from its throat. Somewhere inside, a sac of fluids burst. Sickening gushes drenched the hunters. They stood, red and glistening.

The thunder faded.

The jungle was silent. After the avalanche, a green peace. After the nightmare, morning.

Billings and Kramer sat on the pathway and threw up. Travis and Lesperance stood with smoking rifles, cursing steadily.

In the Time Machine, on his face, Eckels lay shivering. He had found his way back to the Path, climbed into the Machine.

Travis came walking, glanced at Eckels, took cotton gauze from a metal box, and returned to the others, who were sitting on the Path.

"Clean up."

They wiped the blood from their helmets. They began to curse too. The Monster lay, a hill of solid flesh. Within, you could hear the sighs and murmurs as the furthest chambers of it died, the organs **malfunctioning,** liquids running a final instant from pocket to sac to spleen, everything shutting off, closing up forever. It was like standing by a wrecked locomotive or a steam shovel at quitting time, all valves being released or levered tight. Bones cracked; the tonnage of its own flesh, off balance, dead weight, snapped the delicate forearms, caught underneath. The meat settled, quivering.

Another cracking sound. Overhead, a gigantic tree branch broke from its heavy mooring, fell. It crashed upon the dead beast with finality.

"There." Lesperance checked his watch. "Right on time. That's the giant tree that was scheduled to fall and kill this animal originally." He glanced at the two hunters. "You want the trophy picture?"

"What?"

"We can't take a trophy back to the Future. The body has to stay right here where it would have died originally, so the insects, birds, and bacteria can get at it, as they were intended to. Everything in balance. The body stays. But we *can* take a picture of you standing near it."

The two men tried to think, but gave up, shaking their heads.

Comprehension Check

Reread the boxed paragraph. What is the author describing?

_____

_____

_____

Reading Skill

Evaluate Reread the highlighted sentence. The hunters thought they could kill a dinosaur right before it was supposed to die naturally. This would then prevent any changes to future events. Can you think of any problems with their reasoning?

_____

_____

_____

_____

_____

_____

_____

Word Power

malfunctioning (mal´fungk´shən ing) *adj.* not working properly

103

They let themselves be led along the metal Path. They sank wearily into the Machine cushions. They gazed back at the ruined Monster, the stagnating mound, where already strange reptilian birds and golden insects were busy at the steaming armor.

A sound on the floor of the Time Machine stiffened them. Eckels sat there, shivering.

"I'm sorry," he said at last.

"Get up!" cried Travis.

Eckels got up.

"Go out on that Path alone," said Travis. He had his rifle pointed. "You're not coming back in the Machine. We're leaving you here!"

Lesperance seized Travis' arm. "Wait—"

"Stay out of this!" Travis shook his hand away. "This fool nearly killed us. But it isn't *that* so much, no. It's his *shoes*! Look at them! He ran off the Path. That *ruins* us! We'll forfeit! Thousands of dollars of insurance! We guarantee no one leaves the Path. He left it. Oh, the fool! I'll have to report to the government. They might revoke our license to travel. Who knows *what* he's done to Time, to History!"

"Take it easy, all he did was kick up some dirt."

"How do we *know*?" cried Travis. "We don't know anything! It's all a mystery! Get out there, Eckels!"

Eckels fumbled his shirt. "I'll pay anything. A hundred thousand dollars!"

Travis glared at Eckels' checkbook and spat. "Go out there. The Monster's next to the Path. Stick your arms up to your elbows in his mouth. Then you can come back with us."

"That's unreasonable!"

Comprehension Check

Reread the boxed paragraph. Why is Travis so angry with Eckels? Check the correct response.

- [ ] because Eckels brought dirt into the Time Machine
- [ ] because he realizes that Eckels ran off the Path
- [ ] because Travis has no insurance

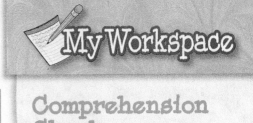
"The Monster's dead, you idiot. The bullets! The bullets can't be left behind. They don't belong in the Past; they might change anything. Here's my knife. Dig them out!"

The jungle was alive again, full of the old tremorings and bird cries. Eckels turned slowly to regard the **primeval** garbage dump, that hill of nightmares and terror. After a long time, like a sleepwalker, he shuffled out along the Path.

He returned, shuddering, five minutes later, his arms soaked and red to the elbows. He held out his hands. Each held a number of steel bullets. Then he fell. He lay where he fell, not moving.

"You didn't have to make him do that," said Lesperance.

"Didn't I? It's too early to tell." Travis nudged the still body. "He'll live. Next time he won't go hunting game like this. Okay." He jerked his thumb wearily at Lesperance. "Switch on. Let's go home."

1492. 1776. 1812.

They cleaned their hands and faces. They changed their caking shirts and pants. Eckels was up and around again, not speaking. Travis glared at him for a full ten minutes.

"Don't look at me," cried Eckels. "I haven't done anything."

"Who can tell?"

"Just ran off the Path, that's all, a little mud on my shoes—what do you want me to do—get down and pray?"

"We might need it. I'm warning you, Eckels, I might kill you yet. I've got my gun ready."

"I'm innocent. I've done nothing."

1999. 2000. 2055.

The Machine stopped.

"Get out," said Travis.

Word Power

primeval (pri mē ′ vəl) *adj.* having to do with the first or earliest age of the world; primitive

Comprehension Check

Reread the boxed paragraph. What does Travis tell Eckels to do? Why does he tell him to do that?

_____

_____

_____

_____

_____

Background Info

Important historical events happened in each of these years. In 1492, Columbus landed in the Americas. In 1776, the American colonies declared their independence from Great Britain. In 1812, a war began between the United States and Great Britain.

Literary Element

Plot Reread the highlighted sentences. How do these story clues hint at the resolution of the story?

_____

_____

_____

_____

_____

The room was there as they had left it. But not the same as they had left it. The same man sat behind the same desk. But the same man did not quite sit behind the same desk.

Travis looked around swiftly. "Everything okay here?" he snapped.

"Fine. Welcome home!"

Travis did not relax. He seemed to be looking at the very atoms of the air itself, at the way the sun poured through the one high window.

"Okay, Eckels, get out. Don't ever come back."

Eckels could not move.

"You heard me," said Travis. "What're you *staring* at?"

Eckels stood smelling of the air, and there was a thing to the air, a chemical taint so subtle, so slight, that only a faint cry of his subliminal senses warned him it was there. The colors, white, gray, blue, orange, in the wall, in the furniture, in the sky beyond the window, were . . . were . . . And there was a feel. His flesh twitched. His hands twitched. He stood drinking the oddness with the pores of his body. Somewhere, someone must have been screaming one of those whistles that only a dog can hear. His body screamed silence in return. Beyond this room, beyond this wall, beyond this man who was not quite the same man seated at this desk that was not quite the same desk . . . lay an entire world of streets and people. What sort of world it was now, there was no telling. He could feel them moving there, beyond the walls, almost, like so many chess pieces blown in a dry wind. . . .

But the immediate thing was the sign painted on the office wall, the same sign he had read earlier today on first entering.

Somehow, the sign had changed:

TYME SEFARI INC.
SEFARIS TU ANY YEER EN THE PAST.
YU NAIM THE ANIMALL.
WEE TAEKYUTHAIR.
YU SHOOT ITT.

Eckels felt himself fall into a chair. He fumbled crazily at the thick slime on his boots. He held up a clod of dirt, trembling, "No, it can't be. Not a *little* thing like that. No!"

Embedded in the mud, glistening green and gold and black, was a butterfly, very beautiful and very dead.

Reading Skill
Evaluate Reread the highlighted text. Why do you think the author uses misspelled words to show that the future has changed?

_____

_____

_____

_____

_____

_____

Comprehension Check

Reread the boxed text. At the beginning of the story, Deutscher is described an "an anti-everything man." How is he described now?

_____

_____

_____

Reading Skill

Predict What did you predict would happen to Eckels? How close was your prediction to what actually happens to Eckels?

_____

_____

_____

_____

_____

"Not a little thing like *that*! Not a butterfly!" cried Eckels.

It fell to the floor, an **exquisite** thing, a small thing that could upset balances and knock down a line of small dominoes and then big dominoes and then gigantic dominoes, all down the years across Time. Eckels' mind whirled. It *couldn't* change things. Killing one butterfly couldn't be *that* important! Could it?

His face was cold. His mouth trembled, asking: "Who—Who won the presidential election yesterday?

The man behind the desk laughed. "You joking? You know very well. Deutscher, of course! Who else? Not that fool weakling Keith. We got an iron man now, a man with guts!" The official stopped. "What's wrong?"

Eckels moaned. He dropped to his knees. He scrabbled at the golden butterfly with shaking fingers. "Can't we," he pleaded to the world, to himself, to the officials, to the Machine, "can't we take it *back*, can't we *make* it alive again? Can't we start over? Can't we—"

He did not move. Eyes shut, he waited, shivering. He heard Travis breathe loud in the room; he heard Travis shift his rifle, click the safety catch, and raise the weapon.

There was a sound of thunder.

Word Power

exquisite (iks kwiz´it) *adj.* beautiful and delicate

Respond to Literature

A Sound of Thunder

A Comprehension Check

Answer the following questions in the spaces provided.

1. How does Eckels react when he sees the *Tyrannosaurus rex*?

   _____

2. What do the men find out when they return from their trip?

   _____

B Reading Skills

Answer the following questions in the spaces provided.

1. **Predict** What clues help the reader predict that the future will be changed by the hunters' safari?

   _____

   _____

   _____

2. **Predict** At the end of the story, the Time Safari sign is misspelled. Use this clue to make a prediction about what life might be like in the "changed" future. _____

   _____

3. **Evaluate** Do you think the sentence "There was a sound of thunder" is a good ending for the story? Explain why or why not. _____

   _____

   _____

C Word Power

Complete each sentence below, using one of the words in the box.

dictatorship	annihilate	expendable
resilient	malfunctioning	primeval	exquisite

1. The _____ flowers popped back up after being flattened by the strong storm.

2. Yolanda took her _____ computer back to the store to get it fixed.

3. The swarm of grasshoppers managed to _____ the farmer's corn crop.

4. The hikers half-expected to see a dinosaur as they passed through the _____ forest.

5. No species is _____ in a rain forest—every plant, insect, and animal is important.

6. After a long civil war, the government changed from a _____ to a democracy.

7. Rachel was so surprised when she opened the gift box and found the _____ diamond ring.

D Literary Element: Plot

Read the passages below from "A Sound of Thunder." As you read, think about what the passages tell you about the plot of the story. Then answer the questions that follow.

"We guarantee nothing," said the official, "except the dinosaurs."[1] He turned.[2] "This is Mr. Travis, your Safari Guide in the Past.[3] He'll tell you what and where to shoot."[4]

"Get me out of here," said Eckels.[5] "It was never like this before.[6] I was always sure I'd come through alive."[7]

Eckels, not looking back, walked blindly to the edge of the Path, his gun limp in his arms, stepped off the Path, and walked, not knowing it, in the jungle.[8]

1. What do sentences 1–4 tell you about the story? How does this exposition help set the story? _____

_____

_____

2. How does the rising action in sentences 5–7 lead to the climax in sentence 8? Why is sentence 8 the turning point? How do you know?

_____

_____

_____

E A Journal Entry

Imagine you are either Billings or Kramer in the story. You are in the Time Machine on your way back to the present. You are writing a journal entry about your experience. Tell what happened on the safari and what you saw when you arrived back home.

Today's date: _____

I stepped into the Time Machine with our guide and two other hunters. I didn't like Eckels. I thought that he was

_____

As we traveled back in time, Travis told us why we couldn't go off the Path. He said that if we did, _____

_____

We stepped onto the Path. Ahead of us we saw the Tyrannosaurus rex. It looked terrifying. It towered thirty feet above half of the trees. It had _____

Eckels was afraid. He _____

_____

I shot the dinosaur with the other hunter. Travis was angry with Eckels. He made him _____
When we arrived back home, things had changed. Eckels had stepped on a butterfly in the past, which changed history. Travis was very angry. As I left the office, I heard the sound of a gun. Surely Travis didn't kill Eckels! But now I must live in this changed world where

_____

_____

Assessment

Fill in the circle next to each correct answer.

1. Why does Eckels want to travel back in time?
   - ○ A. to study dinosaurs
   - ○ B. to kill a dinosaur
   - ○ C. to change the future
   - ○ D. to change the past

2. Which quote from the story helps you predict that the future will be changed?
   - ○ A. "This makes Africa seem like Illinois."
   - ○ B. "If the election had gone badly yesterday, I might be here now running away from the results."
   - ○ C. "Right on time. That's the giant tree that was scheduled to fall and kill this animal originally."
   - ○ D. "The stomp of your foot, on one mouse, could start an earthquake, the effects of which could shake our earth ... ."

3. Who is most to blame for the future changing?
   - ○ A. Eckels, for killing the butterfly
   - ○ B. Travis, for not leaving Eckels in the past
   - ○ C. Keith, for winning the election
   - ○ D. Lesperance, for talking Travis out of leaving Eckels in the past

4. Which statement **best** states the plot of the story "A Sound of Thunder"?
   - ○ A. Eckels is a cowardly hunter who kills a butterfly.
   - ○ B. People elect a bad man as president of the United States instead of a good leader.
   - ○ C. A company brings hunters back in time on a safari to kill dinosaurs.
   - ○ D. A hunter changes history when he goes back in time and accidentally kills a butterfly.

5. Which of the following words means "beautiful and delicate"?
   - ○ A. resilient
   - ○ B. exquisite
   - ○ C. primeval
   - ○ D. expendable

Get Ready to Read!

Through the Tunnel

What You Know

Think of a time when you watched someone try to do something difficult or challenging. Did watching him or her make you want to try it yourself?

Reason to Read

Read this short story to find out how one boy faces a difficult challenge.

Background Info

Underwater diving with no equipment other than goggles is called breath-hold diving or free diving. This type of diving can be very dangerous because of the water pressure. Water is more than a thousand times as dense as air. Most breath-hold divers can stay underwater for less than one minute. With training, some divers can stay underwater for two minutes.

"Through the Tunnel" takes place at a beach resort along the Mediterranean Sea. There are many bays and peninsulas along the coastline that offer good swimming and diving places. Many Europeans and people from other parts of the world spend their vacation in this region.

Word Power

contrition (kən trish′ ən) *n.* a feeling of sorrow for having done something wrong; p. 116
After losing his temper with his sister, Alex apologized out of *contrition*.

idly (īd′ lē) *adv.* without doing any purposeful activity; p. 119
The mothers chatted *idly* while their children played in the park.

beseeching (bi sēch′ ing) *adj.* pleading; begging; p. 121
"Please let me have a party for my birthday!" Randi said, hopeful and *beseeching*.

inquisitive (in kwiz′ ə tiv) *adj.* curious; p. 121
The *inquisitive* kitten squeezed into the pipe and became stuck.

torment (tôr′ ment) *n.* extreme pain or suffering; p. 125
The pizza commercial was a *torment* to Brad, who had just had his tonsils removed.

incredulous (in krej′ ə ləs) *adj.* unwilling to believe something; p. 126
Carmen was *incredulous* when she heard that a UFO had been sighted over her house.

convulsive (kən vul′ siv) *adj.* sudden and violent; p. 127
The man's *convulsive* sneeze made everyone in the movie theater jump.

lapses (laps′ iz) *n.* temporary interruptions; p. 128
Lack of sleep can cause you to have *lapses* in concentration.

Answer the following questions, using one of the new words above. Write your answers in the spaces provided.

1. Which word goes with "brief moments of forgetfulness"? _____

2. Which word goes with "interested in finding out more"? _____

3. Which word goes with "pain and suffering"? _____

4. Which word goes with "violent shaking"? _____

5. Which word goes with "unbelieving"? _____

6. Which word goes with "not doing any work at all"? _____

7. Which word goes with "being sorry after doing something wrong"? _____

8. Which word goes with "asking for something very sincerely"? _____

Through the Tunnel

Doris Lessing

Reading Skill

Predict Reread the title and the highlighted sentence. What do you think the story will be about? Do you think there will be any danger involved?

_____

_____

_____

English Coach

The word *contrition* is formed from the base word *contrite*, which means "feeling very sorry," and the suffix *-tion*, which means "act of" or "condition of." What word then means the "act of connecting"?

_____

Going to the shore on the first morning of the vacation, the young English boy stopped at a turning of the path and looked down at a wild and rocky bay, and then over to the crowded beach he knew so well from other years. His mother walked on in front of him, carrying a bright striped bag in one hand.

Her other arm, swinging loose, was very white in the sun. The boy watched that white, naked arm, and turned his eyes, which had a frown behind them, toward the bay and back again to his mother. When she felt he was not with her, she swung around. "Oh, there you are, Jerry!" she said. She looked impatient, then smiled. "Why, darling, would you rather not come with me? Would you rather—" She frowned, conscientiously worrying over what amusements he might secretly be longing for, which she had been too busy or too careless to imagine. He was very familiar with that anxious, apologetic smile. **Contrition** sent him running after her. And yet, as he ran, he looked back over his shoulder at the wild bay; and all morning, as he played on the safe beach, he was thinking of it.

Word Power

contrition (kən trish´ ən) *n.* a feeling of sorrow for having done something wrong

116

Next morning, when it was time for the routine of swimming and sunbathing, his mother said, "Are you tired of the usual beach, Jerry? Would you like to go somewhere else?"

"Oh, no!" he said quickly, smiling at her out of that unfailing impulse of contrition—a sort of chivalry. Yet, walking down the path with her, he blurted out, "I'd like to go and have a look at those rocks down there."

She gave the idea her attention. It was a wild looking place, and there was no one there; but she said, "Of course, Jerry. When you've had enough, come to the big beach. Or just go straight back to the villa, if you like." She walked away, that bare arm, now slightly reddened from yesterday's sun, swinging. And he almost ran after her again, feeling it unbearable that she should go by herself, but he did not.

She was thinking, Of course he's old enough to be safe without me. Have I been keeping him too close? He mustn't feel he ought to be with me. I must be careful.

He was an only child, eleven years old. She was a widow. She was determined to be neither possessive nor lacking in devotion. She went worrying off to her beach.

As for Jerry, once he saw that his mother had gained her beach, he began the steep descent to the bay. From where he was, high up among red-brown rocks, it was a scoop of moving bluish green fringed with white. As he went lower, he saw that it spread among small promontories and inlets of rough, sharp rock, and the crisping, lapping surface showed stains of purple and darker blue. Finally, as he ran sliding and scraping down the last few yards, he saw an edge of white surf and the shallow, luminous movement of water over white sand, and, beyond that, a solid, heavy blue.

Did You Know?
Promontories are high points of land or rock overlooking the water.

Background Info

Chivalry (shiv´ əl rē) refers to the code of behavior of knights in medieval times. Knights were expected to act with honor and courtesy, especially toward women. In this context, *chivalry* means "an act of courtesy or politeness."

Reading Skill

Evaluate Reread the highlighted paragraph. Do you agree with the mother's reasoning? Should Jerry be given freedom to explore on his own? Why or why not?

_____

_____

_____

_____

Comprehension Check

Reread the boxed paragraph. What is the bay like? Check the correct response.
- ☐ wild and rocky
- ☐ quiet and flat
- ☐ dark with no sand

He ran straight into the water and began swimming. He was a good swimmer. He went out fast over the gleaming sand, over a middle region where rocks lay like discolored monsters under the surface, and then he was in the real sea—a warm sea where irregular cold currents from the deep water shocked his limbs.

When he was so far out that he could look back not only on the little bay but past the promontory that was between it and the big beach, he floated on the buoyant surface and looked for his mother. There she was, a speck of yellow under an umbrella that looked like a slice of orange peel. He swam back to shore, relieved at being sure she was there, but all at once very lonely.

On the edge of a small cape that marked the side of the bay away from the promontory was a loose scatter of rocks. Above them, some boys were stripping off their clothes. They came running, naked, down to the rocks. The English boy swam toward them, but kept his distance at a stone's throw. They were of that coast; all of them were burned smooth dark brown and speaking a language he did not understand. To be with them, of them, was a craving that filled his whole body. He swam a little closer; they turned and watched him with narrowed, alert dark eyes. Then one smiled and waved. It was enough. In a minute, he had swum in and was on the rocks beside them, smiling with a desperate, nervous supplication. They shouted cheerful greetings at him; and then, as he preserved his nervous, uncomprehending smile, they understood that he was a foreigner strayed from his own beach, and they proceeded to forget him. But he was happy. He was with them.

They began diving again and again from a high point into a well of blue sea between rough, pointed rocks. After they had dived and come up, they swam around, hauled themselves up, and waited their turn to dive again. They were big boys—men, to Jerry. He dived, and they watched him; and when he swam around to take his place, they made way for him. He felt he was accepted, and he dived again, carefully, proud of himself.

Connect to the Text

Reread the text boxed in purple. Think of a time you made friends at a beach, a park, or some other place. How did you become part of the group?

_____

_____

_____

_____

Comprehension Check

Reread the paragraph boxed in green. Why does Jerry believe the other boys accept him? Underline the sentence in the paragraph that illustrates this.

Soon the biggest of the boys poised himself, shot down into the water, and did not come up. The others stood about, watching. Jerry, after waiting for the sleek brown head to appear, let out a yell of warning; they looked at him **idly** and turned their eyes back toward the water. After a long time, the boy came up on the other side of a big dark rock, letting the air out of his lungs in a sputtering gasp and a shout of triumph. Immediately the rest of them dived in. One moment, the morning seemed full of chattering boys; the next, the air and the surface of the water were empty. But through the heavy blue, dark shapes could be seen moving and groping.

Jerry dived, shot past the school of underwater swimmers, saw a black wall of rock looming at him, touched it, and bobbed up at once to the surface, where the wall was a low barrier he could see across. There was no one visible; under him, in the water, the dim shapes of the swimmers had disappeared. Then one, and then another of the boys came up on the far side of the barrier of rock, and he understood that they had swum through some gap or hole in it. He plunged down again. He could see nothing through the stinging salt water but the blank rock. When he came up the boys were all on the diving rock, preparing to attempt the feat again. And now, in a panic of failure, he yelled up, in English, "Look at me! Look!" and he began splashing and kicking in the water like a foolish dog.

They looked down gravely, frowning. He knew the frown. At moments of failure, when he clowned to claim his mother's attention, it was with just this grave, embarrassed inspection that she rewarded him. Through his hot shame, feeling the pleading grin on his face like a scar that he could never remove, he looked up at the group of big brown boys on the rock and shouted, "Bonjour! Merci! Au revoir! Monsieur, monsieur!" while he hooked his fingers round his ears and waggled them.

Word Power

idly (īd′ lē) *adv.* without doing any purposeful activity

Background Info

Bonjour! (bôn zhoor′) *Merci!* (mer sē′) *Au revoir!* (ō rə vwä′) *Monsieur!* (mə syœ′) are words in French for "Hello! Thank you! Good-bye! Sir!"

Reread the boxed text. What are the boys able to do that Jerry is not?

_____

_____

_____

_____

Water surged into his mouth; he choked, sank, came up. The rock, lately weighted with boys, seemed to rear up out of the water as their weight was removed. They were flying down past him, now, into the water; the air was full of falling bodies. Then the rock was empty in the hot sunlight. He counted one, two, three...

At fifty, he was terrified. They must all be drowning beneath him, in the watery caves of the rock! At a hundred, he stared around him at the empty hillside, wondering if he should yell for help. He counted faster, faster, to hurry them up, to bring them to the surface quickly, to drown them quickly—anything rather than the terror of counting on and on into the blue emptiness of the morning. And then, at a hundred and sixty, the water beyond the rock was full of boys blowing like brown whales. They swam back to the shore without a look at him.

He climbed back to the diving rock and sat down, feeling the hot roughness of it under his thighs. The boys were gathering up their bits of clothing and running off along the shore to another promontory. They were leaving to get away from him. He cried openly, fists in his eyes. There was no one to see him, and he cried himself out.

Crowded Day at the Beach, 1922. Martha Walter. Oil on board, 16 x 20 in. David David Gallery, Philadelphia.

Why might Jerry not want to go to a beach like this one with his mother?

_____

It seemed to him that a long time had passed, and he swam out to where he could see his mother. Yes, she was still there, a yellow spot under an orange umbrella. He swam back to the big rock, climbed up, and dived into the blue pool among the fanged and angry boulders. Down he went, until he touched the wall of rock again. But the salt was so painful in his eyes that he could not see.

He came to the surface, swam to shore, and went back to the villa to wait for his mother. Soon she walked slowly up the path, swinging her striped bag, the flushed, naked arm dangling beside her. "I want some swimming goggles," he panted, defiant and **beseeching.**

She gave him a patient, **inquisitive** look as she said casually, "Well, of course, darling."

But now, now, now! He must have them this minute, and no other time. He nagged and pestered until she went with him to a shop. As soon as she had bought the goggles, he grabbed them from her hand as if she were going to claim them for herself, and was off, running down the steep path to the bay.

Jerry swam out to the big barrier rock, adjusted the goggles, and dived. The impact of the water broke the rubber-enclosed vacuum, and the goggles came loose. He understood that he must swim down to the base of the rock from the surface of the water. He fixed the goggles tight and firm, filled his lungs, and floated, face down, on the water. Now, he could see. It was as if he had eyes of a different kind—fish eyes that showed everything clear and delicate and wavering in the bright water.

Word Power

beseeching (bi sēch′ ing) *adj.* pleading; begging
inquisitive (in kwiz′ ə tiv) *adj.* curious

Reading Skill

Evaluate Reread the highlighted sentence. The word *defiant* means "challenging or resisting authority." Do you think the author's word choices help show Jerry's struggle here to be independent? Why or why not?

_____

_____

_____

_____

_____

_____

Under him, six or seven feet down, was a floor of perfectly clean, shining white sand, rippled firm and hard by the tides. Two grayish shapes steered there, like long, rounded pieces of wood or slate. They were fish. He saw them nose toward each other, poise motionless, make a dart forward, swerve off, and come around again. It was like a water dance. A few inches above them the water sparkled as if sequins were dropping through it. Fish again—myriads of minute fish, the length of his fingernail, were drifting through the water, and in a moment he could feel the innumerable tiny touches of them against his limbs. It was like swimming in flaked silver. The great rock the big boys had swum through rose sheer out of the white sand—black, tufted lightly with greenish weed. He could see no gap in it. He swam down to its base.

Again and again he rose, took a big chestful of air, and went down. Again and again he groped over the surface of the rock, feeling it, almost hugging it in the desperate need to find the entrance. And then, once, while he was clinging to the black wall, his knees came up, and he shot his feet out forward and they met no obstacle. He had found the hole.

He gained the surface, clambered about the stones that littered the barrier rock until he found a big one, and, with this in his arms, let himself down over the side of the rock. He dropped, with the weight, straight to the sandy floor.

Clinging tight to the anchor of stone, he lay on his side and looked in under the dark shelf at the place where his feet had gone. He could see the hole. It was an irregular, dark gap; but he could not see deep into it. He let go of his anchor, clung with his hands to the edges of the hole, and tried to push himself in.

He got his head in, found his shoulders jammed, moved them in sidewise, and was inside as far as his waist. He could see nothing ahead. Something soft and clammy touched his mouth; he saw a dark frond moving against the grayish rock, and panic filled him. He thought of octopuses, of clinging weed. He pushed himself out backward and caught a glimpse, as he retreated, of a harmless tentacle of seaweed drifting in the mouth of the tunnel. But it was enough. He reached the sunlight, swam to shore, and lay on the diving rock. He looked down into the blue well of water. He knew he must find his way through that cave, or hole, or tunnel, and out the other side.

First, he thought, he must learn to control his breathing. He let himself down into the water with another big stone in his arms, so that he could lie effortlessly on the bottom of the sea. He counted. One, two, three. He counted steadily. He could hear the movement of blood in his chest. Fifty-one, fifty-two... His chest was hurting. He let go of the rock and went up into the air. He saw that the sun was low. He rushed to the villa and found his mother at her supper. She said only, "Did you enjoy yourself?" and he said, "Yes."

Comprehension Check

Reread the boxed sentences. Why does Jerry fail in his first attempt to get through the tunnel? Check the correct response.

- [ ] He runs out of breath.
- [ ] He swallows some seawater.
- [ ] He panics when his shoulders get stuck.
- [ ] He gets frightened by a piece of seaweed.

STOP Stop here for **Break Time** on the next page.

Break Time

Jerry, the main character of "Through the Tunnel," is an eleven-year-old boy. At times he acts maturely, like an adult, and shows that he is growing up and becoming more independent. But at other times, he acts immaturely and shows that in some ways he is still a little boy. Fill in the chart with details from the story that show times when Jerry acts independently and when he acts immaturely.

How Jerry Acts	
How Jerry shows he wants to be independent	**How Jerry shows he is still a young boy**
Jerry wants to leave his mother and go to the rocks.	Jerry at first stays with his mother on her beach.

GO Continue reading on the next page.

All night the boy dreamed of the water-filled cave in the rock, and as soon as breakfast was over he went to the bay.

That night, his nose bled badly. For hours he had been underwater, learning to hold his breath, and now he felt weak and dizzy. His mother said, "I shouldn't overdo things, darling, if I were you."

That day and the next, Jerry exercised his lungs as if everything, the whole of his life, all that he would become, depended upon it. Again his nose bled at night, and his mother insisted on his coming with her the next day. It was a **torment** to him to waste a day of his careful self training, but he stayed with her on that other beach, which now seemed a place for small children, a place where his mother might lie safe in the sun. It was not his beach.

He did not ask for permission, on the following day, to go to his beach. He went, before his mother could consider the complicated rights and wrongs of the matter. A day's rest, he discovered, had improved his count by ten. The big boys had made the passage while he counted a hundred and sixty. He had been counting fast, in his fright. Probably now, if he tried, he could get through that long tunnel, but he was not going to try yet. A curious, most unchildlike persistence, a controlled impatience, made him wait. In the meantime, he lay underwater on the white sand, littered now by stones he had brought down from the upper air, and studied the entrance to the tunnel. He knew every jut and corner of it, as far as it was possible to see. It was as if he already felt its sharpness about his shoulders.

Word Power

torment (tôr´ ment) *n.* extreme pain or suffering

Comprehension Check

Reread the boxed text. What does Jerry decide to do?

_____

_____

He sat by the clock in the villa, when his mother was not near, and checked his time. He was **incredulous** and then proud to find he could hold his breath without strain for two minutes. The words "two minutes," authorized by the clock, brought close the adventure that was so necessary to him.

In another four days, his mother said casually one morning, they must go home. On the day before they left, he would do it. He would do it if it killed him, he said defiantly to himself. But two days before they were to leave—a day of triumph when he increased his count by fifteen—his nose bled so badly that he turned dizzy and had to lie limply over the big rock like a bit of seaweed, watching the thick red blood flow on to the rock and trickle slowly down to the sea. He was frightened. Supposing he turned dizzy in the tunnel? Supposing he died there, trapped? Supposing—his head went around, in the hot sun, and he almost gave up. He thought he would return to the house and lie down, and next summer, perhaps, when he had another year's growth in him—then he would go through the hole.

But even after he had made the decision, or thought he had, he found himself sitting up on the rock and looking down into the water; and he knew that now, this moment, when his nose had only just stopped bleeding, when his head was still sore and throbbing—this was the moment when he would try. If he did not do it now, he never would.

He was trembling with fear that he would not go; and he was trembling with horror at that long, long tunnel under the rock, under the sea. Even in the open sunlight, the barrier rock seemed very wide and very heavy; tons of rock pressed down on where he would go. If he died there, he would lie until one day—perhaps not before next year—those big boys would swim into it and find it blocked.

___

Word Power

incredulous (in krej′ ə ləs) *adj.* unwilling to believe something

He put on his goggles, fitted them tight, tested the vacuum. His hands were shaking. Then he chose the biggest stone he could carry and slipped over the edge of the rock until half of him was in the cool, enclosing water and half in the hot sun. He looked up once at the empty sky, filled his lungs once, twice, and then sank fast to the bottom with the stone. He let it go and began to count. He took the edges of the hole in his hands and drew himself into it, wriggling his shoulders in sidewise as he remembered he must, kicking himself along with his feet.

Soon he was clear inside. He was in a small rock-bound hole filled with yellowish-gray water. The water was pushing him up against the roof. The roof was sharp and pained his back. He pulled himself along with his hands—fast, fast—and used his legs as levers. His head knocked against something; a sharp pain dizzied him. Fifty, fifty-one, fifty-two... He was without light, and the water seemed to press upon him with the weight of rock. Seventy-one, seventy-two... There was no strain on his lungs. He felt like an inflated balloon, his lungs were so light and easy, but his head was pulsing.

He was being continually pressed against the sharp roof, which felt slimy as well as sharp. Again he thought of octopuses, and wondered if the tunnel might be filled with weed that could tangle him. He gave himself a panicky, **convulsive** kick forward, ducked his head, and swam. His feet and hands moved freely, as if in open water. The hole must have widened out. He thought he must be swimming fast, and he was frightened of banging his head if the tunnel narrowed.

Background Info

Divers usually check the seal of their goggles to see that they are tight to prevent water or air from getting in. If the seal is not good, the goggles will not hold securely against the diver's face.

Literary Element

Climax Reread the highlighted sentence and the rest of the text on the page. Underline the phrases that indicate the pain Jerry is feeling.

Word Power

convulsive (kən vul′ siv) *adj.* sudden and violent

A hundred, a hundred and one... The water paled. Victory filled him. His lungs were beginning to hurt. A few more strokes and he would be out. He was counting wildly; he said a hundred and fifteen, and then, a long time later, a hundred and fifteen again. The water was a clear jewel-green all around him. Then he saw, above his head, a crack running up through the rock. Sunlight was falling through it, showing the clean, dark rock of the tunnel, a single mussel shell, and darkness ahead.

Did You Know?
A mussel is a kind of shellfish related to clams, oysters, and scallops.
. . . .

Comprehension Check

Reread the boxed paragraph. Why does Jerry continue to try to swim through the tunnel and not swim back?

_____

_____

_____

He was at the end of what he could do. He looked up at the crack as if it were filled with air and not water, as if he could put his mouth to it to draw in air. A hundred and fifteen, he heard himself say inside his head—but he had said that long ago. He must go on into the blackness ahead, or he would drown. His head was swelling, his lungs cracking. A hundred and fifteen, a hundred and fifteen pounded through his head, and he feebly clutched at rocks in the dark, pulling himself forward, leaving the brief space of sunlit water behind.

He felt he was dying. He was no longer quite conscious. He struggled on in the darkness between **lapses** into unconsciousness. An immense, swelling pain filled his head, and then the darkness cracked with an explosion of green light. His hands, groping forward, met nothing; and his feet, kicking back, propelled him out into the open sea.

Word Power
lapses (laps´ iz) *n.* temporary interruptions

He drifted to the surface, his face turned up to the air. He was gasping like a fish. He felt he would sink now and drown; he could not swim the few feet back to the rock. Then he was clutching it and pulling himself up on to it. He lay face down, gasping. He could see nothing but a red-veined, clotted dark. His eyes must have burst, he thought; they were full of blood. He tore off his goggles and a gout of blood went into the sea. His nose was bleeding, and the blood had filled the goggles.

He scooped up handfuls of water from the cool, salty sea, to splash on his face, and did not know whether it was blood or salt water he tasted. After a time, his heart quieted, his eyes cleared, and he sat up. He could see the local boys diving and playing half a mile away. He did not want them. He wanted nothing but to get back home and lie down.

In a short while, Jerry swam to shore and climbed slowly up the path to the villa. He flung himself on his bed and slept, waking at the sound of feet on the path outside. His mother was coming back. He rushed to the bathroom, thinking she must not see his face with bloodstains, or tearstains, on it. He came out of the bathroom and met her as she walked into the villa, smiling, her eyes lighting up.

"Have a nice morning?" she asked, laying her hand on his warm brown shoulder a moment.

"Oh, yes, thank you," he said.

"You look a bit pale." And then, sharp and anxious, "How did you bang your head?"

"Oh, just banged it," he told her.

Literary Element

Climax Reread the sentences highlighted in blue. What event marks the climax of the story?

_____

_____

_____

_____

Reading Skill

Evaluate Reread the sentences highlighted in green. Do you think Jerry's decision to swim through the tunnel is a good one? Why or why not?

_____

_____

_____

_____

_____

_____

_____

_____

(Rocky Sea Shore), 1916–1919. Edward Hopper. Oil on canvas panel, 9½ x 12¹⁵⁄₁₆ in. Collection of Whitney Museum of American Art, New York. Josephine N. Hopper Bequest. 70.166.

How does the scene shown here affect your understanding of Jerry's beach?

_____

Reading Skill

Predict Reread the highlighted sentences. What do you think Jerry will tell his mother about his experience?

_____

_____

_____

_____

She looked at him closely. He was strained; his eyes were glazed-looking. She was worried. And then she said to herself, Oh, don't fuss! Nothing can happen. He can swim like a fish.

They sat down to lunch together.

"Mummy," he said, "I can stay under water for two minutes— three minutes, at least." It came bursting out of him.

"Can you, darling?" she said. "Well, I shouldn't overdo it. I don't think you ought to swim any more today."

She was ready for a battle of wills, but he gave in at once. It was no longer of the least importance to go to the bay.

Respond to Literature

Through the Tunnel

A Comprehension Check

Answer the following questions in the spaces provided.

1. How is Jerry's beach different from his mother's? _____

_____

_____

2. What must Jerry learn to do before he can try to swim through the tunnel?

_____

_____

B Reading Skills

Answer the following questions in the spaces provided.

1. **Predict** Jerry has proved to himself that he can now swim underwater for an extended time period. What do you think will happen to him after he and his mother leave the beach resort area? Do you think Jerry will change

in any way? _____

_____

_____

2. **Evaluate** Was Jerry's decision to test himself a good one, or did he risk too

much? Explain. _____

_____

_____

_____

C Word Power

Complete each sentence below, using one of the words in the box.

contrition	idly	beseeching	inquisitive
torment	incredulous	convulsive	lapses

1. We took our cat to the vet because of its many _____ in appetite.

2. The _____ of seeing kids play outside while she was inside doing her homework was more than Sara could stand.

3. Her daughter's _____ eyes persuaded Mrs. Anderson to let the stray puppy stay.

4. Chad surfed through the TV channels _____ while he told his father how his math test went that day.

5. Amber was _____ that Mr. Simmons had given the lead role in the school play to Jessica and not to her.

6. Derrick showed his _____ for forgetting his girlfriend's birthday by sending her a bouquet of roses.

7. Everyone stared at Karla because her _____ dance moves made her look like a duck with a broken leg.

8. The _____ child asked one question after another.

D Literary Element: Climax

Read the passages below from "Through the Tunnel." As you read, think about what the sentences reveal about the climax of the story. Then answer the questions that follow.

He felt he was dying.[1] He was no longer quite conscious.[2] He struggled on in the darkness between lapses into unconsciousness.[3] An immense, swelling pain filled his head, and then the darkness cracked with an explosion of green light.[4] His hands, groping forward, met nothing; and his feet, kicking back, propelled him out into the open sea.[5]

He drifted to the surface, his face turned up to the air.[6] He was gasping like a fish.[7] He felt he would sink now and drown; he could not swim the few feet back to the rock.[8] Then he was clutching it and pulling himself up on to it.[9] He lay face down, gasping.[10]

1. In sentences 1–5, how does Jerry feel and what does he see?

_____

_____

_____

2. How do sentences 6–10 show that Jerry is exhausted and that this means the climax is over? _____

_____

_____

E A Letter to Jerry

Imagine that you are Jerry, but are now around four years older. Write a letter to yourself, as the Jerry who was eleven years old. Tell him your opinion about his decision to try to swim through the tunnel. Support your opinion with reasons. Base your reasons on details from the story or on personal experience.

Dear Jerry,

I think your decision to swim by yourself through the tunnel was

very _____

_____

The other boys were able to swim through the tunnel because they were older and more experienced. I think that you should

have _____

_____

But then when you trained to practice holding your breath

underwater, I was _____

_____

_____

I am very happy that you made it through the tunnel. It was a very difficult thing to do.

Sincerely,
Jerry

Assessment

Fill in the circle next to each correct answer.

1. How do the bigger boys make Jerry cry?
   - ○ A. by laughing at him
   - ○ B. by not letting him dive
   - ○ C. by leaving to get away from him
   - ○ D. by not laughing at his clowning around

2. What happens when Jerry practices holding his breath underwater?
   - ○ A. He gets nosebleeds.
   - ○ B. He gets scared and has bad dreams.
   - ○ C. He enjoys swimming even more.
   - ○ D. His appetite improves.

3. Which quote from the story helps you predict that Jerry is going to try to swim through the tunnel?
   - ○ A. "I want some swimming goggles."
   - ○ B. "Look at me! Look!"
   - ○ C. "How did you bang your head?"
   - ○ D. "I shouldn't overdo things, darling, if I were you."

4. What part of the story is the climax?
   - ○ A. when Jerry decides to swim through the tunnel
   - ○ B. when Jerry agrees not to go swimming
   - ○ C. when Jerry buys goggles
   - ○ D. when Jerry makes it through the tunnel

5. Which of the following words means "curious"?
   - ○ A. convulsive
   - ○ B. inquisitive
   - ○ C. beseeching
   - ○ D. incredulous

Get Ready to Read!

Marigolds

Meet Eugenia W. Collier

Eugenia Collier was born in Baltimore, Maryland, in 1928. She taught English at colleges and universities near Baltimore and Washington until she retired in 1996. In 1969, Collier won the Gwendolyn Brooks Award for Fiction for "Marigolds." Many people believe that the story is based on Collier's experiences growing up. However, she does point out that the work is not autobiographical. "Marigolds" was first published in 1969.

What You Know

Have you ever done something in anger that you later felt ashamed of doing?

Reason to Read

Read this short story to find out how a young girl discovers compassion and learns to respect people.

Background Info

From 1929 to about 1939, there was a terrible economic and cultural depression in the United States. During this time, many factories shut down, stock prices dropped, and people lost their jobs and could not find work. Some banks closed their doors, and people lost their life savings. Businesses failed all across the country. Life was difficult for almost all Americans during this time period, which was called the Great Depression.

It is this Depression that is the setting for this short story. Even though the story tells about people being poor and how the lack of money affects families, it also is about the passage from childhood into adulthood for a young girl. This type of struggle can often be more difficult than overcoming economic hardships.

Word Power

futile (fū′ til) *adj.* hopeless; useless; not likely to have results; p. 138
Ms. Brown made a *futile* attempt to cheer up the team after they lost the game.

innocence (in′ ə səns) *n.* the condition of being simple; free from guilt or evil; p. 139
Many parents try to protect their children's *innocence* by not allowing them to watch violent movies.

sophisticated (sə fis′ tə kā′ tid) *adj.* having worldly knowledge and experience; p. 141
As a young girl, Ana was too *sophisticated* to believe in the tooth fairy.

reinforce (rē′ in fôrs′) *v.* to strengthen by repairing or adding something; p. 141
The town used sandbags to *reinforce* the river's levee to keep it from breaking.

preoccupied (prē ok′ yə pīd′) *adj.* absorbed in doing something and not noticing other things; p. 142
Julia was so *preoccupied* with her puzzle that she did not hear her father calling her.

fitful (fit′ fəl) *adj.* not regular or steady; p. 143
Every now and then, they heard the *fitful* crying of the restless baby.

smoldering (smōl′ dər ing) *adj.* feeling anger or hate but keeping it under control; p. 147
Laura looked calm, but inside she had a *smoldering* anger that was building up.

squalor (skwol′ ər) *n.* filth; misery from a state of poverty; p. 148
The family could not live in the *squalor* of the house after the flood ruined it.

**Answer the following questions, using one of the new words above.
Write your answers in the spaces provided.**

1. Which word goes with "keeping angry feelings inside"? _____

2. Which word goes with "living in miserable conditions"? _____

3. Which word goes with "being very experienced and cultured"? _____

4. Which word goes with "sleeping restlessly"? _____

5. Which word goes with "making a hopeless attempt"? _____

6. Which word goes with "thinking of other things all the time"? _____

7. Which word goes with "keeping a fence from falling down"? _____

8. Which word goes with "a simple, childlike person"? _____

Adapted from

Marigolds

Eugenia W. Collier

When I think of the hometown of my youth, all that I seem to remember is dust—the brown, crumbly dust of late summer. I don't know why I should remember only the dust. There must have been lush green lawns and paved streets under leafy shade trees somewhere in town. But memory does not present things as they are, but rather as they _feel._ One other thing I remember, another mismatching memory—a bright splash of sunny yellow against the dust—Miss Lottie's marigolds.

Whenever the memory of those marigolds flashes across my mind, I feel again the confused emotions of adolescence. Joy and rage and wild animal gladness and shame become tangled together in the complicated feelings of fourteen-going-on-fifteen. I recall that awful moment when I was suddenly more woman than child, years ago in Miss Lottie's yard.

I suppose that **futile** waiting was the sad background music of our poor little community when I was young. The Depression that gripped the nation was no new thing to us. The black workers of rural Maryland had always been depressed. I don't know what it was that we were waiting for. Certainly not for the wealth that was "just around the corner." Those were white folks' words, which we never believed. Perhaps we waited for a miracle. But God was not generous with miracles in those days, and so we waited—and waited.

Word Power

futile (fū´ til) _adj._ hopeless; useless; not likely to have results

We children, of course, were only vaguely aware of how poor we were. Having no radios, few newspapers, and no magazines, we were somewhat unaware of the world outside our community. In those days everybody we knew was just as hungry and poorly clothed as we were. Poverty was the cage in which we all were trapped.

By the time I was fourteen, my brother Joey and I were the only children left at our house. Joey was three years younger than I, and a boy and therefore vastly inferior. Each morning our mother and father walked wearily down the dirt road. She to her housekeeping job, he to his daily unsuccessful search for work. After our few chores Joey and I were free to run wild in the sun with other children.

For the most part, those days are unclear in my memory. I do remember, that year, a strange restlessness of body and of spirit. A feeling that something old and familiar was ending, and something unknown and therefore terrifying was beginning.

One day returns to me with special clarity, perhaps because it was the beginning of the experience that in some mysterious way marked the end of **innocence.** I was loafing under the great oak tree in our yard deep in some daydream which I have now forgotten. Joey and a bunch of kids were bored now with the old tire suspended from an oak limb, which had kept them entertained for a while.

"Hey, Lizabeth," Joey yelled. He never talked when he could yell. "Hey, Lizabeth, let's go somewhere."

I came reluctantly from my private world. "Where you want to go? What you want to do?"

The truth was that we were becoming tired of our formless summer days which had become an almost desperate effort to fill up the empty midday hours.

Word Power

innocence (in′ ə səns) *n.* the condition of being simple; free from guilt or evil

Reading Skill

Predict Reread the highlighted sentences. Think about how the narrator has described her childhood. Based on what you have read so far, what do you think will happen to her?

_____

_____

_____

_____

_____

English Coach

The prefix *mid-* in *midday* means "middle." So, *midday* means "the middle of the day." What does *midway* mean? What other words do you know that begin with *mid-*?

_____

_____

_____

_____

How is the house in this picture similar to the description of Miss Lottie's house in the story?

Reading Skill

Evaluate Reread the highlighted paragraph. What is your opinion of the way the narrator treats Miss Lottie? Do you approve of her behavior? Why or why not?

_____

_____

_____

English Coach

The suffix *-less* means "without" or "not capable of being." How is John Burke *ageless* and *mindless*? Check the correct response.

☐ He is very old and thinks very hard all day.

☐ He doesn't seem to age, and he seems to think of nothing all the time.

☐ No one knows how old he is or pays him any attention.

"Let's us go over to Miss Lottie's," said Joey, his eyes sparkling.

The idea caught on at once. Annoying Miss Lottie was always fun. I was still child enough to follow along with the group, back to where Miss Lottie lived.

When Miss Lottie's house came into view we stopped. Miss Lottie's house was the most rundown of all our rundown homes. The boards seemed to remain upright not from being nailed together but rather from leaning together, like a house that a child might have built from cards. The fact that it was still standing suggested a kind of charm that was stronger than the elements. There it stood, a gray, rotting thing with no porch, no shutters, no steps, on a cramped lot with no grass, not even any weeds—a monument to decay.

In front of the house in a squeaky rocking chair sat Miss Lottie's son, John Burke. John Burke was not quite right in the head. Black and ageless, he sat rocking day in and day out in a mindless daze.

Miss Lottie seemed to be at least a hundred years old. Her big frame still held traces of the tall, powerful woman she must have been in youth. Her face had Indian-like features and a lack of emotion that one associates with Indian faces. Miss Lottie didn't like intruders, especially children. She never left her yard, and nobody ever visited her. When we were tiny children, we thought Miss Lottie was a witch. We were far too **sophisticated** now, of course, to believe the witch nonsense. But old fears have a way of clinging like cobwebs. So when we saw her house, we had to stop to **reinforce** our nerves.

"Look, there she is," I whispered, forgetting that Miss Lottie could not possibly have heard me from that distance. "She's fooling with them crazy flowers."

Miss Lottie's marigolds were perhaps the strangest part of the picture. Certainly they did not fit in with the crumbling decay of the rest of her yard. Beyond the dusty brown yard, in front of the sorry gray house, rose suddenly and shockingly a dazzling strip of bright blossoms, clumped together in enormous mounds. They were warm and passionate and sun-golden. The old black witch-woman worked on them all summer, every summer. For some reason, we children hated those marigolds. They interfered with the perfect ugliness of the place. They were too beautiful. They said too much that we could not understand. They did not make sense.

There was something in the energy with which the old woman destroyed the weeds that frightened us. It should have been a comical sight—the old woman with the man's hat on her head, leaning over the bright mounds, her big backside in the air—but it wasn't comical. It was something we could not name.

Word Power

sophisticated (sə fis′ tə kā′ tid) *adj.* having worldly knowledge and experience

reinforce (rē′ in fôrs′) *v.* to strengthen by repairing or adding something

---

Comprehension Check

Reread the boxed sentences. Why do the children get nervous when they see Miss Lottie's house? Check the correct response.

- ☐ She is the neighborhood witch.
- ☐ They are afraid of the cobwebs in the house.
- ☐ They have been afraid of her since they were younger.

Reading Skill

Predict Reread the highlighted sentences. Think about how the children feel about Miss Lottie and her marigolds. What do you think the children will do next?

_____

_____

_____

_____

Reading Skill

Predict Look back at the prediction you made on the last page. Did you predict that the children would tease Miss Lottie or harm her flowers? (Don't worry if your prediction doesn't match! You can change your prediction as you get new information from the story.) Do you think Lizabeth will participate? Revise your prediction as needed below.

_____

_____

_____

_____

English Coach

The word *beheaded* means "cut off the head of" and is an expression from old English. The prefix *be-* here means "away from." Today this prefix can have slightly different meanings, such as "make" or "to treat as." What then does *befriend* mean?

_____

_____

_____

We had to annoy her by throwing a pebble into her flowers or by yelling a dirty word, then dancing away from her rage, celebrating our youth and mocking her age. Actually, I think it was the flowers we wanted to destroy, but nobody had the nerve to try it.

"Y'all git some stones," commanded Joey. Everyone except me began to gather pebbles from the dusty ground. "Come on, Lizabeth."

I just stood there, torn between wanting to join the fun and feeling that it was all a bit silly.

"You scared, Lizabeth?"

I cursed and spat on the ground—my favorite gesture of phony bravery. "Y'all children get the stones, I'll show you how to use 'em."

I said before that we children were not aware of how thick were the bars of our cage. Perhaps we had some dim notion of what we were, and how little chance we had of being anything else. Otherwise, why would we have been so **preoccupied** with destruction? Anyway, the pebbles were collected quickly, and everybody looked at me to begin the fun.

We crept to the edge of the bushes that bordered the narrow road in front of Miss Lottie's place. She was working calmly, kneeling over the flowers. Suddenly *zing*—a well-aimed stone cut the head off one of the blossoms.

"Who out there?" Miss Lottie's backside came down and her head came up as her sharp eyes searched the bushes. "You better git!"

We had crouched down out of sight in the bushes, where we held back the giggles that insisted on coming. Miss Lottie gazed across the road for a moment, then carefully returned to her weeding. *Zing*—Joey sent a pebble into the blooms, and another marigold was beheaded.

Word Power

preoccupied (prē ok´ yə pīd´) *adj.* absorbed in doing something and not noticing other things

Miss Lottie was furious now. She began struggling to her feet shouting, "Y'all git! Go on home!" Then the rest of the kids let loose with their pebbles, attacking the flowers and laughing wildly and senselessly at Miss Lottie's powerless rage. She shook her stick at us and started shakily toward the road crying, "Git 'long! John Burke! John Burke, come help!"

Then I lost my head entirely, mad with the power of causing such rage. I ran out of the bushes, straight toward Miss Lottie, chanting madly, "Old witch, fell in a ditch, picked up a penny and thought she was rich!" The children screamed with delight, dropped their pebbles, and swarmed around Miss Lottie like bees chanting, "Old lady witch!" while she screamed curses at us. The madness lasted only a moment. John Burke, startled at last, jumped out of his chair. We dashed for the bushes just as Miss Lottie's cane went whizzing at my head.

I did not join the celebration when the kids gathered again under the oak in our bare yard. Suddenly I was ashamed, and I did not like being ashamed. The child in me sulked and said it was all in fun. But the woman in me drew back at the thought of the cruel attack that I had led. When we ate supper that night, I did not notice my father's silence, for he was always silent these days. Nor did I notice my mother's absence, for she always worked until well into evening. Joey and I had a particularly nasty argument after supper. Finally I stretched out upon the small bed in the room we shared and fell into a **fitful** doze.

 Stop here for **Break Time** on the next page.

Word Power

fitful (fit′ fəl) *adj.* not regular or steady

Comprehension Check

Reread the paragraph boxed in green. What do the children do to Miss Lottie?

_____

_____

_____

_____

Connect to the Text

Reread the sentences boxed in purple. Think about a time when you did something that later made you ashamed. Why did you feel bad about it? What did you do about it?

_____

_____

_____

_____

_____

Break Time

In "Marigolds," Miss Lottie's house seems to be in poor condition, but her garden of marigolds offers a bright contrast to the home. How do you picture her house and garden? In the box below, draw her house and garden as you would imagine them, based on the information you have read up to now. Include any characters from the story if you wish.

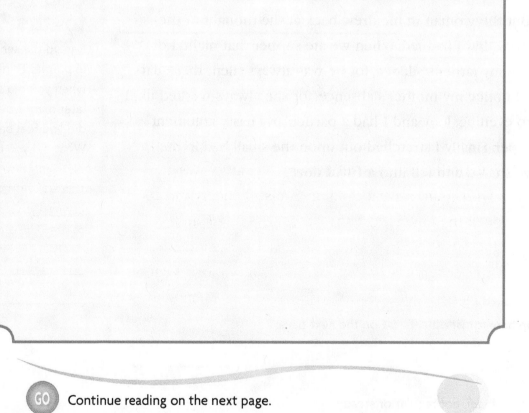

GO Continue reading on the next page.

When I awoke, somewhere in the middle of the night, my mother had returned. I listened to the conversation through the thin walls that separated our rooms. At first I heard no words, only voices. My mother's voice was like a cool, dark room in summer—peaceful, soothing, quiet. But my father's voice cut through hers, shattering the peace.

"Twenty-two years, Maybelle," he was saying, "and I got nothing for you, nothing, nothing."

"It's all right, honey, you'll get something. Everybody out of work now, you know that."

"It ain't right. Ain't no man ought to eat his woman's food year in and year out, and see his children running wild."

"Honey, you took good care of us when you had it. Ain't nobody got nothing nowadays."

"I ain't talking about nobody else, I'm talking about *me*. God knows I try." My mother said something I could not hear, and my father cried out louder, "What must a man do, tell me that?"

"Look, we ain't starving. I git paid every week, and Mrs. Ellis is real nice about giving me things. She gonna let me have Mr. Ellis's old coat for you this winter—"

"Damn Mr. Ellis's coat! You think I want white folks' leftovers? Damn, Maybelle"—and suddenly he sobbed, loudly and painfully. I had never heard a man cry before. I did not know men ever cried. I covered my ears with my hands but could not cut off the sound of my father's harsh, despairing sobs. My father was a strong man who could carry a child upon his shoulders and go singing through the house. My father made toys for us, and laughed so loud that the great oak seemed to laugh with him. How could it be that my father was crying? But the sobs went on until I could hear my mother's voice, deep and rich, humming softly as she used to hum to a frightened child.

Comprehension Check

Reread the boxed sentences. Why is Lizabeth's father upset?

_____

_____

_____

_____

Reading Skill

Evaluate Reread the highlighted sentences. Lizabeth hears her father crying. Do you think it's realistic for a man to behave this way? Explain why or why not.

_____

_____

_____

_____

My Workspace

Connect to the Text

Reread the boxed sentences. Think of a time when you felt scared and confused. Explain how you felt and what you found to comfort yourself.

_____

_____

_____

Reading Skill

Predict Reread the sentences highlighted in green. Think about what has happened in the story so far. Where do you think Lizabeth is going? What do you think she will do there?

_____

_____

_____

_____

Literary Element

Climax Reread the sentences highlighted in blue. Underline the details in the passage that help build the feeling of suspense leading to the climax.

Did You Know?

An accordion is a handheld musical instrument with keyboards or buttons on each side and bellows (special folds) in the middle. It is played by pressing the keys, squeezing the bellows together, and pulling them apart.

. . . .

My mother, who was small and soft, was now the strength of the family. My father, who was the rock on which the family had been built, was sobbing like the tiniest child. Everything was suddenly out of tune, like a broken accordion. Where did I fit into this crazy picture? I do not now remember my thoughts, only a feeling of great confusion and fear.

Long after the sobbing and humming had stopped, I lay on the bed, still as stone, wishing that I too could cry and be comforted. The night was silent now except for the sound of the crickets and of Joey's soft breathing. But the room was too crowded with fear to allow me to sleep. Feeling the terrible aloneness of 4 A.M., I decided to awaken Joey.

"Come on, wake up."

"What for? Go 'way."

I could not say, "I'm scared and I don't want to be alone," so I merely said, "I'm going out. If you want to come, come on."

The promise of adventure awoke him. "Going out now? Where to, Lizabeth? What you going to do?"

I was pulling my dress over my head. Until now I had not thought of going out. "Just come on," I replied.

I was out the window and halfway down the road before Joey caught up with me.

"Wait, Lizabeth, where you going?"

I ran furiously until I came to where I had half known I was headed: to Miss Lottie's yard.

The old house was like the ruin that my world had become. It looked haunted, but I was not afraid, because I was haunted too.

146

"Lizabeth, you lost your mind?" panted Joey.

I had indeed lost my mind, for all the **smoldering** emotions of that summer swelled in me and burst. The great need for my mother who was never there, the hopelessness of our poverty, the confusion of being neither child nor woman and yet both at once, the fear let loose by my father's tears. And these feelings combined in one great impulse toward destruction.

Comprehension Check

Reread the boxed paragraph. Underline the things that are causing Lizabeth to feel that she needs to possibly destroy something.

Word Power

smoldering (smōl´ dər ing) *adj.* feeling anger or hate but keeping it under control

Literary Element

Climax Remember that the climax of a story is the emotional high point, or turning point. Reread the highlighted sentences. Underline the words in the text that express the intense emotion and wild actions shown by Lizabeth.

Comprehension Check

Reread the boxed sentences. Why are the flowers so important to Miss Lottie?

_____

_____

_____

_____

"Lizabeth!"

I leaped furiously into the mounds of marigolds and pulled madly, trampling and pulling and destroying the perfect yellow blooms. The fresh smell of early morning and the marigolds urged me on as I went tearing and mangling and sobbing while Joey tugged my dress crying, "Lizabeth, stop, please stop!"

And then I was sitting in the ruined little garden among the ruined flowers, crying and crying. It was too late to undo what I had done. Joey was sitting beside me, silent and frightened, not knowing what to say. Then, "Lizabeth, look."

I opened my swollen eyes and saw in front of me a pair of large feet. My gaze lifted to the swollen legs, the age-distorted body in a tight cotton nightdress, and then the shadowed Indian face surrounded by stubby white hair. And there was no rage in the face now, now that the garden was destroyed and there was nothing any longer to be protected.

"M-miss Lottie!" I scrambled to my feet and just stood there and stared at her. That was the moment when childhood faded and womanhood began. That violent, crazy act was the last act of childhood. For as I gazed at the still face with the sad, weary eyes, I gazed upon a kind of reality which is hidden to childhood. The witch was no longer a witch but only a broken old woman who had dared to create beauty in the middle of ugliness and lifelessness. She had been born in **squalor** and lived in it all her life. Now at the end of that life she had nothing except a falling-down hut, a wrecked body, and John Burke, the mindless son of her passion. Whatever energy there was left in her, whatever love and beauty and joy had not been squeezed out by life, had been there in the marigolds she had so tenderly cared for.

Word Power

squalor (skwol´ ər) *adj.* filth; misery from a state of poverty

Of course I could not express the things that I knew about Miss Lottie as I stood there awkward and ashamed. The years have put words to the things I knew in that moment. As I look back upon it, I know that that moment marked the end of innocence. Innocence involves an ignorance of the area below the surface. In that moment I looked beyond myself and into the depths of another person. This was the beginning of compassion, and one cannot have both compassion and innocence.

The years have taken me worlds away from that time and that place. Miss Lottie died long ago and many years have passed since I last saw her hut. Despite my wild apologies she never planted marigolds again. Yet, there are times when the image of those passionate yellow mounds returns with a painful significance. For one does not have to be ignorant and poor to find that his life is as empty as the dusty yards of our town. And I too have planted marigolds.

Reading Skill

Evaluate Reread the highlighted sentences. Lizabeth says that a person cannot be innocent, or childlike, once he or she sees the deep troubles of others. Do you think Lizabeth is right? Why or why not?

_____

_____

_____

_____

_____

Comprehension Check

Reread the boxed sentences. Why does Lizabeth make "wild apologies" to Miss Lottie? Check the correct response.

☐ She feels sorry that Miss Lottie was going to die.

☐ She feels sorry that she hasn't seen the hut in many years.

☐ She feels sorry for destroying the marigolds.

Respond to Literature

Marigolds

A Comprehension Check

Answer the following questions in the spaces provided.

1. Why do the children go to Miss Lottie's house? _____

_____

2. What does Lizabeth do to the marigolds and how does she feel about her

actions? _____

_____

B Reading Skills

Answer the following questions in the spaces provided.

1. **Predict** What do you think will happen to Lizabeth years later? Do you
   think she will plant a garden like the one Miss Lottie had? Explain.

_____

_____

_____

2. **Evaluate** Should Lizabeth be punished for what she does to Miss Lottie's
   flowers, or are the results of her action punishment enough? Explain.

_____

_____

_____

_____

C Word Power

Complete each sentence below, using one of the words in the box.

futile	innocence	sophisticated	reinforce
preoccupied	fitful	smoldering	squalor

1. The teenagers looked very grown up and _____ in their prom clothes.

2. Jessica made several _____ attempts to call Chin Sook on her cell phone before she gave up trying to reach her.

3. Ellen was so _____ with reading the recipe that she did not notice that the water was boiling over.

4. Derrick gave some strong reasons to _____ his request to buy new sneakers.

5. Alfonso lost his childlike _____ when he found out that someone stole his bike.

6. After a night of _____ sleep, Moishe had a hard time staying awake at school.

7. Amanda's red face and clenched jaw made it clear that her

_____ hatred toward Cyrus was about to erupt.

8. "How can you live in this _____?!" was the first thing most people said upon entering Ralph's messy bedroom.

D Literary Element: Climax

Read the passage below from "Marigolds." As you read, think about what the sentences reveal about the climax of the story. Then answer the questions that follow.

> I had indeed lost my mind, for all the smoldering emotions of that summer swelled in me and burst.[1] The great need for my mother who was never there, the hopelessness of our poverty, the confusion of being neither child nor woman and yet both at once, the fear let loose by my father's tears.[2] And these feelings combined in one great impulse toward destruction.[3]
>
> "Lizabeth!"[4]
>
> I leaped furiously into the mounds of marigolds and pulled madly, trampling and pulling and destroying the perfect yellow blooms.[5] The fresh smell of early morning and the marigolds urged me on as I went tearing and mangling and sobbing while Joey tugged my dress crying, "Lizabeth, stop, please stop!"[6]

1. How does the tension in sentences 1–3 build to the climax of the story?

_____

_____

_____

_____

2. Sentences 5–6 are the climax of the story. Explain why and tell what words illustrate this. _____

_____

_____

E A Letter of Apology

Imagine that you are Lizabeth. You are going to make one more attempt at apologizing to Miss Lottie for what you did. Write Miss Lottie a letter in which you tell her how sorry you are and explain why you destroyed her marigolds.

Dear Miss Lottie,

My name is Lizabeth. I am the girl who destroyed your marigolds the other day. I am writing to tell you that

_____

I don't know for sure why I did it. It could be because

_____

But I think most likely it was because _____

_____

But no matter why I did it, it was a _____

_____

I hope that one day you will be able to find it in your heart to forgive me. Even if you don't, I hope that you will decide to

_____

You are a wonderful gardener, and your marigolds were beautiful.

Sincerely,
Lizabeth

Assessment

Fill in the circle next to each correct answer.

1. What did the children do for fun at Miss Lottie's?
   - ○ A. helped her pick her flowers
   - ○ B. threw stones at her flowers
   - ○ C. talked with John Burke
   - ○ D. pulled weeds in her garden

2. Why does Lizabeth's father start to cry?
   - ○ A. He is afraid his children are running wild.
   - ○ B. He is sad because Lizabeth has to work.
   - ○ C. He is upset because he can't find work.
   - ○ D. He is upset because Lizabeth destroyed the flowers.

3. Which sentence from the story **best** helps the reader predict that Lizabeth will learn a lesson about growing up?
   - ○ A. I don't know what it was that we were waiting for.
   - ○ B. But memory does not present things as they are, but rather as they *feel*.
   - ○ C. When I think of the hometown of my youth, all that I seem to remember is dust.
   - ○ D. I recall that awful moment when I was suddenly more woman than child, years ago in Miss Lottie's yard.

4. Which of the following is the climax of the story?
   - ○ A. when Lizabeth destroys the marigolds
   - ○ B. when Lizabeth hears her father cry
   - ○ C. when the children yell at Miss Lottie
   - ○ D. when John Burke chases the children away

5. Which of the following words means "completely caught up in doing something"?
   - ○ A. futile
   - ○ B. smoldering
   - ○ C. preoccupied
   - ○ D. sophisticated

UNIT 2 **Wrap-up**

Compare and Contrast

Climax is an important literary element in "Through the Tunnel" and "Marigolds." Although the events in these stories are very different, the suspense in each story builds to an important climax. Think about the climax in each story. Then think about what each character learns at this moment.

Complete the Venn diagram. In the left circle, describe the climax in "Through the Tunnel." Then tell what lesson Jerry learns. In the right circle, describe the climax in "Marigolds" and tell what lesson Lizabeth learns. In the overlapping part, tell what similar lesson both characters learn.

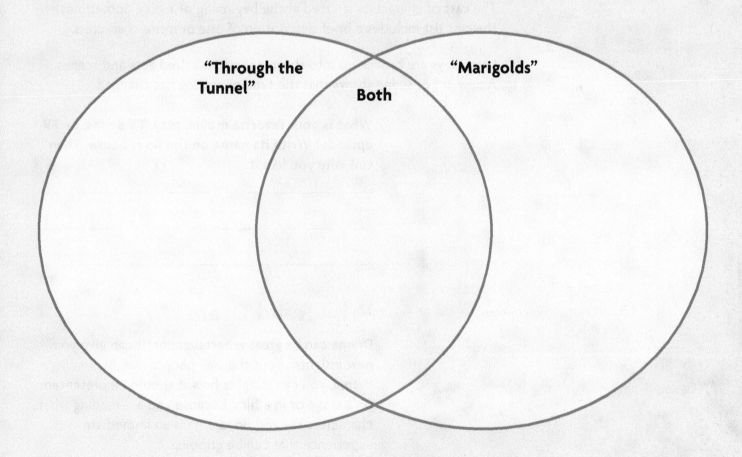

UNIT 3 Drama

What's Drama?

A **drama** is a story told mainly through the words and actions of characters. A drama, also called a play, is meant to be performed on stage or screen for an audience. Writers include stage directions in the lines of the script. These directions tell the characters how to speak their lines and where they should move on the stage. They may also give details about the setting and scenery.

The cast of characters is listed at the beginning of a play. Sometimes the cast list includes a brief description of one or more characters.

Long plays are broken up into shorter sections called acts and scenes. A new act or scene shows that the time or setting has changed.

What is your favorite movie, play, TV series, or TV episode? Write its name on the lines below. Then tell why you like it.

_____

_____

_____

Why Read Drama?

Drama can be great entertainment. It can give you new insights about the way people live. By reading a drama, you can imagine how it should be presented on a stage or in a film. Because you are reading what characters say and do, drama is an immediate experience that can be gripping.

How Do I Read Drama?

Focus on the key **literary element** and **reading skills** to get the most out of reading the drama in this unit. Here are one key literary element and two key reading skills that you will practice in this unit.

Key Literary Element

Character

A **character** is an actor in a play. The main characters have the most important parts. You can understand characters by looking at what they do and say, as well as what other characters say about them. Characters may change because of events that occur in the story. A play can include descriptions of a character's appearance and tell how a character feels and thinks. A character who speaks lines *wearily* may feel defeated and hopeless.

Key Reading Skills

• Visualize

When you **visualize** a person, a place, an object, or an event, you see it in your mind. Try to imagine the person or thing or scene described in the words. Build on any details the writer provides. Pay special attention to the stage directions in a drama, which give descriptions of the setting and characters. Trying to visualize what you are reading can give you a feeling of being part of the story. "See" in your mind what a character is doing on the stage.

• Draw Conclusions

Sometimes you must figure out what the author means or wants you to know by drawing conclusions. When you **draw conclusions,** you use clues in the story to gather evidence and make general statements about characters and events. You can draw conclusions about characters by noting how they are described, what they say and do, and how other characters respond to them.

Get Ready to Read!

A Raisin in the Sun

Meet Lorraine Hansberry

Lorraine Hansberry was born in Chicago, Illinois, in 1930. It is likely that the past experience of racial prejudice influenced Hansberry as she wrote *A Raisin in the Sun*, in which the dream of owning a home plays a major role in the lives of the Younger family. Hansberry died in 1965. *A Raisin in the Sun* was first performed in 1959 and was awarded the New York Drama Critics Circle Award for Best Play of the Year.

What You Know

Do you have a dream of one day achieving a difficult goal? How do you think you will feel when you achieve it? What will you do if circumstances keep you from achieving your dream?

Reason to Read

Read this drama to find out how one family reacts when they are faced with the chance of finally achieving dreams that have always seemed just beyond their reach.

Background Info

The title of the play *A Raisin in the Sun* comes from the poem "Dream Deferred" by celebrated African American writer Langston Hughes: *What happens to a dream deferred?/Does it dry up/like a raisin in the sun?*

In the 1950s, when Lorraine Hansberry wrote this play, African Americans faced widespread prejudice in the United States. Restaurants, movie theaters, and public schools were segregated. The schools that African American children attended were supposedly "separate but equal," but, in fact, their schools were greatly inferior to the schools that white children attended. Due to the prejudice they faced in society, some young African American people had a very difficult time achieving their dreams.

Word Power

stupor (stōo′ pər) *n.* a dazed condition in which a person can barely think, feel, or act; p. 162
The long, boring movie put Vincent into a *stupor*.

indifference (in dif′ ər əns) *n.* complete lack of concern or interest; p. 164
Students expressed *indifference* and ignored Tamara's campaign for student council.

exasperated (ig zas′ pə rāt′ id) *adj.* extremely annoyed and irritated; p. 165
Jason was *exasperated* by his little brother's constant questions.

mutual (mū′ chōo əl) *adj.* expressing the same feelings toward each other; p. 168
The tennis players showed their *mutual* respect by shaking hands after the match.

anguish (ang′ gwish) *n.* great suffering or pain; agony; p. 171
Miranda cried out in *anguish* as the splinter pierced her finger.

vengeance (ven′ jəns) *n.* the act of getting even with someone; revenge; p. 174
Sara showed *vengeance* when she hid her brother's homework after he didn't help.

dissected (di sekt′ id) *v.* took or cut apart to examine; p. 174
Thomas *dissected* his watch to find out what made it run.

ledger (lej′ ər) *v.* a book in which records are kept, usually of income and expenses; p. 181
Mario's mother, an accountant, kept a *ledger* of her son's allowance.

Answer the following questions, using one of the new words above.
Write your answers in the spaces provided.

1. Which word goes with "keeping track of the income of a business"? _____

2. Which word goes with "acting out of anger"? _____

3. Which word goes with "cut apart to look at the insides of a frog"? _____

4. Which word goes with "not caring much"? _____

5. Which word goes with "feelings that two people share for each other"? _____

6. Which word goes with "feeling torment and pain"? _____

7. Which word goes with "being half-asleep"? _____

8. Which word goes with "feeling impatient and irritated"? _____

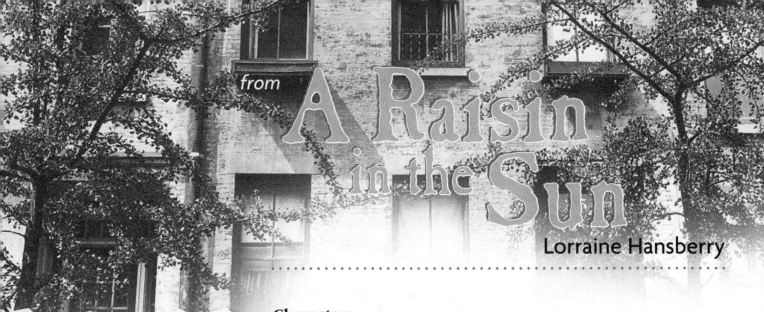

from

A Raisin in the Sun

Lorraine Hansberry

Reading Skill

Visualize Reread the highlighted text and the rest of the first two paragraphs. What details help you form a picture of the Youngers' living room in your mind? Underline the words and phrases that help you form this picture.

Characters

RUTH YOUNGER

TRAVIS YOUNGER

WALTER LEE YOUNGER (BROTHER)

BENEATHA YOUNGER

LENA YOUNGER (MAMA)

Act 1, Scene 1

The YOUNGER living room would be a comfortable and well-ordered room if it were not for a number of indestructible contradictions to this state of being. Its furnishings are typical and undistinguished and their primary feature now is that they have clearly had to accommodate the living of too many people for too many years—and they are tired. Still, we can see that at some time, a time probably no longer remembered by the family (except perhaps for MAMA), the furnishings of this room were actually selected with care and love and even hope—and brought to this apartment and arranged with taste and pride.

That was a long time ago. Now the once loved pattern of the couch upholstery has to fight to show itself from under acres of crocheted doilies and couch covers which have themselves finally come to be more important than the upholstery. And here a table or a chair has been moved to disguise the worn places in the carpet; but the carpet has fought back by showing its weariness, with depressing uniformity, elsewhere on its surface.

Weariness has, in fact, won in this room. Everything has been polished, washed, sat on, used, scrubbed too often.

All pretenses but living itself have long since vanished from the very atmosphere of this room.

Moreover, a section of this room, for it is not really a room unto itself, though the landlord's lease would make it seem so, slopes backward to provide a small kitchen area, where the family prepares the meals that are eaten in the living room proper, which must also serve as dining room. The single window that has been provided for these "two" rooms is located in this kitchen area. The sole natural light the family may enjoy in the course of a day is only that which fights its way through this little window.

At left, a door leads to a bedroom which is shared by MAMA and her daughter, BENEATHA. At right, opposite, is a second room (which in the beginning of the life of this apartment was probably a breakfast room) which serves as a bedroom for WALTER and his wife, RUTH.

TIME: *Sometime between World War II and the present.*
PLACE: *Chicago's Southside.*
AT RISE: *It is morning dark in the living room. TRAVIS is asleep on the* make-down bed *at center. An alarm clock sounds from within the bedroom at right, and presently RUTH enters from that room and closes the door behind her. She crosses sleepily toward the window. As she passes her sleeping son she reaches down and shakes him a little. At the window she raises the shade and a dusky Southside morning light comes in feebly. She fills a pot with water and puts it on to boil. She calls to the boy, between yawns, in a slightly muffled voice.*

RUTH is about thirty. We can see that she was a pretty girl, even exceptionally so, but now it is apparent that life has been little that she expected, and disappointment has already begun to hang in her face. In a few years, before thirty-five even, she will be known among her people as a "settled woman." She crosses to her son and gives him a good, final, rousing shake.

Background Info

A make-down bed refers to a sofa that is used as a bed only at night. Pillows and bedding are put on the sofa for sleeping, and then taken off for the daytime.

Reading Skill

Visualize Reread the highlighted sentences to form a picture of Ruth in your mind. What do you think she looks like? Check the **best** response below.

☐ attractive but tired-looking
☐ glamorous and expensively dressed
☐ dressed poorly

How did you visualize the character of Ruth?

Connect to the Text

Reread the boxed sentences. Think about a time when you had to wake up for school but did not get enough sleep the night before. How did you feel? What was your mood like that morning?

_____

_____

_____

_____

Literary Element

Character Reread the highlighted sentences. What is the author telling you about Ruth's character? Check the **best** response below.

☐ She is careless and forgets to wake her family at the right time.

☐ She is responsible and tries her best to take care of the family.

☐ She is impatient and hates the frantic, busy mornings.

RUTH. Come on now, boy, it's seven thirty! [_Her son sits up at last, in a **stupor** of sleepiness._] I say hurry up, Travis! You ain't the only person in the world got to use a bathroom! [_The child, a sturdy, handsome little boy of ten or eleven, drags himself out of the bed and almost blindly takes his towels and "today's clothes" from drawers and a closet and goes out to the bathroom, which is in an outside hall and which is shared by another family or families on the same floor. RUTH crosses to the bedroom door at right and opens it and calls in to her husband._] Walter Lee! . . . It's after seven thirty! Lemme see you do some waking up in there now! [_She waits._] You better get up from there, man! It's after seven thirty I tell you. [_She waits again._] All right, you just go ahead and lay there and next thing you know Travis be finished and Mr. Johnson'll be in there and you'll be fussing and cussing round here like a madman! And be late too! [_She waits, at the end of patience._] Walter Lee—it's time for you to GET UP!

Word Power

stupor (stoo′ pər) _n._ a dazed condition in which a person can barely think, feel, or act

[*She waits another second and then starts to go into the bedroom, but is apparently satisfied that her husband has begun to get up. She stops, pulls the door to, and returns to the kitchen area. She wipes her face with a moist cloth and runs her fingers through her sleep-disheveled hair in a vain effort and ties an apron around her housecoat. The bedroom door at right opens and her husband stands in the doorway in his pajamas, which are rumpled and mismated. He is a lean, intense young man in his middle thirties, inclined to quick nervous movements and erratic speech habits—and always in his voice there is a quality of indictment.*]

WALTER. Is he out yet?

RUTH. What you mean *out*? He ain't hardly got in there good yet.

WALTER. [*wandering in, still more oriented to sleep than to a new day*] Well, what was you doing all that yelling for if I can't even get in there yet? [*stopping and thinking*] Check coming today?

RUTH. They *said* Saturday and this is just Friday and I hopes to God you ain't going to get up here first thing this morning and start talking to me 'bout no money—'cause I 'bout don't want to hear it.

WALTER. Something the matter with you this morning?

RUTH. No—I'm just sleepy as the devil. What kind of eggs you want?

WALTER. Not scrambled. [*RUTH starts to scramble eggs.*] Paper come? [*Ruth points impatiently to the rolled up* Tribune *on the table, and he gets it and spreads it out and vaguely reads the front page.*] Set off another bomb yesterday.

English Coach

The prefix *mis-* can mean "wrongly," "badly," or "poorly." *Mismated* is another word for *mismatched*, or "wrongly matched." Write another word that begins with the prefix *mis-* below.

_____

_____

_____

Reading Skill
Draw Conclusions
Reread the highlighted sentences. Think about Ruth's and Walter's actions here. What conclusion can you draw about their relationship?

_____

_____

_____

_____

Background Info

A tea party is a formal afternoon gathering at which people drink tea and eat fancy foods. It was a ritual of the wealthy upper classes. By showing *tea-party interest*, Ruth is speaking to Walter in a formal, overly polite way and pretending to be interested.

Comprehension Check

Reread the boxed sentences. According to Ruth, why can't Travis go to bed earlier?

_____

_____

_____

_____

_____

RUTH. [*maximum **indifference***] Did they?

WALTER. [*looking up*] What's the matter with you?

RUTH. Ain't nothing the matter with me. And don't keep asking me that this morning.

WALTER. Ain't nobody bothering you. [*reading the news of the day absently again*] Say Colonel McCormick is sick.

RUTH. [*affecting* tea-party interest] Is he now? Poor thing.

WALTER. [*sighing and looking at his watch*] Oh, me. [*He waits.*] Now what is that boy doing in that bathroom all this time? He just going to have to start getting up earlier. I can't be being late to work on account of him fooling around in there.

RUTH. [*turning on him*] Oh, no he ain't going to be getting up no earlier no such thing! It ain't his fault that he can't get to bed no earlier nights 'cause he got a bunch of crazy good-for-nothing clowns sitting up running their mouths in what is supposed to be his bedroom after ten o'clock at night...

WALTER. That's what you mad about, ain't it? The things I want to talk about with my friends just couldn't be important in your mind, could they? [*He rises and finds a cigarette in her handbag on the table and crosses to the little window and looks out, smoking and deeply enjoying this first one.*]

RUTH. [*almost matter of factly, a complaint too automatic to deserve emphasis*] Why you always got to smoke before you eat in the morning?

WALTER. [*at the window*] Just look at 'em down there... Running and racing to work... [*He turns and faces his wife and watches her a moment at the stove, and then, suddenly.*] You look young this morning, baby.

RUTH. [*indifferently*] Yeah?

Word Power

indifference (in dif ʹ ər əns) *n.* complete lack of concern or interest

WALTER. Just for a second—stirring them eggs. Just for a second it was—you looked real young again. [*He reaches for her; she crosses away. Then, drily*] It's gone now—you look like yourself again!

RUTH. Man, if you don't shut up and leave me alone.

WALTER. [*looking out to the street again*] First thing a man ought to learn in life is not to make love to no colored woman first thing in the morning. You all some eeeevil people at eight o'clock in the morning.

[TRAVIS *appears in the hall doorway, almost fully dressed and quite wide awake now, his towels and pajamas across his shoulders. He opens the door and signals for his father to make the bathroom in a hurry.*]

TRAVIS. [*watching the bathroom*] Daddy, come on!

[WALTER *gets his bathroom utensils and flies out to the bathroom.*]

RUTH. Sit down and have your breakfast, Travis.

TRAVIS. Mama, this is Friday. [*gleefully*] Check coming tomorrow, huh?

RUTH. You get your mind off money and eat your breakfast.

TRAVIS. [*eating*] This is the morning we supposed to bring the fifty cents to school.

RUTH. Well, I ain't got no fifty cents this morning.

TRAVIS. Teacher say we have to.

RUTH. I don't care what teacher say. I ain't got it. Eat your breakfast, Travis.

TRAVIS. I *am* eating.

RUTH. Hush up now and just eat!

[*The boy gives her an **exasperated** look for her lack of understanding, and eats grudgingly.*]

Word Power

exasperated (ig zas′ pə rāt′ id) *adj*. extremely annoyed and irritated

Literary Element

Character Reread the highlighted sentences. What can you tell about Walter from his actions and dialogue? Check the **best** response below.

☐ He loves his wife, but is growing irritated with her.

☐ He no longer loves his wife because she is too old.

☐ He thinks his wife is too young for him.

Connect to the Text

Reread the boxed sentences. Think about a time when you felt that a parent or other adult was not listening to you or was not being understanding. What did you say or do? How did you feel?

_____

_____

_____

_____

My Workspace

How does Ruth help Travis get ready for school? Does it compare to your morning preparation for school?

TRAVIS. You think Grandmama would have it?

RUTH. No! And I want you to stop asking your grandmother for money, you hear me?

TRAVIS. [*outraged*] Gaaaleee! I don't ask her, she just gimme it sometimes!

RUTH. Travis Willard Younger—I got too much on me this morning to be—

TRAVIS. Maybe Daddy—

RUTH. *Travis!*

[*The boy hushes abruptly. They are both quiet and tense for several seconds.*]

TRAVIS. [*presently*] Could I maybe go carry some groceries in front of the supermarket for a little while after school then?

RUTH. Just hush, I said. [*TRAVIS jabs his spoon into his cereal bowl viciously, and rests his head in anger upon his fists.*] If you through eating, you can get over there and make up your bed.

[*The boy obeys stiffly and crosses the room, almost mechanically, to the bed and more or less folds the bedding into a heap, then angrily gets his books and cap.*]

TRAVIS. [*sulking and standing apart from her unnaturally*] I'm gone.

Connect to the Text

Reread the boxed words. Think about the last time someone called you by your full name (first, middle, and last). Why did this person call you by your full name? Was this person angry at you?

_____

_____

_____

_____

_____

RUTH. [*looking up from the stove to inspect him automatically*] Come here. [*He crosses to her and she studies his head.*] If you don't take this comb and fix this here head, you better! [*TRAVIS puts down his books with a great sigh of oppression, and crosses to the mirror. His mother mutters under her breath about his "slubbornness."*] 'Bout to march out of here with that head looking just like chickens slept in it! I just don't know where you get your slubborn ways... And get your jacket, too. Looks chilly out this morning.

TRAVIS. [*with conspicuously brushed hair and jacket*] I'm gone.

RUTH. Get carfare and milk money—[*waving one finger*]—and not a single penny for no caps, you hear me?

TRAVIS. [*with sullen politeness*] Yes'm.

[*He turns in outrage to leave. His mother watches after him as in his frustration he approaches the door almost comically. When she speaks to him, her voice has become a very gentle tease.*]

RUTH. [*mocking; as she thinks he would say it*] Oh, Mama makes me so mad sometimes, I don't know what to do! [*She waits and continues to his back as he stands stock-still in front of the door.*] I wouldn't kiss that woman good-bye for nothing in this world this morning! [*The boy finally turns around and rolls his eyes at her, knowing the mood has changed and he is vindicated; he does not, however, move toward her yet.*] Not for nothing in this world! [*She finally laughs aloud at him and holds out her arms to him and we see that it is a way between them, very old and practiced. He crosses to her and allows her to embrace him warmly but keeps his face fixed with masculine rigidity. She holds him back from her presently and looks at him and runs her fingers over the features of his face. With utter gentleness—*] Now—whose little old angry man are you?

TRAVIS. [*The masculinity and gruffness start to fade at last.*] Aw gaalee—Mama...

Comprehension Check

Reread the boxed sentences. Why doesn't Ruth want Travis to carry bags outside the supermarket after school?

_____

_____

_____

_____

_____

Literary Element

Character Reread the highlighted sentences. What do Walter's actions tell you about his character? Check the **best** response below.

☐ He can be forgetful and careless.

☐ He can be generous and defiant.

☐ He can be thoughtful and clever.

RUTH. [*mimicking*] Aw gaaaaalleeeee, Mama! [*She pushes him, with rough playfulness and finality, toward the door.*] Get on out of here or you going to be late.

> **TRAVIS.** [*in the face of love, new aggressiveness*] Mama, could I *please* go carry groceries?
>
> **RUTH.** Honey, it's starting to get so cold evenings.
>
> **WALTER.** [*coming in from the bathroom and drawing a make-believe gun from a make-believe holster and shooting at his son*] What is it he wants to do?
>
> **RUTH.** Go carry groceries after school at the supermarket.

WALTER. Well, let him go . . .

TRAVIS. [*quickly, to the ally*] I *have* to—she won't gimme the fifty cents . . .

WALTER. [*to his wife only*] Why not?

RUTH. [*simply, and with flavor*] 'Cause we don't have it.

WALTER. [*to RUTH only*] What you tell the boy things like that for? [*reaching down into his pants with a rather important gesture*] Here, son—

[*He hands the boy the coin, but his eyes are directed to his wife's. TRAVIS takes the money happily.*]

TRAVIS. Thanks, Daddy.

[*He starts out. RUTH watches both of them with murder in her eyes. WALTER stands and stares back at her with defiance, and suddenly reaches into his pocket again on an afterthought.*]

WALTER. [*without even looking at his son, still staring hard at his wife*] In fact, here's another fifty cents . . . Buy yourself some fruit today—or take a taxicab to school or something!

TRAVIS. Whoopee—

[*He leaps up and clasps his father around the middle with his legs, and they face each other in **mutual** appreciation; slowly WALTER LEE peeks around the boy to catch the violent rays from his wife's eyes and draws his head back as if shot.*]

Word Power

mutual (mū´ chŏŏ əl) *adj.* expressing the same feelings toward each other

WALTER. You better get down now—and get to school, man.

TRAVIS. [*at the door*] O.K. Good-bye.

[*He exits.*]

WALTER. [*after him, pointing with pride*] That's my boy.
[*RUTH looks at him in disgust and turns back to her work.*]
You know what I was thinking 'bout in the bathroom
this morning?

RUTH. No.

WALTER. How come you always try to be so pleasant!

RUTH. What is there to be pleasant 'bout!

WALTER. You want to know what I was thinking 'bout in the
bathroom or not!

RUTH. I know what you thinking 'bout.

WALTER. [*ignoring her*] 'Bout what me and Willy Harris was
talking about last night.

RUTH. [*immediately—a refrain*] Willy Harris is a good-for-
nothing loudmouth.

WALTER. Anybody who talks to me has got to be a good-for-
nothing loudmouth, ain't he? And what you know about who
is just a good-for-nothing loudmouth? Charlie Atkins was just a
"good-for-nothing loudmouth" too, wasn't he! When he wanted
me to go in the dry-cleaning business with him. And now—
he's grossing a hundred thousand a year. A hundred thousand
dollars a year! You still call *him* a loudmouth!

RUTH. [*bitterly*] Oh, Walter Lee . . .

[*She folds her head on her arms over the table.*]

WALTER. [*rising and coming to her and standing over her*]
You tired, ain't you? Tired of everything. Me, the boy, the way
we live—this beat-up hole—everything. Ain't you? [*She
doesn't look up, doesn't answer.*] So tired—moaning and
groaning all the time, but you wouldn't do nothing to help,
would you! You couldn't be on my side that long for nothing,
could you?

Reading Skill
Draw Conclusions
Reread the highlighted passage. What conclusion can you draw about Ruth's feelings about Walter's friends? Does she think that Willy Harris would be a good business partner for Walter?

_____

_____

_____

_____

Connect to the Text
Reread the boxed sentence. Think about a time when you felt that someone was not "on your side." How did you react? Did you try to convince this person to be on your side?

_____

_____

_____

Comprehension Check

Reread the boxed passage. What is Walter trying to get Ruth to do? Check the **best** response below.

☐ He wants Ruth to tell Mama that the liquor store will be a good idea.

☐ He wants Ruth to think about drinking less coffee.

☐ He wants Ruth to tell Mama about Willy and Bobo.

Background Info

In this context, graft refers to an illegal or corrupt gain, such as one gotten through bribery. Walter is saying that if he gives the local officials money, they will speed up the process to get him a liquor license.

RUTH. Walter, please leave me alone.

WALTER. A man needs for a woman to back him up...

RUTH. Walter—

WALTER. Mama would listen to you. You know she listen to you more than she do me and Bennie. She think more of you. All you have to do is just sit down with her when you drinking your coffee one morning and talking 'bout things like you do and—[*He sits down beside her and demonstrates graphically what he thinks her methods and tone should be.*]—you just sip your coffee, see, and say easy like that you been thinking 'bout that deal Walter Lee is so interested in, 'bout the store and all, and sip some more coffee, like what you saying ain't really that important to you— And the next thing you know, she be listening good and asking you questions and when I come home—I can tell her the details. This ain't no fly-by-night proposition, baby. I mean we figured it out, me and Willy and Bobo.

RUTH. [*with a frown*] Bobo?

WALTER. Yeah. You see, this little liquor store we got in mind cost seventy-five thousand and we figured the initial investment on the place be 'bout thirty thousand, see. That be ten thousand each. Course, there's a couple of hundred you got to pay so's you don't spend your life just waiting for them clowns to let your license get approved—

RUTH. You mean graft?

WALTER. [*frowning impatiently*] Don't call it that. See there, that just goes to show you what women understand about the world. Baby, don't *nothing* happen for you in this world 'less you pay *somebody* off!

What seems to be the main problem that causes Walter to be angry?

_____

RUTH. Walter, leave me alone! [*She raises her head and stares at him vigorously—then says, more quietly.*] *Eat* your eggs, they gonna be cold.

WALTER. [*straightening up from her and looking off*] That's it. There you are. Man say to his woman: I got me a dream. His woman say: Eat your eggs. [*sadly, but gaining in power*] Man say: I got to take hold of this here world, baby! And a woman will say: Eat your eggs and go to work. [*passionately now*] Man say: I got to change my life, I'm choking to death, baby! And his woman say—[*in utter **anguish** as he brings his fists down on his thighs*]—Your eggs is getting cold!

RUTH. [*softly*] Walter, that ain't none of our money.

Word Power

anguish (ang´ gwish) *n.* great suffering or pain; agony

Connect to the Text

Reread the boxed passage. Think about a time when you were trying to discuss something important, but the person you were speaking to kept changing the subject. What did you do or say? How did it make you feel?

_____

_____

_____

_____

_____

Reading Skill
Draw Conclusions

Reread the highlighted sentences. Think about the events in the story, such as Ruth's reaction to Walter's friends, and the conversation between Ruth and Walter up to this point. What conclusion can you draw about why Walter is so angry?

_____

_____

_____

_____

_____

Background Info

Rough-dried refers to laundry that has been washed and dried, but not ironed. A pile of rough-dried clothes would be wrinkled and not yet ready to wear.

WALTER. [*not listening at all or even looking at her*] This morning, I was lookin' in the mirror and thinking about it... I'm thirty-five years old; I been married eleven years and I got a boy who sleeps in the living room—[*very quietly*]—and all I got to give him is stories about how rich white people live...

RUTH. Eat your eggs, Walter.

WALTER. [*slams the table and jumps up*]—DAMN MY EGGS— DAMN ALL THE EGGS THAT EVER WAS!

RUTH. Then go to work.

WALTER. [*looking up at her*] See—I'm trying to talk to you 'bout myself—[*shaking his head with the repetition*]—and all you can say is eat them eggs and go to work.

RUTH. [*wearily*] Honey, you never say nothing new. I listen to you every day, every night and every morning, and you never say nothing new. [*shrugging*] So you would rather *be* Mr. Arnold than be his chauffeur. So—I would *rather* be living in Buckingham Palace.

WALTER. That is just what is wrong with the colored woman in this world... Don't understand about building their men up and making 'em feel like they somebody. Like they can do something.

RUTH. [*drily, but to hurt*] There *are* colored men who do things.

WALTER. No thanks to the colored woman.

RUTH. Well, being a colored woman, I guess I can't help myself none.
[*She rises and gets the ironing board and sets it up and attacks a huge pile of rough-dried clothes, sprinkling them in preparation for the ironing and then rolling them into tight fat balls.*]

WALTER. [*mumbling*] We one group of men tied to a race of women with small minds!

 Stop here for **Break Time** on the next page.

Break Time

Just like any work of fiction, a drama has story elements: setting, characters, plot, and themes. Complete the story map with details from the play. In the Setting circle, write details about where the scene takes place. In the Characters circle, write the names of the characters you've met so far and a few words to describe them. In the Plot circle, write a short summary of what has happened so far in the story. In the Themes circle, write important ideas from the story; think about a message the author is trying to make.

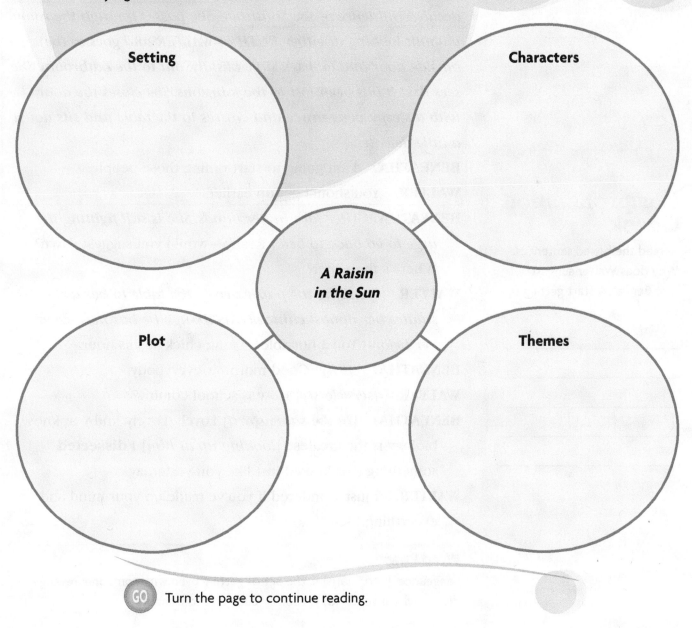

Setting

Characters

A Raisin in the Sun

Plot

Themes

GO Turn the page to continue reading.

Reading Skill

Visualize Reread the highlighted sentences. Use the details from the text to form a picture of Beneatha in your mind. Draw how you picture her in the box below.

Your Sketch

Comprehension Check

Reread the boxed sentences. Why does Walter suggest that Beneatha start getting up earlier?

_____

_____

_____

_____

[*His sister BENEATHA enters. She is about twenty, as slim and intense as her brother. She is not as pretty as her sister-in-law, but her lean, almost intellectual face has a handsomeness of its own. She wears a bright-red flannel nightie, and her thick hair stands wildly about her head. Her speech is a mixture of many things; it is different from the rest of the family's insofar as education has permeated her sense of English—and perhaps the Midwest rather than the South has finally—at last—won out in her inflection; but not altogether, because over all of it is a soft slurring and transformed use of vowels which is the decided influence of the Southside. She passes through the room without looking at either RUTH or WALTER and goes to the outside door and looks, a little blindly, out to the bathroom. She sees that it has been lost to the Johnsons. She closes the door with a sleepy **vengeance** and crosses to the table and sits down a little defeated.*]

BENEATHA.   I am going to start timing those people.

WALTER.   You should get up earlier.

BENEATHA.   [*Her face in her hands. She is still fighting the urge to go back to bed.*] Really—would you suggest dawn? Where's the paper?

WALTER.   [*pushing the paper across the table to her as he studies her almost clinically, as though he has never seen her before*] You a horrible-looking chick at this hour.

BENEATHA.   [*drily*] Good morning, everybody.

WALTER.   [*senselessly*] How is school coming?

BENEATHA.   [*in the same spirit*] Lovely. Lovely. And you know, biology is the greatest. [*looking up at him*] I **dissected** something that looked just like you yesterday.

WALTER.   I just wondered if you've made up your mind and everything.

Word Power

vengeance (ven´ jəns) *n.* the act of getting even with someone; revenge
dissected (di sekt´ id) *v.* took or cut apart to examine

BENEATHA. [*gaining in sharpness and impatience*] And what did I answer yesterday morning—and the day before that?

RUTH. [*from the ironing board, like someone disinterested and old*] Don't be so nasty, Bennie.

BENEATHA. [*still to her brother*] And the day before that and the day before that!

WALTER. [*defensively*] I'm interested in you. Something wrong with that? Ain't many girls who decide—

WALTER and BENEATHA. [*in unison*]—"to be a doctor."

[*silence*]

WALTER. Have we figured out yet just exactly how much medical school is going to cost?

RUTH. Walter Lee, why don't you leave that girl alone and get out of here to work?

BENEATHA. [*exits to the bathroom and bangs on the door*] Come on out of there, please!

[*She comes back into the room.*]

WALTER. [*looking at his sister intently*] You know the check is coming tomorrow.

BENEATHA. [*turning on him with a sharpness all her own*] That money belongs to Mama, Walter, and it's for her to decide how she wants to use it. I don't care if she wants to buy a house or a rocket ship or just nail it up somewhere and look at it. It's hers. Not ours—*hers.*

WALTER. [*bitterly*] Now ain't that fine! You just got your mother's interest at heart, ain't you, girl? You such a nice girl—but if Mama got that money she can always take a few thousand and help you through school too—can't she?

BENEATHA. I have never asked anyone around here to do anything for me!

Literary Element

Character Reread the highlighted sentences. Think about Beneatha's decision to become a doctor at a time when not many women (especially African Americans) dreamed of becoming one. What does this tell you about her character? Check all the responses that apply.

☐ She is smart and determined.

☐ She is indecisive and unsure.

☐ She is ambitious.

Comprehension Check

Reread the boxed passage. What does Beneatha want Mama to do with her money? Check the **best** response below.

☐ give it all to charity

☐ look at it but not spend it

☐ anything she wants, because it belongs to her

Reading Skill
Draw Conclusions

Reread the highlighted sentences. What conclusion can you draw about who has been paying for Beneatha's education so far?

_____

_____

_____

_____

Connect to the Text

Reread the boxed passage. Think about a time when you had an important goal that other people were not supportive of, or didn't think you could reach. Did you keep at it? How did it turn out?

_____

_____

_____

WALTER. No! And the line between asking and just accepting when the time comes is big and wide—ain't it!

BENEATHA. [*with fury*] What do you want from me, Brother— that I quit school or just drop dead, which!

WALTER. I don't want nothing but for you to stop acting holy 'round here. Me and Ruth done made some sacrifices for you—why can't you do something for the family?

RUTH. Walter, don't be dragging me in it.

WALTER. You are in it— Don't you get up and go work in somebody's kitchen for the last three years to help put clothes on her back?

RUTH. Oh, Walter—that's not fair . . .

WALTER. It ain't that nobody expects you to get on your knees and say thank you, Brother; thank you, Ruth; thank you, Mama—and thank you, Travis, for wearing the same pair of shoes for two semesters—

BENEATHA. [*dropping to her knees*] Well—I *do*—all right?— thank everybody! And forgive me for ever wanting to be anything at all! [*pursuing him on her knees across the floor*] FORGIVE ME, FORGIVE ME, FORGIVE ME!

RUTH. Please stop it! Your mama'll hear you.

WALTER. Who the hell told you you had to be a doctor? If you so crazy 'bout messing 'round with sick people—then go be a nurse like other women—or just get married and be quiet . . .

BENEATHA. Well—you finally got it said . . . It took you three years but you finally got it said. Walter, give up; leave me alone—it's Mama's money.

How does the way Beneatha act toward her brother, Walter, help reveal her character?

WALTER. *He was my father, too!*

BENEATHA. So what? He was mine, too—and Travis's grand-father—but the insurance money belongs to Mama. Picking on me is not going to make her give it to you to invest in any liquor stores—[*underbreath, dropping into a chair*]—and I for one say, God bless Mama for that!

WALTER. [*to RUTH*] See—did you hear? Did you hear?

RUTH. Honey, please go to work.

WALTER. Nobody in this house is ever going to understand me.

BENEATHA. Because you're a nut.

WALTER. Who's a nut?

BENEATHA. You—you are a nut. Thee is mad, boy.

WALTER. [*looking at his wife and his sister from the door, very sadly*] The world's most backward race of people, and that's a fact.

BENEATHA. [*turning slowly in her chair*] And then there are all those prophets who would lead us out of the wilderness—[*WALTER slams out of the house.*]—into the swamps!

RUTH. Bennie, why you always gotta be pickin' on your brother? Can't you be a little sweeter sometimes? [*Door opens. WALTER walks in. He fumbles with his cap, starts to speak, clears throat, looks everywhere but at RUTH. Finally:*]

WALTER. [*to RUTH*] I need some money for carfare.

Reading Skill
Draw Conclusions
Reread the highlighted text. Beneatha mentions money and her father. What conclusion can you draw about where the money is coming from? Check the correct response.
- [ ] lottery winnings
- [ ] a life insurance policy
- [ ] a lost bank account

Background Info

Thee is a very formal and old-fashioned word for "you" or "yourself." In this context, Beneatha is using the word to be overly formal and sarcastic with her brother.

Reading Skill

Visualize Reread the highlighted sentences. Underline the words in the text that help you form a picture of Mama in your mind.

Background Info

The Hereros are an African people. Today, they live mostly in Namibia, Botswana, and Angola. In 1883, German settlers moved into Namibia and made it a German colony, called German South-West Africa. The Hereros rebelled, resulting in wars and many deaths.

RUTH. [*looks at him, then warms; teasing, but tenderly*] Fifty cents! [*She goes to her bag and gets money.*] Here—take a taxi!

[*WALTER exits. MAMA enters. She is a woman in her early sixties, full-bodied and strong. She is one of those women of a certain grace and beauty who wear it so unobtrusively that it takes a while to notice. Her dark-brown face is surrounded by the total whiteness of her hair, and, being a woman who has adjusted to many things in life and overcome many more, her face is full of strength. She has, we can see, wit and faith of a kind that keep her eyes lit and full of interest and expectancy. She is, in a word, a beautiful woman. Her bearing is perhaps most like the noble bearing of the women of the* Hereros of Southwest Africa—*rather as if she imagines that as she walks she still bears a basket or a vessel upon her head. Her speech, on the other hand, is as careless as her carriage is precise—she is inclined to slur everything—but her voice is perhaps not so much quiet as simply soft.*]

MAMA. Who that 'round here slamming doors at this hour? [*She crosses through the room, goes to the window, opens it, and brings in a feeble little plant growing doggedly in a small pot on the windowsill. She feels the dirt and puts it back out.*]

RUTH. That was Walter Lee. He and Bennie was at it again.

MAMA. My children and they tempers. Lord, if this little old plant don't get more sun than it's been getting it ain't never going to see spring again. [*She turns from the window.*] What's the matter with you this morning, Ruth? You looks right peaked. You aiming to iron all them things? Leave some for me. I'll get to 'em this afternoon. Bennie honey, it's too drafty for you to be sitting 'round half dressed. Where's your robe?

BENEATHA.   In the cleaners.

MAMA.   Well, go get mine and put it on.

BENEATHA.   I'm not cold, Mama, honest.

MAMA.   I know—but you so thin . . .

BENEATHA.   [*irritably*] Mama, I'm not cold.

MAMA.   [*seeing the make-down bed as TRAVIS has left it*] Lord have mercy, look at that poor bed. Bless his heart—he tries, don't he?

[*She moves to the bed TRAVIS has sloppily made up.*]

RUTH.   No—he don't half try at all 'cause he knows you going to come along behind him and fix everything. That's just how come he don't know how to do nothing right now—you done spoiled that boy so.

MAMA.   [*folding bedding*] Well—he's a little boy. Ain't supposed to know 'bout housekeeping. My baby, that's what he is. What you fix for his breakfast this morning?

RUTH.   [*angrily*] I feed my son, Lena!

MAMA.   I ain't meddling—[*underbreath; busy-bodyish*] I just noticed all last week he had cold cereal, and when it starts getting this chilly in the fall a child ought to have some hot grits or something when he goes out in the cold—

RUTH.   [*furious*] I gave him hot oats—is that all right!

MAMA.   I ain't meddling. [*pause*] Put a lot of nice butter on it? [RUTH *shoots her an angry look and does not reply.*] He likes lots of butter.

RUTH.   [*exasperated*] Lena—

MAMA.   [*To BENEATHA. MAMA is inclined to wander conversationally sometimes.*] What was you and your brother fussing 'bout this morning?

English Coach

Busy-bodyish is made up of two smaller words: *busy* and *body*, with the suffix *-ish*, meaning "having the characteristic of." What do you think a busybody is? Check the correct response below.

☐ a very busy person

☐ a person who gets involved in other people's business

☐ a person who takes care of other people

Connect to the Text

Reread the boxed passage. Think about a time when someone was being nosy, or telling you how to do something that you felt was your business. What did you say to this person?

_____

_____

_____

English Coach

To have your *heart set on* something means "to want something very badly." What other expressions with *heart* do you know?

_____

_____

_____

Literary Element

Character Reread the text highlighted in blue. Characters can change throughout a story or drama. Think about Ruth's attitude about Walter's goals earlier in the scene. How has she changed since then? Do you think she now supports Walter? Why or why not?

_____

_____

_____

_____

_____

BENEATHA. It's not important, Mama.

[*She gets up and goes to look out at the bathroom, which is apparently free, and she picks up her towels and rushes out.*]

MAMA. What was they fighting about?

RUTH. Now you know as well as I do.

MAMA. [*shaking her head*] Brother still worrying hisself sick about that money?

RUTH. You know he is.

MAMA. You had breakfast?

RUTH. Some coffee.

MAMA. Girl, you better start eating and looking after yourself better. You almost thin as Travis.

RUTH. Lena—

MAMA. Un-hunh?

RUTH. What are you going to do with it?

MAMA. Now don't you start, child. It's too early in the morning to be talking about money. It ain't Christian.

RUTH. It's just that he got his heart set on that store—

MAMA. You mean that liquor store that Willy Harris want him to invest in?

RUTH. Yes—

MAMA. We ain't no business people, Ruth. We just plain working folks.

RUTH. Ain't nobody business people till they go into business. Walter Lee say colored people ain't never going to start getting ahead till they start gambling on some different kinds of things in the world—investments and things.

MAMA. What done got into you, girl? Walter Lee done finally sold you on investing.

RUTH. No. Mama, something is happening between Walter and me. I don't know what it is—but he needs something—something I can't give him anymore. He needs this chance, Lena.

If you were the character of Mama, would you give the money to your children or spend it on yourself?

_____

MAMA. [_frowning deeply_] But liquor, honey—

RUTH. Well—like Walter say—I spec people going to always be drinking themselves some liquor.

MAMA. Well—whether they drinks it or not ain't none of my business. But whether I go into business selling it to 'em *is*, and I don't want that on my **ledger** this late in life. [_stopping suddenly and studying her daughter-in-law_] Ruth Younger, what's the matter with you today? You look like you could fall over right there.

RUTH. I'm tired.

MAMA. Then you better stay home from work today.

RUTH. I can't stay home. She'd be calling up the agency and screaming at them, "My girl didn't come in today—send me somebody! My girl didn't come in!" Oh, she just have a fit...

MAMA. Well, let her have it. I'll just call her up and say you got the flu—

RUTH. [_laughing_] Why the flu?

MAMA. 'Cause it sounds respectable to 'em. Something white people get, too. They know 'bout the flu. Otherwise they think you been cut up or something when you tell 'em you sick.

RUTH. I got to go in. We need the money.

Word Power

ledger (lĕj′ ər) *v.* a book in which records are kept, usually of income and expenses

181

MAMA. Somebody would of thought my children done all but starved to death the way they talk about money here late. Child, we got a great big old check coming tomorrow.

RUTH. [*sincerely, but also self-righteously*] Now that's your money. It ain't got nothing to do with me. We all feel like that—Walter and Bennie and me—even Travis.

MAMA. [*thoughtfully, and suddenly very far away*] Ten thousand dollars—

RUTH. Sure is wonderful.

MAMA. Ten thousand dollars.

RUTH. You know what you should do, Miss Lena? You should take yourself a trip somewhere. To Europe or South America or someplace—

MAMA. [*throwing up her hands at the thought*] Oh, child!

RUTH. I'm serious. Just pack up and leave! Go on away and enjoy yourself some. Forget about the family and have yourself a ball for once in your life—

MAMA. [*drily*] You sound like I'm just about ready to die. Who'd go with me? What I look like wandering 'round Europe by myself?

RUTH. Shoot—these here rich white women do it all the time. They don't think nothing of packing up they suitcases and piling on one of them big steamships and—swoosh!—they gone, child.

MAMA. Something always told me I wasn't no rich white woman.

RUTH. Well—what are you going to do with it then?

MAMA. I ain't rightly decided. [*Thinking. She speaks now with emphasis.*] Some of it got to be put away for Beneatha and her schoolin'—and ain't nothing going to touch that part of it. Nothing. [*She waits several seconds, trying to make up her mind about something, and looks at RUTH a little tentatively before going on.*] Been thinking that we maybe could meet the notes on a little old two-story somewhere, with a yard where Travis could play in the summertime, if we use part of the insurance for a down payment and everybody kind of pitch in. I could maybe take on a little day work again, few days a week—

RUTH. [*studying her mother-in-law furtively and concentrating on her ironing, anxious to encourage without seeming to*] Well, Lord knows, we've put enough rent into this here rat trap to pay for four houses by now . . .

MAMA. [*looking up at the words "rat trap" and then looking around and leaning back and sighing—in a suddenly reflective mood—*] "Rat trap"—yes, that's all it is. [*smiling*] I remember just as well the day me and Big Walter moved in here. Hadn't been married but two weeks and wasn't planning on living here no more than a year. [*She shakes her head at the dissolved dream.*] We was going to set away, little by little, don't you know, and buy a little place out in Morgan Park. We had even picked out the house. [*chuckling a little*] Looks right dumpy today. But Lord, child, you should know all the dreams I had 'bout buying that house and fixing it up and making me a little garden in the back—[*She waits and stops smiling.*] And didn't none of it happen. [*dropping her hands in futile gesture*]

RUTH. [*keeps her head down, ironing*] Yes, life can be a barrel of disappointments, sometimes.

English Coach

Rat trap means a "run-down, unattractive place." It implies that it is a place where rats would live. What would a room that was a *pigpen* look like?

_____

_____

_____

Reading Skill

Visualize Reread the highlighted sentences. Think about the home Mama describes here. Then think about the description of the Youngers' home given in the beginning of the scene. Picture both places in your mind. What differences do you see?

_____

_____

_____

_____

_____

_____

MAMA. Honey, Big Walter would come in here some nights back then and slump down on that couch there and just look at the rug, and look at me and look at the rug and then back at me—and I'd know he was down then . . . really down. [*After a second very long and thoughtful pause; she is seeing back to times that only she can see.*] And then, Lord, when I lost that baby—little Claude—I almost thought I was going to lose Big Walter too. Oh, that man grieved hisself! He was one man to love his children.

RUTH. Ain't nothin' can tear at you like losin' your baby.

MAMA. I guess that's how come that man finally worked hisself to death like he done. Like he was fighting his own war with this here world that took his baby from him.

RUTH. He sure was a fine man, all right. I always liked Mr. Younger.

MAMA. Crazy 'bout his children! God knows there was plenty wrong with Walter Younger—hard-headed, mean, kind of wild with women—plenty wrong with him. But he sure loved his children. Always wanted them to have something—be something. That's where Brother gets all these notions, I reckon. Big Walter used to say, he'd get right wet in the eyes sometimes, lean his head back with the water standing in his eyes and say, "Seem like God didn't see fit to give the black man nothing but his dreams—but He did give us children to make them dreams seem worthwhile." [*She smiles.*] He could talk like that, don't you know.

RUTH. Yes, he sure could. He was a good man, Mr. Younger.

MAMA. Yes, a fine man—just couldn't never catch up with his dreams, that's all.

Respond to Literature

A Raisin in the Sun

A Comprehension Check

Answer the following questions in the spaces provided.

1. Why is the Younger family looking forward to Saturday?

   _____

   _____

2. What is a topic that comes up in all the Younger family conversations
   during the morning? _____

   _____

B Reading Skills

Answer the following questions in the spaces provided.

1. **Visualize** How do you picture the Youngers' apartment?

   _____

   _____

   _____

2. **Draw Conclusions** Does the rest of the Younger family support Walter's
   idea of investing Mama's insurance money in a liquor store? What details
   support your conclusion? _____

   _____

   _____

C Word Power

Complete each sentence below, using one of the words in the box.

stupor	indifference	exasperated	mutual
anguish	vengeance	dissected	ledger

1. The crowd at the basketball game howled in _____ when the home team lost the championship game.

2. Mrs. Lee and Mrs. Ruiz shared a _____ dislike for one another after they both wore the same dress to a party.

3. By the sound of her father's _____ grunts, Kara could tell that he was getting frustrated putting her bike together.

4. Henry and his lab partner _____ an earthworm in their biology class.

5. After running into the other skier, Max was in a _____ and had to sit down for a moment to clear his head.

6. Brianna's _____ to gardening showed in the overgrown weeds.

7. After Alberto read that his girlfriend no longer wanted to see him, he tore up the letter with a _____.

8. Tiara's savings account _____ showed that she had made two deposits to her account and one withdrawal in the past month.

D Literary Element: Character

Read the passage below from *A Raisin in the Sun*. As you read, think about what the lines reveal about the characters of Walter and Ruth. Then answer the questions that follow.

RUTH.   Walter, leave me alone![1] [*She raises her head and stares at him vigorously—then says, more quietly.*] *Eat* your eggs, they gonna be cold.[2]

WALTER.   [*straightening up from her and looking off*] That's it.[3] There you are.[4] Man say to his woman: I got me a dream.[5] His woman say: Eat your eggs.[6] [*sadly, but gaining in power*] Man say: I got to take hold of this here world, baby![7] And a woman will say: Eat your eggs and go to work.[8] [*passionately now*] Man say: I got to change my life, I'm choking to death, baby![9] And his woman say—[*in utter anguish as he brings his fists down on his thighs*]—Your eggs is getting cold![10]

RUTH.   [*softly*] Walter, that ain't none of our money.[11]

1. Read sentences 3–10. What do they tell you about Walter and how he feels about his dreams? _____

_____

_____

2. Read sentences 1–2 and 11. How do these sentences help you understand what kind of person Ruth is? _____

_____

_____

E The Drawing

Imagine that Mama cannot make up her mind about how to spend the insurance money. She has decided that each member of the Younger family will write down how he or she thinks the money should be spent and why on slips of paper. Write what each person would write on his or her slip of paper.

I think the insurance money should be spent on _____ because _____ _____ _____

— Walter

I think the insurance money should be spent on _____ because _____ _____ _____

—Ruth

I think the insurance money should be spent on _____ because _____ _____

—Beneatha

I think the insurance money should be spent on _____ _____ because _____ _____ _____ _____

—Mama

Assessment

Fill in the circle next to each correct answer.

1. Where is the money Mama is expecting coming from?
   - ○ A. the insurance policy of her late husband
   - ○ B. the sale of her and her husband's house
   - ○ C. the investment she made in a liquor store
   - ○ D. the rent from the other families in the building

2. Which sentence from the play **best** helps you visualize Mama's appearance?
   - ○ A. She is, in a word, a beautiful woman.
   - ○ B. She is a woman who has adjusted to many things in life.
   - ○ C. Her dark brown face is surrounded by the total whiteness of her hair.
   - ○ D. Her speech, on the other hand, is as careless as her carriage is precise.

3. What conclusion can you draw about how Ruth feels about Willy Harris and his ability to own a liquor store?
   - ○ A. He will talk too loudly to the customers.
   - ○ B. He will be a poor businessman.
   - ○ C. He will be an excellent businessman.
   - ○ D. He will be better than Charlie Atkins.

4. Which word **best** describes Beneatha's character?
   - ○ A. greedy
   - ○ B. carefree
   - ○ C. exasperated
   - ○ D. determined

5. Which of the following words means "great suffering or pain"?
   - ○ A. stupor
   - ○ B. anguish
   - ○ C. vengeance
   - ○ D. indifference

UNIT 4

Legend and Folktale

What's a Legend? What's a Folktale?

Legends are set in particular times and places, and they focus on people who may have existed. Although these stories may contain exaggerated, magical, or supernatural elements, they are historically based. Robin Hood was a real person. King Arthur may have been a real man too, although no one knows for sure.

Originally, legends were passed on from generation to generation by word of mouth. Because legends were not written down and were retold by different storytellers, they changed with each retelling. This might explain why stories based on actual people and events end up containing very little information based on historical fact.

Folktales are also stories that have been passed down through generations by word of mouth. Unlike legends, which may be based on real people, folktale characters can be animals or people who have unusual powers or experiences. The characters can also be ordinary people who face unusual problems. Folktales reflect the traditional beliefs, customs, stories, songs, and dances of a culture.

Coyote the trickster is a character in many Native American folktales. King Arthur is a hero from a legend. What other characters from legends and folktales can you think of? Write your response below.

_____

Why Read Legends and Folktales?

People today read these kinds of tales to enjoy a good story! But these stories can also tell you about the cultures they come from. Readers then can learn about the values and concerns of various cultures.

How Do I Read Legends and Folktales?

Focus on key **literary elements** and **reading skills** to get the most out of reading the legends and folktale in this unit. Here are two key literary elements and two key reading skills that you will practice in this unit.

Key Literary Elements

• Dialogue

Dialogue is the conversation between characters in a story. The reader learns about what is happening and how the characters think and feel through dialogue. Dialogue reveals the characters' personalities, gives information to the reader, and moves the story forward.

• Setting

Setting is the time and place in which the events of a story occur. The setting includes the values and beliefs of the time and place. The setting of a story often helps to create a particular atmosphere or mood. A story that takes place today in New England on a peaceful farm will have a very different atmosphere from a story that takes place during a battle between Native Americans and U.S. soldiers in the 1880s in Montana.

Key Reading Skills

• Paraphrase

When you **paraphrase** part of a story, you restate a text or passage. You simplify the idea to make a passage clearer. When you use your own words to restate what you have read, you understand the author's meaning better. You can paraphrase just part of a story, or the whole story.

• Infer

When you **infer,** you make an educated guess about information you have read. You draw logical conclusions, combining clues from the text with what you already know from experience or other reading. A writer does not always state things directly. For example, instead of telling you that a character is strong, the writer may use details and actions that show the character doing something that takes great strength.

Get Ready to Read!

Where the Girl Rescued Her Brother

Meet Joseph Bruchac and Gayle Ross

Joseph Bruchac (broo shak´), a Native American writer and storyteller, was born in 1942. Bruchac learned the art of storytelling from his grandfather.

Native American storyteller and writer Gayle Ross was born in 1951. She is a direct descendent of Chief John Ross, a Cherokee nation leader during the 1800s. "Where the Girl Rescued Her Brother" first appeared in *The Girl Who Married the Moon* in 1994.

What You Know

Have you heard or read about someone who responded heroically in a time of crisis? What made his or her actions heroic?

Reason to Read

Read to find out how a young woman responds heroically in a time of crisis.

Background Info

The characters and events described in this story are based on fact. The battle that sparked these events took place on June 17, 1876, at Rosebud Creek in southern Montana.

When gold was found in the Black Hills of South Dakota in the early 1870s, miners rushed into the area, even though a treaty had guaranteed the Sioux people ownership of the land. There were many conflicts between the miners and the Sioux. This led to Brigadier General George Crook of the U.S. Army ordering the Sioux to leave the area. Sioux chiefs Sitting Bull and Crazy Horse ignored the order. After several attacks on his people, Sitting Bull summoned the Sioux, Cheyenne, and some Arapaho to Montana. They surprised Crook's troops at Rosebud Creek. This is the setting for "Where the Girl Rescued Her Brother."

Word Power

allies (al´ īz) *n.* persons, groups, or nations joined together to help and support each other; p. 195
Julia's classmates became her *allies* in helping her convince Mr. Brown to take the class on a field trip.

confronted (kən frun´ tid) *v.* faced someone or something in a challenge; p. 196
Edgar's dad *confronted* the skunk and ran it out of the campsite.

reared up (rērd up) *v.* rose up on hind legs; p. 198
The circus trainer was frightened when the elephant *reared up*.

vaulted (vôl´ tid) *v.* leaped or jumped quickly over or onto something; p. 198
The racer *vaulted* onto his motorcycle and sped back to the racetrack.

ferocity (fə ros´ ə tē) *n.* fierceness; intensity; p. 198
Few things in nature match the *ferocity* of a mother bear defending her cubs.

strategic (strə tē´ jik) *adj.* highly important to an intended goal; p. 200
The coach made the *strategic* decision to call a time-out so that the players could take a short break.

**Answer the following questions that contain the new words above.
Write your answers in the spaces provided.**

1. Would a *strategic* decision usually be essential or not essential at all?

   _____

2. If a girl on her way to school *vaulted* onto her bicycle, would she be taking her time

   or trying to hurry? _____

3. Should a beginning rider or an expert rider ride a horse that *reared up* all the time?

   _____

4. If a boy *confronted* a bully at school, would he stand up to him or run away

   from him? _____

5. Would *allies* help you or stand in your way if you tried to raise money for a

   new park? _____

6. Would you find a lion's *ferocity* frightening or amusing? _____

Where the Girl Rescued Her Brother

Joseph Bruchac and Gayle Ross

Background Info

Native Americans often use full moons and important natural events that happen at a regular time each year to tell when something will happen. Here, it is the month of July or August.

Reading Skill

Paraphrase Reread the highlighted sentence. Responsibility is often compared to a weight or burden. What is another way of saying this sentence?

_____

_____

_____

_____

It was the moon when the choke-cherries were ripe. A young woman rode out of a Cheyenne camp with her husband and her brother. The young woman's name was Buffalo Calf Road Woman. Her husband, Black Coyote, was one of the chiefs of the Cheyenne, the people of the plains who call themselves Tsis-tsis-tas, meaning simply "The People." Buffalo Calf Road Woman's brother, Comes-in-Sight, was also one of the Cheyenne chiefs, and it was well known how close he was to his sister.

Like many of the other young women of the Cheyenne, Buffalo Calf Road Woman was respected for her honorable nature. Although it was the men who most often went to war to defend the people—as they were doing on this day—women would accompany their husbands when they went to battle. If a man held an important position among the Cheyenne, such as the keeper of the Sacred Arrows, then his wife, too, would have to be of the highest moral character, for she shared the weight of his responsibility.

Buffalo Calf Road Woman was well aware of this, and as she rode by her husband she did so with pride. She knew that today they were on their way to meet their old **allies,** the Lakota. They were going out to try to drive back the *veho*, the spider people who were trying to claim all the lands of the Native peoples.

The Cheyenne had been worried about the *veho*, the white people, for a long time. They had given them that name because, like the black widow spider, they were very beautiful but it was dangerous to get close to them. And unlike the Cheyenne, they seemed to follow a practice of making promises and not keeping them. Although their soldier chief Custer had promised to be friendly with the Cheyenne, now he and the others had come into their lands to make war upon them.

Buffalo Calf Road Woman wore a robe embroidered with porcupine quills. The clothing of her brother and her husband, Black Coyote, was also beautifully decorated with those quills, which had been flattened, dyed in different colors, folded, and sewed on in patterns. Buffalo Calf Road Woman was proud that she belonged to the Society of Quilters. As with the men's societies, only a few women—those of the best character—could join. Like the men, the women had to be strong, honorable, and brave. Buffalo Calf Road Woman had grown up hearing stories of how Cheyenne women would defend their families when the men were away. The women of the Cheyenne were brave, and those in the Society of Quilters were the bravest of all.

Did You Know?

Porcupine quills were the most popular decoration for clothing and other items among Native Americans until glass beads were introduced by European American traders.

. . . .

Comprehension Check

Reread the boxed passage. Why were Buffalo Calf Road Woman and her husband and brother riding out of their camp? Check the correct response.

☐ They were going to hunt with the Lakota.

☐ They were going to drive out the white people.

☐ They were meeting their allies, the white people.

Background Info

In 1876, Lieutenant Colonel George A. Custer of the U.S. Cavalry regiment led an attack to drive out the Sioux and Cheyenne along the Rosebud River. His troops were outnumbered by three to one. Custer and about 200 men died in the battle led by Crazy Horse and Sitting Bull. The battle became known as "Custer's Last Stand."

Word Power

allies (al´ īz) *n.* persons, groups, or nations joined together to help and support each other

Background Info

The Plains Indians used the names of full moons to name the months. Here Buffalo Calf Road Woman is most likely remembering the month of October because of the falling leaves.

Literary Element

Setting Reread the sentence highlighted in blue. What is an important detail about the camp on this day when the grizzly bear arrives?

_____

_____

_____

_____

Reading Skill

Infer Reread the sentences highlighted in green. What can you infer about Buffalo Calf Road Woman and the others from their actions?

_____

_____

_____

_____

Buffalo Calf Road Woman smiled as she remembered one day when the women of the Society of Quilters showed such bravery. It was during the Moon of Falling Leaves. A big hunt had been planned. The men who acted as scouts had gone out and located the great buffalo herd. They had seen, too, that there were no human enemies anywhere near their camp. So almost none of the men remained behind.

On that day, when all the men were away, a great grizzly bear came into the camp. Such things seldom happened, but this bear was one that had been wounded in the leg by a white fur-trapper's bullet. It could no longer hunt as it had before, and hunger brought it to the Cheyenne camp, where it smelled food cooking.

When the huge bear came walking into the camp, almost everyone scattered. Some women grabbed their little children. Old people shut the door flaps of their tepees, and the boys ran to find their bows and arrows. Only a group of seven women who had been working on the embroidery of an elk-skin robe did not run. They were members of the Society of Quilters, and Buffalo Calf Road Woman was among them. The seven women put down their work, picked up the weapons they had close to hand, and stood to face the grizzly bear.

Now of all of the animals of the plains, the only one fierce enough and powerful enough to attack a human was the grizzly. But **confronted** by that determined group of women, the grizzly bear stopped in its tracks. It had come to steal food, not fight. The head of the Society of Quilters stepped forward a pace and spoke to the bear.

"Grandfather," she said, her voice low and firm, "we do not wish to harm you, but we will protect our camp. Go back to your own home."

Word Power

confronted (kən frun′ tid) v. faced someone or something in a challenge

196

Cheyenne Woman. Greg Perillo.

In what way does the image of this Cheyenne woman remind you of Buffalo Calf Road Woman?

The grizzly shook its head and then turned and walked out of the camp. The women stood and watched it as it went down through the cottonwoods and was lost from sight along the bend of the stream.

Buffalo Calf Road Woman turned her mind away from her memories. They were close to Rosebud Creek. The scouts had told them that a great number of the *veho* soldiers would be there and that the Gray Fox, General George Crook, was in command. The Cheyenne had joined up now with the Oglala, led by Crazy Horse. The Lakota people were always friends to the Cheyenne, but this man, Crazy Horse, was the best friend of all. Some even said that he was one of their chiefs, too, as well as being a war leader of his Oglala.

There were Crow and Shoshone scouts with Crook, and the *veho* had many cannons. The Lakota and the Cheyenne were outnumbered by the two thousand men in Crook's command. But they were prepared to fight. They had put on their finest clothes, for no man should risk his life without being dressed well enough so that if he died, the enemy would know a great warrior had fallen. Some of the men raised their headdresses three times, calling out their names and the deeds they had done.

Background Info

Also a Sioux people, the Oglala (ō glä′ lə) lived in what is now South Dakota. The Crow and Shoshone (shə shō′ nē) peoples lived primarily in the Rocky Mountains.

English Coach

The prefix *out-* means "better or more than." Was the number of soldiers in Crook's army greater than or less than the number of Lakota and Cheyenne?

Literary Element

Setting Reread the highlighted sentence and the rest of the paragraph. Underline the words and phrases the author uses in this paragraph to help the reader picture the setting.

English Coach

The *odds* here means "the chances of." If the odds in the battle were almost even, the two sides had an equal chance of winning—or of losing. What is another expression you know that includes "odds"?

_____

_____

Those headdresses of eagle feathers were thought to give magical protection to a warrior. Other men busied themselves painting designs on their war ponies.

Now they could hear Crook's army approaching. The rumble of the horses' hooves echoed down the valley, and there was the sound of trumpets. War ponies **reared up** and stomped their feet. Many of the Cheyenne men found it hard to put on the last of their paint as their hands shook from the excitement of the coming battle.

Crazy Horse **vaulted** onto his horse and held up one arm. "*Hoka Hey*," he cried. "It is a good day to die."

Buffalo Calf Road Woman watched from a hill as the two lines of men—the blue soldiers to one side, and the Lakota and Cheyenne to the other—raced toward each other. The battle began. It was not a quick fight or an easy one. There were brave men on both sides. Two Moons, Little Hawk, Yellow Eagle, Sitting Bull, and Crazy Horse were only a few of the great warriors who fought for the Cheyenne and the Lakota. And Crook, the Gray Fox general of the whites, was known to be a tough fighter and a worthy enemy.

Buffalo Calf Road Woman's husband, Black Coyote, and her brother, Comes-in-Sight, were in the thick of the fight. The odds in the battle were almost even. Although the whites had more soldiers and guns, the Lakota and the Cheyenne were better shots and better horsemen. Had it not been for the Crow and Shoshone scouts helping Crook, the white soldiers might have broken quickly from the **ferocity** of the attack.

Word Power

reared up (rērd up) *v.* rose up on hind legs
vaulted (vôl´ tid) *v.* leaped or jumped quickly over or onto something
ferocity (fə ros´ ə tē) *n.* fierceness, intensity

From one side to the other, groups of men attacked and retreated as the guns cracked, cannons boomed, and smoke filled the air. The war shouts of the Lakota and the Cheyenne were almost as loud as the rumble of the guns. The sun moved across the sky as the fight went on, hour after hour, while the confusion of battle swirled below.

Then Buffalo Calf Road Woman saw something that horrified her. Her brother had been drawn off to one side, surrounded by Crow scouts. He tried to ride free of them, but his pony went down, struck by a rifle bullet and killed. Now he was on foot, still fighting. The Crow warriors were trying to get close, to count coup on him. It was more of an honor to touch a living enemy, so they were not firing their rifles at him. And he was able to keep them away with his bow and arrows. But it was clear that soon he would be out of ammunition and would fall to the enemy.

Buffalo Calf Road Woman waited no longer. She dug her heels into her pony's sides and galloped down the hill. Her head low, her braids streaming behind her, she rode into the heart of the fight. Some men moved aside as they saw her coming, for there was a determined look in her eyes. She made the long howling cry that Cheyenne women used to urge on the warriors. This time, however, she was the one going into the fight. Her voice was as strong as an eagle's. Her horse scattered the ponies of the Crow scouts who were closing in on her brother, Comes-in-Sight. She held out a hand; her brother grabbed it and vaulted onto the pony behind her. Then she wheeled, ducking the arrows of the Crow scouts, and heading back up the hill.

Reading Skill

Paraphrase Reread the highlighted sentence. Check the box next to the sentence that **best** paraphrases the highlighted sentence.

☐ The sun fought against the sky.

☐ The battle lasted for an hour.

☐ The battle went on for many hours.

Background Info

Among some Native Americans, to *count coup* (ko͞o) was to touch a living enemy and get away safely. This act required both skill and courage.

Comprehension Check

Reread the boxed paragraph. How does Buffalo Calf Road Woman save her brother?

_____

_____

_____

_____

_____

Reading Skill

Infer Reread the highlighted sentence. What do you think the men are thinking as they watch Buffalo Calf Road Woman?

_____

_____

_____

_____

Comprehension Check

Reread the boxed sentence. How does the battle end?

_____

_____

_____

_____

That was when it happened. For a moment, it seemed as if all the shooting stopped. The Cheyenne and the Lakota, and even the veho soldiers, lowered their guns to watch this act of great bravery. A shout went up, not from one side but from both, as Buffalo Calf Road Woman reached the safety of the hilltop again, her brother safe behind her on her horse. White men and Indians cheered her.

So it was that Buffalo Calf Road Woman performed the act for which the people would always remember her. Inspired by her courage, the Cheyenne and Lakota drove back the Gray Fox—Crook made a **strategic** withdrawal.

"Even the *veho* general was impressed," said the Cheyenne people. "He saw that if our women were that brave, he would stand no chance against us in battle."

So it is that to this day, the Cheyenne and the Lakota people do not refer to the fight as the Battle of the Rosebud. Instead, they honor Buffalo Calf Road Woman by calling the fight Where the Girl Rescued Her Brother.

Word Power

strategic (strə te´ jik) *adj.* highly important to an intended goal

200

Respond to Literature

Where the Girl Rescued Her Brother

A Comprehension Check

Answer the following questions in the spaces provided.

1. Who are Black Coyote, Comes-in-Sight, and Buffalo Calf Road Woman going to meet? _____

_____

2. What do the Cheyenne believe is the reason for the outcome of the battle?

_____

_____

B Reading Skills

Answer the following questions in the spaces provided.

1. **Infer** What can you infer from the fact that Buffalo Calf Road Woman smiles when she remembers the story of the women defending the camp from a grizzly bear? _____

_____

2. **Infer** What can you infer from the battle preparations of the Native Americans in the story about their attitude toward fighting and battle?

_____

_____

3. **Paraphrase** How would you paraphrase this sentence from the story: "But confronted by that determined group of women, the grizzly bear stopped in its tracks"? _____

_____

C Word Power

Complete each sentence below, using one of the words in the box.

| allies | confronted | reared p |
| vaulted | ferocity | strategic |

1. The boys _____ over the fence and ran down the street.

2. Scientists worry about the spread of killer bees, which are known for their _____.

3. It is important for a country to help its _____ when they need support.

4. When the bear _____ to its full height, it stood over ten feet tall.

5. In the middle of the movie, Ahmed turned around in his seat and _____ a woman talking on her cell phone.

6. Anne's _____ move kept Leon from capturing her queen and winning the chess game.

D Literary Element: Setting

Read the passages below from "Where the Girl Rescued Her Brother." As you read, think about what the sentences reveal about the setting of the story. Then answer the questions that follow.

When the huge bear came walking into the camp, almost everyone scattered.[1] Some women grabbed their little children.[2] Old people shut the door flaps of their tepees, and the boys ran to find their bows and arrows.[3] Only a group of seven women who had been working on the embroidery of an elk-skin robe did not run.[4]

The grizzly shook its head and then turned and walked out of the camp.[5] The women stood and watched it as it went down through the cottonwoods and was lost from sight along the bend of the stream.[6]

1. What details in sentences 1–4 tell you that the setting is a Native American camp? _____

_____

_____

2. What details in sentences 5 and 6 describe the setting of the camp?

_____

_____

_____

E A Newspaper Article

Imagine that you are a reporter who saw the battle take place in "Where the Girl Rescued Her Brother." Write a newspaper article about the battle. Include details about Buffalo Calf Road Woman's heroic rescue of her brother.

Headline: _____

On June 17, 1876, a terrible battle took place at Rosebud Creek in southern Montana. The battle was fought by

_____

_____

The fighting was fierce. Although General Crook had more men, the Cheyenne and Lakota were _____

_____

The fight went on for hours. Suddenly, a Cheyenne woman named Buffalo Calf Road Woman came riding down the hill. She _____

_____

_____

Together they rode back up the hill. Everyone stood and watched. The battle stopped for a moment, and men on both sides cheered.

When he saw her bravery, General Crook _____

_____

Respond to Literature

Assessment

Fill in the circle next to each correct answer.

1. What do the Cheyenne think about the *veho*, the white people?
   - ○ A. They are good friends.
   - ○ B. They are dangerous and can't be trusted.
   - ○ C. They are not good-looking.
   - ○ D. They make good neighbors for everyone.

2. What can you infer from Crazy Horse's cry before the battle: "*Hoka Hey*. It is a good day to die"?
   - ○ A. Crazy Horse hopes to ward off evil spirits.
   - ○ B. Crazy Horse hopes that no one is killed in battle.
   - ○ C. Crazy Horse is afraid of dying.
   - ○ D. Crazy Horse is prepared to die if he must.

3. Which of the following **best** paraphrases the sentence below?
   "Although their soldier chief Custer had promised to be friendly with the Cheyenne, now he and the others had come into their lands to make war upon them."
   - ○ A. Custer said he would be friends with the Cheyenne for a long time.
   - ○ B. Custer and others broke their promises to be friendly.
   - ○ C. Custer broke his promise to be friendly and had come to fight.
   - ○ D. Custer was coming with others into their lands to make war.

4. Where was Buffalo Calf Road Woman as she watched the battle?
   - ○ A. on the banks of a stream
   - ○ B. at the bottom of the valley
   - ○ C. at the top of a hill
   - ○ D. behind some cottonwood trees

5. Which of the following words means "faced someone or something in a challenge"?
   - ○ A. confronted
   - ○ B. vaulted
   - ○ C. reared up
   - ○ D. ferocity

Get Ready to Read!

Yuki-Onna

Meet Lafcadio Hearn

Lafcadio Hearn was born in Greece in 1850. His father was Irish and English, and his mother was Greek. In 1890 he traveled to Japan. He found that he loved the Japanese culture, and decided to stay. He took on a Japanese name: Yakumo Koizumi. He stayed in Japan for the rest of his life, and wrote many books about Japanese culture for English speakers. Hearn died in 1904. "Yuki-Onna" was first published in 1904.

What You Know

Have you ever made a promise to keep a secret? Did you keep your promise? Why or why not? What happened as a result?

Reason to Read

Read this folktale to find out how one man's mysterious secret follows him throughout his life.

Background Info

This folktale is a traditional Japanese ghost story, or kaidan (kī dan´). In Japan, people traditionally told ghost stories in the summertime. This was a great way to escape from the heat—since scary stories can send a chill down your spine! The Japanese people's interest in ghost stories was at its height during the Edo period (1603–1867), named after the city where the government was located. "Yuki-Onna," or "The Snow Woman," is a retelling of one of these ancient Japanese legends.

Word Power

utter (ut´ ər) *v.* to speak or make a sound with the voice; p. 209
I was so surprised and speechless that I couldn't *utter* a sound.

gleam (glēm) *n.* reflected brightness; p. 210
The *gleam* of Alice's smile made everyone in the room notice her.

senseless (sens´ lis) *adj.* not being able to think or feel; unconscious; p. 210
The boxer was knocked *senseless* by his opponent's powerful punch.

confidences (kon´ fə dəns iz) *n.* secrets; p. 211
My best friend and I share *confidences* that we would never tell anyone else.

hesitation (hez´ ə tā´ shən) *n.* the act of holding back because of feeling unsure;
p. 211
After a little *hesitation,* I finally got up the nerve to audition for the school play.

Answer the following questions that contain the new words above.
Write your answers in the spaces provided.

1. Would you share *confidences* with someone you trust or someone you do not trust?

   _____

2. If you showed *hesitation* about asking a question, did you ask it right away or pause

   before you asked it? _____

3. If you *utter* a few words, are you speaking out loud or being silent?

   _____

4. If someone is lying *senseless* in a bed, is that person asleep or awake?

   _____

5. Would the *gleam* of a new car be seen or heard? _____

Adapted from

Yuki-Onna

Lafcadio Hearn

Literary Element

Setting Reread the highlighted passage. Is this story set in a city or the country? Is the climate calm or sometimes severe? How can you tell?

_____

_____

_____

_____

_____

_____

_____

In a village of Musashi Province, there lived two woodcutters: Mosaku and Minokichi. At the time of which I am speaking, Mosaku was an old man and Minokichi, his assistant, was eighteen years old. Every day they went together to a forest located about five miles from their village. On the way to that forest there is a wide river to cross, but there is a ferryboat. Several times a bridge was built where the ferry is, but the bridge was each time washed away by a flood. No ordinary bridge can resist the current there when the river rises.

Mosaku and Minokichi were on their way home, one very cold evening, when a great snowstorm overtook them. When they reached the river, they found that the boatman had gone away, leaving his boat on the other side of the river. It was no day for swimming, so the woodcutters took shelter in the boatman's hut—thinking themselves lucky to find any shelter at all. There was no place in which to make a fire.

Did You Know?

A two-mat hut is a very small, primitive house. *Two-mat* means that the surface of the floor is only about thirty-six square feet.

It was only a two-mat hut, with a single door, but no window. Mosaku and Minokichi locked the door and lay down to rest, with their straw raincoats over them. At first they did not feel very cold and they thought that the storm would soon be over.

The old man almost immediately fell asleep. But the boy, Minokichi, lay awake a long time. He listened to the awful wind and the continual slashing of the snow against the door. The river was roaring and the hut swayed and creaked like a boat at sea. It was a terrible storm. The air was every moment becoming colder. Minokichi shivered under his raincoat. But at last, in spite of the cold, he too fell asleep.

He was awakened by a showering of snow in his face. The door of the hut had been forced open. By the light reflected on the snow, he saw a woman in the room—a woman all in white. She was bending above Mosaku, and blowing her breath upon him. Her breath was like a bright white smoke. Almost in the same moment she turned to Minokichi, and stooped over him. He tried to scream, but found that he could not **utter** any sound. The white woman bent down over him, lower and lower, until her face almost touched him. He saw that she was very beautiful, though her eyes made him afraid.

For a little time she continued to look at him. Then she smiled and whispered, "I intended to treat you like the other man. But I cannot help feeling some pity for you, because you are so young. You are a pretty boy, Minokichi, and I will not hurt you now. But, if you ever tell anybody—even your own mother—about what you have seen this night, I shall know it. And then I will kill you. Remember what I say!"

Word Power

utter (ut′ ər) *v.* to speak or make a sound with the voice

Literary Element

Dialogue Reread the sentences highlighted below. What does this dialogue tell you about the snow woman?

_____

_____

_____

_____

_____

Reading Skill

Infer Reread the sentences highlighted in green. You already know that the woman just blew her breath on Mosaku. What do you think has happened to Mosaku? Why do you think so?

_____

_____

_____

_____

_____

_____

With these words, she turned from him and passed through the doorway. Then he found himself able to move. He jumped up and looked out. But the woman was nowhere to be seen. The snow was blowing furiously into the hut. Minokichi closed the door and secured it by fixing several pieces of wood against it. He wondered if the wind had blown it open. He thought that he might have been only dreaming, and might have mistaken the **gleam** of the light in the doorway for the figure of a white woman. But he could not be sure. He called to Mosaku, and was frightened because the old man did not answer. He put out his hand in the dark, and touched Mosaku's face, and found that it was ice! Mosaku was stiff and dead...

By dawn the storm was over. When the boatman returned to his station, a little after sunrise, he found Minokichi lying **senseless** beside the frozen body of Mosaku. Minokichi was promptly cared for, and soon came to. But he remained a long time ill from the effects of the cold of that terrible night. He had been greatly frightened also by the old man's death, but he said nothing about the vision of the woman in white. As soon as he got well again, he returned to his job. He went alone every morning to the forest and came back at nightfall with his bundles of wood, which his mother helped him to sell.

One evening, in the winter of the following year, as he was on his way home, he passed a girl who happened to be traveling on the same road. She was a tall, slim girl, very good-looking. She answered Minokichi's greeting in a voice as pleasant to the ear as the voice of a songbird. Then he walked beside her and they began to talk.

English Coach

The phrase *came to* means "woke up." Rewrite this sentence to use the new phrase: *I was asleep, but I heard my alarm and woke up.* Write the new sentence below.

_____

_____

_____

_____

Word Power

gleam (glēm) *n.* reflected brightness

senseless (sens´ lis) *adj.* not being able to think or feel; unconscious

The girl said that her name was O-Yuki, that she had lately lost both of her parents, and that she was going to Yedo. There she happened to have some poor relatives, who might help her to find a position as a servant. Minokichi soon felt charmed by this strange girl. The more that he looked at her, the more attractive she appeared to be. He asked her whether she was yet engaged to be married. She answered, laughingly, that she was free. Then, in her turn, she asked Minokichi whether he was married, or pledged to marry. He told her that, although he had only a widowed mother to support, the question of an "honorable daughter-in-law" had not yet been considered, because he was very young. After these **confidences,** they walked on for a long while without speaking. But, as the saying goes, *Ki ga areba, me mo kuchi hodo ni mono wo iu:* ("When the wish is there, the eyes can say as much as the mouth.") By the time they reached the village, they had become very fond of each other. Then Minokichi asked O-Yuki to rest awhile at his house. After some shy **hesitation,** she went there with him. His mother made her welcome, and prepared a warm meal for her. O-Yuki behaved so nicely that Minokichi's mother took a sudden liking to her and persuaded her to delay her journey to Yedo. The natural end of the matter was that O-Yuki never went to Yedo at all. She remained in the house as an "honorable daughter-in-law."

Comprehension Check

Reread the boxed sentences. Why is O-Yuki going to Yedo?

_____

_____

_____

_____

_____

Reading Skill

Paraphrase Reread the highlighted sentence. Which sentence below **best** paraphrases the saying from the story? Check the correct response.

☐ If you wish hard enough, you can achieve your dreams.

☐ If you feel something deeply, you don't need to speak—it will show in your eyes.

☐ If you close your eyes and make a wish, it will come true.

Word Power

confidences (kon´ fə dəns iz) *n.* secrets
hesitation (hez´ ə tā´ shən) *n.* the act of holding back because of feeling unsure

211

Comprehension Check

Reread the boxed paragraph. Was O-Yuki well liked by her mother-in-law? How does O-Yuki's family situation change?

_____

_____

_____

_____

_____

Reading Skill

Infer Reread the highlighted paragraph. Think about clues the author gives, such as the fact that O-Yuki never seems to grow older. What do you think the author wants you to know about her?

_____

_____

_____

_____

Spring Water Tea House. Ando Hiroshige. 14 x 9 in. The Newark Museum, Newark, NJ. John Cotton Dana Collection.

How does this picture show what life might have been like for O-Yuki and Minokichi?

_____

O-Yuki proved a very good daughter-in-law. When Minokichi's mother came to die—some five years later—her last words were words of affection and praise for the wife of her son. And O-Yuki bore Minokichi ten children, boys and girls. They were all handsome children and very fair-skinned.

The country folk thought O-Yuki a wonderful person, by nature different from themselves. Most of the peasant women age early, but O-Yuki, even after having become the mother of ten children, looked as young and fresh as on the day when she had first come to the village.

One night, after the children had gone to sleep, O-Yuki was sewing by the light of a paper lamp. Minokichi, watching her, said:

"To see you sewing there, with the light on your face, makes me think of a strange thing that happened when I was eighteen. I then saw somebody as beautiful and white as you are now—indeed, she was very like you."

Without lifting her eyes from her work, O-Yuki responded:

"Tell me about her. Where did you see her?"

Then Minokichi told her about the terrible night in the boatman's hut, and about the White Woman that had stooped above him, smiling and whispering, and about the silent death of old Mosaku. And he said:

"Asleep or awake, that was the only time that I saw a being as beautiful as you. Of course, she was not a human being. I was afraid of her—very much afraid—and she was so white! Indeed, I have never been sure whether it was a dream that I saw or the Woman of the Snow."

O-Yuki flung down her sewing, arose, and bowed above Minokichi where he sat, and shrieked into his face:

"It was I—I—I! Yuki it was! And I told you then that I would kill you if you ever said one word about it! If it were not for those children asleep there, I would kill you this moment! And now you had better take very, very good care of them. For if ever they have reason to complain of you, I will treat you as you deserve!"

Even as she screamed, her voice became thin, like a crying of wind. Then she melted into a bright white mist that rose to the roof beams, and disappeared through the chimney. Never again was she seen.

Reading Skill

Paraphrase Reread the highlighted sentence. Paraphrase the sentence and rewrite it below.

_____
_____
_____
_____
_____

English Coach

Thin in this context means "weak." Write another meaning for _thin_ and use it in a sentence.

_____
_____
_____
_____

Respond to Literature

Yuki-Onna

A Comprehension Check

Answer the following questions in the spaces provided.

1. What happens to Mosaku and Minokichi inside the hut? _____

   _____

   _____

2. Why does O-Yuki stay in the village instead of going to Yedo?

   _____

B Reading Skills

Answer the following questions in the spaces provided.

1. **Infer** When Minokichi first sees the woman in white, he sees that she blows her breath upon Mosaku, and her eyes make him afraid. What inference can you make about the woman based on these clues?

   _____

   _____

2. **Infer** When Minokichi meets the young girl, they each ask if the other is free to marry. What inference can you draw about how they feel about each other? _____

   _____

3. **Paraphrase** Paraphrase this sentence from the story: "The country folk thought O-Yuki a wonderful person, by nature different from themselves."

   _____

   _____

Respond to Literature

C Word Power

Complete each sentence below, using one of the words in the box.

utter	gleam	senseless	confidences	hesitation

1. Once the lifeguard told us the water was safe, we were all able to jump in without _____.

2. Our librarian is very strict about talking, so make sure not to _____ a sound!

3. The two best friends whispered _____ to one another.

4. Once my little brother falls asleep, it's no use trying to wake him up—he's absolutely _____.

5. A bright _____ of light shined through the window.

Circle the word that best completes each sentence.

6. The blast of the cannon made the soldiers **(senseless, hesitation)** for several minutes.

7. Did you hear the bird **(utter, gleam)** a loud and lonely cry?

8. The **(gleam, hesitation)** from Mike's new bicycle made everyone take notice.

9. The little boy shared his **(senseless, confidences)** with his favorite toy bear each night.

10. The runners showed no **(confidences, hesitation)** as they left their starting positions at the sound of the gun.

D Literary Element: Dialogue

Read the passage below from "Yuki-Onna." As you read, think about the dialogue in the story. Then answer the questions that follow.

> "Asleep or awake, that was the only time I saw a being as beautiful as you. [1] Of course, she was not a human being. [2] I was afraid of her—very much afraid—and she was so white! [3] Indeed, I have never been sure that it was a dream I saw or the Woman of the Snow." [4]

1. Reread sentences 1–3. What clues does the author give to show that the White Woman in "Yuki-Onna" was frightening?

   _____

   _____

   _____

   _____

2. In sentences 3–4, what clues from Minokichi's dialogue tell you that he had confronted the Woman of the Snow, Yuki-Onna?

   _____

   _____

   _____

   _____

E Diary of a Scary Day

Imagine that you are Minokichi, and you are writing an entry in your diary about your experience in the boatman's hut. Write to tell about what happened and how you felt.

Dear Diary,

I had such a strange day! I was walking home from work with Mosaku when _____

_____

We went inside the boatman's hut, locked the door, and eventually we both fell asleep.

But when I woke up, _____

_____

She was all in white, and as she bent over Mosaku, she

_____

The next thing I knew, she was standing over me! I felt

_____

_____

At last she left, and I tried to wake up Mosaku. But I couldn't, because _____
I don't know if the woman was real or a dream, but either way, today was _____

_____

Assessment

Fill in the circle next to each correct answer.

1. Where does Minokichi first see the "Woman of the Snow"?
   - ○ A. on the bridge
   - ○ B. in the boatman's hut
   - ○ C. on a walk with his mother
   - ○ D. at Mosaku's house

2. Which sentence **best** explains why Minokichi keeps the White Woman a secret for so long?
   - ○ A. He thinks no one will believe him.
   - ○ B. He is sorry for Mosaku.
   - ○ C. He is afraid that the spirit will kill him.
   - ○ D. He no longer remembers what happened.

3. Which of the choices below is the **best** paraphrase for the term "honorable daughter-in-law"?
   - ○ A. a son's honest and good wife
   - ○ B. a girl whose father is trustworthy
   - ○ C. a mother who can keep a secret
   - ○ D. a daughter who never breaks the law

4. Which of the following sentences tells you about the setting in "Yuki-Onna"?
   - ○ A. The old man almost immediately fell asleep.
   - ○ B. She was a tall, slim girl, very good-looking.
   - ○ C. After these confidences, they walked on for a long time without speaking.
   - ○ D. Every day they went together to a forest located about five miles from their village.

5. Which of the following words means the same thing as "not being able to think or feel"?
   - ○ A. utter
   - ○ B. senseless
   - ○ C. hesitation
   - ○ D. gleam

Wrap-up

Compare and Contrast

Setting is an important literary element in "Where the Girl Rescued Her Brother" and "Yuki-Onna." Although the settings in these short stories are different, they both have an important effect on the characters. Think about how the settings impact the characters and events. Then think about how the settings reflect important cultural and historical periods.

Complete the chart below. In the column labeled "Alike," tell how the setting is alike in each story. In the column labeled "Different," tell how the setting is different in each story.

Alike	Different

UNIT 5 Nonfiction

What's Nonfiction?

Pick up a newspaper or magazine or check out many Web sites, and you will find writing that is nonfiction.

Nonfiction is the name for writing that is about real people and real events. Many types of nonfiction are meant to inform or to relate experiences. Nonfiction can tell facts and include the use of vivid descriptions. There are many kinds of nonfiction: biographies, autobiographies, memoirs, essays, letters, and feature articles.

A **biography** is the story of a person's life written by someone other than the subject. An **autobiography** is the story of a person's life written by that person. **Memoirs** are stories of the narrator's personal experience. An **essay** is a short piece of nonfiction about a single topic.

Nonfiction can deal with many topics. This list mentions some of them. **Check one subject below that you like to read about or write a subject of your own.**

☐ the experiences of a traveler
☐ the causes of violent weather
☐ how people live in a distant part of the world
☐ the history of a sport
☐ the life story of a famous person

_____

Why Read Nonfiction?

Read nonfiction to learn about new places, new people, and new ideas. By reading nonfiction and learning new things, you can better understand the world around you. Nonfiction can even help you better understand yourself.

How Do I Read Nonfiction?

Focus on key **literary elements** and **reading skills** to get the most out of reading the nonfiction in this unit. Here are two key literary elements and two key reading skills that you will practice in this unit.

Key Literary Elements

• Tone

Tone is the writer's attitude toward the subject. The writer uses specific words and details to help create the tone. For example, the writer might describe a desert as "sunny, hot, filled with unexpected flowers" or as "scorching, extremely dry, dangerous." In the first description, the tone is cheerful and appreciative. In the second, the tone is fearful.

• Autobiography

In an **autobiography,** a writer tells his or her life story from the first-person point of view and uses the pronoun *I.* Writers create autobiographies to share memories of events, people, and feelings that are important to them. The event may have happened when the author was a child, or it may be recent. Writers may describe not only the events that occurred, but also their reactions to these events. Some autobiographies can also give readers an idea of what society was like during the author's lifetime.

Key Reading Skills

• Problem and Solution

Characters in stories often come up against problems that they need to solve. To focus on **problems and solutions,** ask yourself these questions: What is the main problem? Who has the problem? What solutions do the characters try? What happens as a result?

• Respond

When you stop and think about your thoughts and feelings about something you've read, you are responding. Active readers **respond** to what they are reading. Think about what you have read and how you feel about it. As you read, you can ask yourself, How does this make me feel? and What does this mean to me? Thinking about and answering these questions will help you understand what you have read.

Get Ready to Read!

The Angry Winter

Meet Loren Eiseley

Writer Loren Eiseley was born in Nebraska in 1907 and died in 1977. Eiseley once compared the brain of a writer to an attic in which pictures of the past are collected. Eiseley filled his "attic" with pictures from the Nebraska prairie land, his observations of nature, and his work with fossils. In his lifetime Eiseley was an anthropologist, a university professor, an essayist, and a poet. "The Angry Winter" first appeared in a collection of Eiseley's essays in 1969.

What You Know

Are you affected today by what happened in the past? How might past events—either from the recent past or long ago—influence your behavior in the present?

Reason to Read

Read this nonfiction essay to discover how a man and his dog are influenced by the past.

Background Info

Dogs belong to the same animal family as wolves, coyotes, jackals, and foxes. Scientists think that the animals in this family have been a part of people's lives for thousands of years. The fossilized bones of wolves have been discovered along with human bones at sites dating back 400,000 years. Scientists believe that some wolves may have wandered into campsites looking for food scraps. When humans realized that wolves could give useful warning of approaching danger, they accepted them into their communities. The dogs we keep as family pets today are descendants of those wolves first kept as pets about 14,000 years ago.

Word Power

appraise (ə prāz´) v. to estimate someone's ability or the value of something; p. 224
The wrestlers had only moments to *appraise* each other before the whistle blew and their match began.

diverted (di vur´ tid) v. drew away someone's attention; changed the direction of something; p. 224
A knock on the door *diverted* me from my reading.

utterance (ut´ ər əns) n. words that are said or sounds that are made; p. 225
"Hello!" was the first *utterance* made by Adrian's parrot.

diminished (di min´ isht) v. became less or smaller; p. 227
The rain *diminished*, and we put away our umbrellas.

receded (ri sēd´ id) v. moved back or away; p. 227
People returned to their homes once the water finally *receded*.

**Answer the following questions that contain the new words above.
Write your answers in the spaces provided.**

1. If the sound of the police siren *receded*, did it get louder or fade away?

   _____

2. Would a driver whose attention was easily *diverted* be a safe or an unsafe driver?

   _____

3. If someone made an *utterance*, would you see it or hear it? _____

4. If an athlete's skills *diminished*, would he or she be better or worse than before?

   _____

5. Who would be most likely to *appraise* a dog, a cat owner or a judge at a dog show?

   _____

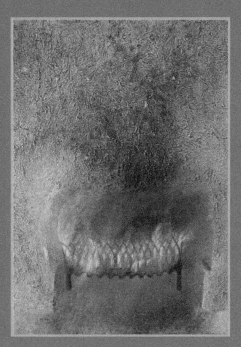

Hearth, 1957. Loren McIver. Oil on plaster on Masonite, 49⅝ x 34⅝ in. Metropolitan Museum of Art, New York. Museum purchase, Marie-Gaetana Matisse Gift, 1993. 1993.280.

Adapted from

The Angry Winter

Loren Eiseley

Background Info

An ice age refers to periods when large areas of Earth were covered by sheets of ice. A million or more years ago, mountain glaciers formed on all continents and vast glaciers spread across much of North America.

A time comes when creatures whose destinies have crossed somewhere in the remote past are forced to **appraise** each other as though they were total strangers. I had been huddled beside the fire one winter night, with the wind prowling outside and shaking the windows. The big shepherd dog on the hearth before me occasionally glanced up affectionately, sighed, and slept. I was working. On my desk lay the lance points of ice age hunters and the heavy leg bone of a fossil bison. No remains of flesh attached to these relics. As I worked on in my little circle of light, I absently laid the bone beside me on the floor. The hour had crept toward midnight. A grating noise, a heavy rasping of big teeth **diverted** me. I looked down.

The dog had risen. That rock-hard fragment of a vanished beast was in his jaws and he was mouthing it with a fierceness I had never seen exhibited by him before.

Word Power

appraise (ə prāz´) *v.* to estimate someone's ability or the value of something

diverted (di vur´ tid) *v.* drew away someone's attention; changed the direction of something

"Wolf," I exclaimed, and stretched out my hand. The dog backed up but did not yield. A low and steady rumbling began to rise in his chest, something out of a long-gone midnight. There was nothing in that bone to taste, but ancient shapes were moving in his mind and determining his **utterance.** Only fools gave up bones. He was warning me.

"Wolf," I said again.

As I advanced, his teeth showed and his mouth wrinkled to strike. The rumbling rose to a direct snarl. His flat head swayed low and wickedly as a reptile's above the floor. I was the most loved object in his universe, but the past was fully alive in him now. Its shadows were whispering in his mind. I knew he was not bluffing. If I made another step he would strike.

Yet his eyes were strained and desperate. "Do not," something pleaded in the back of them, some affectionate thing that had followed at my heel all the days of his mortal life, "do not force me. I am what I am and cannot be otherwise because of the shadows. Do not reach out. You are a man, and my very god. I love you, but do not put out your hand. It is midnight. We are in another time, in the snow."

"The *other* time," the steady rumbling continued while I paused, "the other time in the snow, the big, the final, the terrible snow, when the shape of this thing I hold spelled life. I will not give it up. I cannot. The shadows will not permit me. Do not put out your hand."

Comprehension Check

Reread the boxed text. Why is the dog growling at his master? Check the correct response.

☐ The dog is tired.

☐ The dog is upset with his food.

☐ The dog is protecting a bone.

Reading Skill

Respond Reread the highlighted sentence and the rest of the paragraph. How did you feel when you read this paragraph? How would you feel if you were the narrator?

_____

_____

_____

_____

English Coach

Here the word *spelled* means "meant." What other phrase could you use that would also have the same meaning?

☐ used magical powers

☐ added up to

☐ said the letters of a word

Word Power

utterance (ut′ ər əns) *n.* words that are said or sounds that are made

Literary Element

Tone In your opinion, what does the scene in this picture tell you about the tone of the story thus far?

_____

_____

_____

_____

_____

_____

_____

_____

Snowy Mountains, artist unknown.

I stood silent, looking into his eyes, and heard his whisper through. Slowly I drew back in understanding. The snarl **diminished,** ceased. As I retreated, the bone slumped to the floor. He placed a paw upon it, warningly.

And were there no shadows in my own mind, I wondered. Had I not for a moment, in the grip of that savage utterance, been about to respond, to hurl myself upon him over a bone ten thousand years removed? Even to me the shadows had whispered—to me, the scholar in his study.

"Wolf," I said, but this time, holding a familiar leash, I spoke from the door indifferently. "A walk in the snow." Instantly from his eyes that visitor from another time **receded.** The bone was left lying. He came eagerly to my side, accepting the leash and taking it in his mouth as always.

A blizzard was raging when we went out, but he paid no heed. On his thick fur the driving snow was soon clinging heavily. He played a little—though usually he was a serious dog—making up to me for something still receding in his mind. I felt the snowflakes fall upon my face, and stood thinking of another time, and another time still, until I was moving from midnight to midnight under ever more remote and deeper snows. Wolf came to my side with a little whimper. It was he who was civilized now. "Come back to the fire," he nudged gently, "or you will be lost." Automatically I took the leash he offered. He led me safely home and into the house.

Reading Skill
Problem and Solution Reread the highlighted paragraph. How does the narrator solve the problem with his dog?

_____

_____

_____

_____

Comprehension Check

Reread the boxed sentences. The narrator is lost in thought before the dog nudges him. What is the narrator thinking about? Check the correct response.

☐ He is thinking back to the worst winters he has seen.

☐ He is thinking back to what he was doing at midnight.

☐ He is thinking back to thousands of years ago when dogs and people were wild.

Word Power
diminished (di min´ isht) *v.* became less or smaller
receded (ri sēd´ id) *v.* moved back or away

Literary Element

Tone Reread the highlighted sentence and the rest of the paragraph. Which word **best** describes the tone of this paragraph? Check the correct response.

☐ peaceful
☐ weary
☐ excited

"We have been very far away," I told him solemnly. "I think there is something in us that we had both better try to forget." Sprawled on the rug, Wolf made no response except to thump his tail feebly out of courtesy. Already he was mostly asleep and dreaming. By the movement of his feet I could see he was running far upon some errand in which I played no part.

Softly I picked up his bone—our bone, rather—and replaced it high on a shelf in my cabinet. As I snapped off the light the white glow from the window seemed to shine with a deep, glacial blue. As far as I could see, nothing moved in the long aisles of my neighbor's woods. There was no visible track, and certainly no sound from the living. The snow continued to fall steadily, but the wind, and the shadows it had brought, had vanished.

Respond to Literature

The Angry Winter

A Comprehension Check

Answer the following questions in the spaces provided.

1. What are the narrator and the dog doing at the start of the essay?

   _____

   _____

2. Why is the dog unwilling to give up the bone? _____

   _____

   _____

B Reading Skills

Answer the following questions in the spaces provided.

1. **Respond** How did you feel when the narrator realizes that his dog will

   attack if he steps closer? Explain. _____

   _____

   _____

2. **Problem and Solution** What problem does the narrator face in the story?

   How does the narrator finally solve the problem? _____

   _____

   _____

C Word Power

Complete each sentence below, using one of the words in the box.

appraise	diverted	utterance	diminished	receded

1. When the basketball star gave a speech at the school, the students paid great attention to his every _____.

2. The teacher was _____ from grading papers by a loud noise in the hall.

3. After the floodwaters _____, many people saw that their homes were gone.

4. The woodpile slowly _____ as we threw the logs into the bonfire.

5. Before the swim meet began, Harold glanced around the pool to _____ the other swimmers.

Circle the word that best completes each sentence.

6. The airplane passengers sighed with relief as the baby's crying **(utterance, diminished)**.

7. The border collie waited for the **(utterance, appraise)** from his master that would send him running toward the sheep.

8. Mr. Arroyo was **(receded, diverted)** from his golf swing by a bumblebee and hit the ball into a pond.

9. Walking between tables filled with pastries, the judge paused to **(appraise, diminished)** a raspberry pie.

10. As the train made its way through the valley, the view of the mountains **(diverted, receded)** into the distance.

D Literary Element: Tone

Read the passages below from "The Angry Winter." As you read, think about what the sentences reveal about the tone of the story. Then answer the questions that follow.

As I advanced, his teeth showed and his mouth wrinkled to strike.[1] The rumbling rose to a direct snarl.[2] His flat head swayed low and wickedly as a reptile's above the floor.[3]

And were there no shadows in my own mind, I wondered.[4] Had I not for a moment, in the grip of that savage utterance, been about to respond, to hurl myself upon him over a bone ten thousand years removed?[5] Even to me the shadows had whispered—to me, the scholar in his study.[6]

1. In sentences 1–3, the narrator approaches his dog to try to take away a bone. What details contribute to the tone of danger and excitement?

_____

_____

_____

2. In sentences 4–6, what words and phrases express the tone of thoughtfulness and surprise in this passage? _____

_____

_____

_____

E Pet Psychologist

Imagine that Wolf, the dog in the essay, felt terrible about how he acted toward his owner and did not understand what made him behave the way he did. Write the conversation that may have occurred when Wolf went to talk with Dr. Reedy, a pet psychologist.

WOLF: So, Doc, I caught sight of this bone that my master had placed on the floor. . .

DR. REEDY: What did the bone look like?

WOLF: _____

DR. REEDY: How did it make you feel when you saw the bone, Wolf?

WOLF: _____

DR. REEDY: What did you do after you saw the bone?

WOLF: _____

_____

DR. REEDY: What did your master do?

WOLF: _____

DR. REEDY: Why did you finally give up the bone?

WOLF: _____

DR. REEDY: Our time is up now. I'll see you next week.

Assessment

Fill in the circle next to each correct answer.

1. What did the dog grab and refuse to give up?
   - ○ A. a ham bone
   - ○ B. a rock
   - ○ C. a fossil bone
   - ○ D. a chunk of ice

2. What does the narrator do that leads to the main problem of the story?
   - ○ A. He shows the dog his leash.
   - ○ B. He places a bone on the floor.
   - ○ C. He tries to give a bone to his dog.
   - ○ D. He lets the dog lead him back to the house.

3. What does the narrator think about doing **first** to solve the problem?
   - ○ A. taking the dog for a walk
   - ○ B. placing the bone on a shelf
   - ○ C. keeping the bone on his desk
   - ○ D. taking the bone away by force

4. Which words describe the overall tone of the story?
   - ○ A. sad, then happy
   - ○ B. threatening, then thoughtful
   - ○ C. playful, then serious
   - ○ D. serious, then silly

5. Which of the following words means "moved back or away"?
   - ○ A. receded
   - ○ B. diverted
   - ○ C. utterance
   - ○ D. diminished

Get Ready to Read!

An American Childhood

What You Know

Think of someone you know who has a great sense of humor about life. What makes this person so funny?

Reason to Read

Read this autobiographical selection to learn about a person with a sense of humor.

Background Info

This selection is set in Pittsburgh, Pennsylvania, in the 1950s. Most middle-class women in the 1950s did not work outside the home or have their own careers. Women who could afford to go to college were generally assumed to be looking for a husband. Even a well-educated married woman of the 1950s was expected to concentrate on taking care of her husband and children.

Word Power

improvised (im′ prə vīzd′) *adj.* made up or invented on the spot; p. 236
I hadn't been paying attention when my teacher called on me, so I gave an *improvised* answer to his question.

scenario (si när′ ē ō′) *n.* a sequence of events that might happen in a particular situation; p. 239
Yasir knew his mother would be angry at him for missing dinner, and this was a *scenario* he wanted to avoid.

galled (gôld) *v.* irritated; annoyed; got on one's nerves; p. 239
It *galled* me that most of the players who made the soccer team weren't any better than I was.

tedious (tē′ dē əs) *adj.* tiring and boring; p. 241
Mowing the lawn is one of my most *tedious* chores.

conformity (kən fôr′ mə tē) *n.* behavior that matches everyone else's; p. 244
Tired of *conformity*, the band member decided to dye his hair purple.

ostracism (os′ trə siz′ əm) *n.* exclusion from a group or society; p. 244
I knew I was risking *ostracism* by speaking up, but I decided to tell my friends that I thought they were wrong.

**Answer the following questions that contain the new words above.
Write your answers in the spaces provided.**

1. If a job is *tedious,* is it interesting or not interesting? _____

2. If you want to avoid *conformity,* would you wear the same kinds of clothes as your friends or wear clothes that are different? _____

3. If you are *galled* by someone's behavior, do you find it funny or annoying?

   _____

4. If you gave an *improvised* speech, did you write it out beforehand or make it up as you went along? _____

5. If someone is facing *ostracism,* is that person being accepted by a group or being pushed out of it? _____

6. If you imagine a likely *scenario,* is it something that already happened or something you think might happen? _____

from

An American Childhood

Annie Dillard

Background Info

Here, *utility* means "useful generally rather than in a specialized function." A utility infielder is capable of playing shortstop or first, second, or third base.

Connect to the Text

Reread the boxed text. Think about an unusual phrase or sentence that fascinates you, or that you think is particularly funny. What is it, and why do you react to it that way?

_____

_____

_____

One Sunday afternoon Mother wandered through our kitchen, where Father was making a sandwich and listening to the ball game. The Pirates were playing the New York Giants at Forbes Field. In those days, the Giants had a utility infielder named Wayne Terwilliger. Just as Mother passed through, the radio announcer cried—with undue drama—"Terwilliger bunts one!"

"Terwilliger bunts one?" Mother cried back, stopped short. She turned. "Is that English?"

"The player's name is Terwilliger," Father said. "He bunted."

"That's marvelous," Mother said. "'Terwilliger bunts one.' No wonder you listen to baseball. 'Terwilliger bunts one.'"

For the next seven or eight years, Mother made this surprising string of syllables her own. Testing a microphone, she repeated, "Terwilliger bunts one"; testing a pen or a typewriter, she wrote it. If, as happened surprisingly often in the course of various **improvised** gags, she pretended to whisper something else in my ear, she actually whispered, "Terwilliger bunts one." Whenever someone used a French phrase, or a Latin one, she answered solemnly, "Terwilliger bunts one."

Word Power

improvised (im´ prə vīzd´) *adj.* made up or invented on the spot

If Mother had had, like Andrew Carnegie, the opportunity to cook up a motto for a coat of arms, hers would have read simply and tellingly, "Terwilliger bunts one." (Carnegie's was "Death to Privilege.")

She served us with other words and phrases. On a Florida trip, she repeated tremulously, "That . . . is a royal poinciana." I don't remember the tree; I remember the thrill in her voice. She pronounced it carefully, and spelled it. She also liked to say "portulaca."

The drama of the words "Tamiami Trail" stirred her, we learned on the same Florida trip. People built Tampa on one coast, and they built Miami on another. Then—the height of visionary ambition and folly—they piled a slow, tremendous road through the terrible Everglades to connect them. To build the road, men stood sunk in muck to their armpits. They fought off cottonmouth moccasins and six-foot alligators. They slept in boats, wet. They blasted muck with dynamite, cut jungle with machetes; they laid logs, dragged drilling machines, hauled dredges, heaped limestone. The road took fourteen years to build up by the shovelful, a Panama Canal in reverse, and cost hundreds of lives from tropical, mosquito-carried diseases. Then, capping it all, some genius thought of the word Tamiami: they called the road from Tampa to Miami, this very road under our spinning wheels, the Tamiami Trail. Some called it Alligator Alley. Anyone could drive over this road without a thought.

Hearing this, moved, I thought all the suffering of road building was worth it (it wasn't my suffering), now that we had this new thing to hang these new words on—Alligator Alley for those who like things cute, and, for connoisseurs like Mother, for lovers of the human drama in all its boldness and terror, the Tamiami Trail.

Reading Skill

Problem and Solution Reread the highlighted sentences. The narrator's mother's problem is that her children think they "know it all." What is her solution to this problem?

_____

_____

_____

_____

_____

_____

Background Info

In the 1950s and 1960s, stores used to give customers a certain number of stamps per dollar spent. These stamps were saved up and later exchanged for merchandise.

Back home, Mother cut clips from reels of talk, as it were, and played them back at leisure. She noticed that many Pittsburghers confuse "leave" and "let." One kind relative brightened our morning by mentioning why she'd brought her son to visit: "He wanted to come with me, so I left him." Mother filled in Amy and me on locutions we missed. "I can't do it on Friday," her pretty sister told a crowded dinner party, "because Friday's the day I lay in the stores."

(All unconsciously, though, we ourselves used some pure Pittsburghisms. We said "tele pole," pronounced "telly pole," for that splintery sidewalk post I loved to climb. We said "slippy"—the sidewalks are "slippy." We said, "That's all the farther I could go." And we said, as Pittsburghers do say, "This glass needs washed," or "The dog needs walked"—a usage our father eschewed; he knew it was not standard English, nor even comprehensible English, but he never let on.)

"Spell 'poinsettia,'" Mother would throw out at me, smiling with pleasure. "Spell 'sherbet.'" The idea was not to make us whizzes, but, quite the contrary, to remind us—and I, especially, needed reminding—that we didn't know it all just yet.

"There's a deer standing in the front hall," she told me one quiet evening in the country.

"Really?"

"No. I just wanted to tell you something once without your saying, 'I know.'"

Supermarkets in the middle 1950s began luring, or bothering, customers by giving out Top Value Stamps or Green Stamps. When, shopping with Mother, we got to the head of the checkout line, the checker, always a young man, asked, "Save stamps?"

"No," Mother replied genially, week after week, "I build model airplanes." I believe she originated this line. It took me years to determine where the joke lay.

Anyone who met her verbal challenges she adored. She had surgery on one of her eyes. On the operating table, just before she conked out, she appealed feelingly to the surgeon, saying, as she had been planning to say for weeks, "Will I be able to play the piano?" "Not on me," the surgeon said. "You won't pull that old one on me."

It was, indeed, an old one. The surgeon was supposed to answer, "Yes, my dear, brave woman, you will be able to play the piano after this operation," to which Mother intended to reply, "Oh, good, I've always wanted to play the piano." This pat **scenario** bored her; she loved having it interrupted. It must have **galled** her that usually her acquaintances were so predictably unalert; it must have galled her that, for the length of her life, she could surprise everyone so continually, so easily, when she had been the same all along. At any rate, she loved anyone who, as she put it, saw it coming, and called her on it.

She regarded the instructions on bureaucratic forms as straight lines. "Do you advocate the overthrow of the United States government by force or violence?" After some thought she wrote, "Force." She regarded children, even babies, as straight men. When Molly learned to crawl, Mother delighted in buying her gowns with drawstrings at the bottom, like Swee'pea's, because, as she explained energetically, you could easily step on the drawstring without the baby's noticing, so that she crawled and crawled and crawled and never got anywhere except into a small ball at the gown's top.

© 1996 King Features Syndicate, Inc.
TM of the Hearst Corporation.

Did You Know?
Swee'pea is the baby in "Popeye" cartoons.

My Workspace

Literary Element

Tone Reread the highlighted sentences. Think about the words and phrases that add to the tone of the passage, such as "my dear, brave woman." What choice below **best** describes this tone? Check the correct response.

☐ serious and heartfelt
☐ amused and sarcastic
☐ annoyed and fed up

English Coach

Straight lines are the setups for jokes provided by straight men who assist comedians. What are other phrases or expressions you know that contain the word *straight*?

_____

_____

_____

_____

Word Power

scenario (si när′ ē ō′) *n.* a sequence of events that might happen in a particular situation

galled (gôld) *v.* irritated; annoyed; got on one's nerves

Gathering Fruit, c. 1895. Mary Cassatt. Courtesy Library of Congress Prints & Photography Division.

The artist of this painting uses colors and shapes to set a certain mood. How does this painting reflect the mood of the story? Explain.

_____

Reading Skill

Respond Reread the highlighted sentences. Think about the narrator's mother's practical jokes and how she gets her children to participate in them. How do you feel about this? How would you react if you were the narrator?

_____

_____

_____

_____

_____

_____

When we children were young, she mothered us tenderly and dependably; as we got older, she resumed her career of anarchism. She collared us into her gags. If she answered the phone on a wrong number, she told the caller, "Just a minute," and dragged the receiver to Amy or me, saying, "Here, take this, your name is Cecile," or, worse, just, "It's for you." You had to think on your feet. But did you want to perform well as Cecile, or did you want to take pity on the wretched caller?

During a family trip to the Highland Park Zoo, Mother and I were alone for a minute. She approached a young couple holding hands on a bench by the seals, and addressed the young man in dripping tones: "Where have you been? Still got those baby-blue eyes; always did slay me. And this"—a swift nod at the dumbstruck young woman, who had removed her hand from the man's—"must be the one you were telling me about. She's not so bad, really, as you used to make out. But listen, you know how I miss you, you know where to reach me, same old place. And there's Ann over there—see how she's grown? See the blue eyes?"

And off she sashayed, taking me firmly by the hand, and leading us around briskly past the monkey house and away. She cocked an ear back, and both of us heard the desperate man begin, in a high-pitched wail, "I swear, I never saw her before in my life. . . ."

On a long, sloping beach by the ocean, she lay stretched out sunning with Father and friends, until the conversation gradually grew **tedious,** when without forethought she gave a little push with her heel and rolled away. People were stunned. She rolled deadpan and apparently effortlessly, arms and legs extended and tidy, down the beach to the distant water's edge, where she lay at ease just as she had been, but half in the surf, and well out of earshot.

She dearly loved to fluster people by throwing out a game's rules at whim—when she was getting bored, losing in a dull sort of way, and when everybody else was taking it too seriously. If you turned your back, she moved the checkers around on the board. When you got them all straightened out, she denied she'd touched them; the next time you turned your back, she lined them up on the rug or hid them under your chair. In a betting rummy game called *Michigan,* she routinely played out of turn, or called out a card she didn't hold, or counted backward, simply to amuse herself by causing an uproar and watching the rest of us do double takes and have fits. (Much later, when serious suitors came to call, Mother subjected them to this fast card game as a trial by ordeal; she used it as an intelligence test and a measure of spirit. If the poor man could stay a round without breaking down or running out, he got to marry one of us, if he still wanted to.)

Comprehension Check

Reread the paragraph boxed in green. What did the narrator's mother do at the beach? Why did she do it?

_____

_____

_____

_____

Connect to the Text

Reread the sentence boxed in purple. When you play a game, how seriously do you take the rules? How seriously do you expect other players to take them?

_____

_____

_____

_____

Word Power

tedious (tē′ dē əs) *adj.* tiring and boring

Reading Skill

Problem and Solution Reread the highlighted paragraph. What problem does the narrator's mother have when the family's address changes? How does she solve the problem?

_____

_____

_____

_____

_____

_____

Comprehension Check

Reread the boxed paragraph. Why doesn't the narrator's mother actually create any of the inventions she thinks up? Check the correct response.

☐ She doesn't think anyone will buy new corkscrews.

☐ She feels that running a business is not as interesting as making up ideas.

☐ She doesn't want to sell anything unless people can pay her a lot of money.

She excelled at bridge, playing fast and boldly, but when the stakes were low and the hands dull, she bid slams for the devilment of it, or raised her opponents' suit to bug them, or showed her hand, or tossed her cards in a handful behind her back in a characteristic swift motion accompanied by a vibrantly innocent look. It drove our stolid father crazy. The hand was over before it began, and the guests were appalled. How do you score it, who deals now, what do you do with a crazy person who is having so much fun? Or they were down seven, and the guests were appalled. "Pam!" "Dammit, Pam!" He groaned. What ails such people? What on earth possesses them? He rubbed his face.

She was an unstoppable force; she never let go. When we moved across town, she persuaded the U.S. Post Office to let her keep her old address—forever—because she'd had stationery printed. I don't know how she did it. Every new post office worker, over decades, needed to learn that although the Doaks' mail is addressed to here, it is delivered to there.

Mother's energy and intelligence suited her for a greater role in a larger arena—mayor of New York, say—than the one she had. She followed American politics closely; she had been known to vote for Democrats. She saw how things should be run, but she had nothing to run but our household. Even there, small minds bugged her; she was smarter than the people who designed the things she had to use all day for the length of her life.

"Look," she said. "Whoever designed this corkscrew never used one. Why would anyone sell it without trying it out?" So she invented a better one. She showed me a drawing of it. The spirit of American enterprise never faded in Mother. If capitalizing and tooling up had been as interesting as theorizing and thinking up, she would have fired up a new factory every week, and chaired several hundred corporations.

"It grieves me," she would say, "it grieves my heart," that the company that made one superior product packaged it poorly, or took the wrong tack in its advertising. She knew, as she held the thing mournfully in her two hands, that she'd never find another. She was right. We children wholly sympathized, and so did Father; what could she do, what could anyone do, about it? She was Samson in chains. She paced.

She didn't like the taste of stamps so she didn't lick stamps; she licked the corner of the envelope instead. She glued sandpaper to the sides of kitchen drawers, and under kitchen cabinets, so she always had a handy place to strike a match. She designed, and hounded workmen to build against all norms, doubly wide kitchen counters and elevated bathroom sinks. She drew plans for an over-the-finger toothbrush for babies, an oven rack that slid up and down, and—the family favorite—Lendalarm. Lendalarm was a beeper you attached to books (or tools) you loaned friends. After ten days, the beeper sounded. Only the rightful owner could silence it.

She repeatedly reminded us of P.T. Barnum's dictum: You could sell anything to anybody if you marketed it right. The adman who thought of making Americans believe they needed underarm deodorant was a visionary. So, too, was the hero who made a success of a new product, Ivory soap. The executives were horrified, Mother told me, that a cake of this stuff floated. Soap wasn't supposed to float. Anyone would be able to tell it was mostly whipped-up air. Then some inspired adman made a leap: Advertise that it floats. Flaunt it. The rest is history.

My Workspace

Background Info

In the Bible, Samson told Delilah that the secret of his great strength was that his hair had never been cut. He fell asleep, she got out her clippers, and Samson's enemies soon had him chained up in prison.

Reading Skill

Respond Reread the highlighted sentences. Do you think the "Lendalarm" beeper is a good idea? Would you use the invention? Why or why not?

_____

_____

_____

Background Info

In the 1800s, Barnum founded what is now the Ringling Bros. and Barnum & Bailey Circus. Barnum was also known for staging publicity stunts. The actual words of his saying (dictum) were: "There's a sucker born every minute."

My Workspace

Comprehension Check

Reread the boxed paragraph. What statement below **best** describes the narrator's mother's opinion? Check the correct response.

- [ ] You should always be original and stand up for your own ideas.
- [ ] It's better not to struggle against a mighty stream.
- [ ] If you take too many risks, the world would be a better place without you.

Literary Element

Tone Reread the highlighted paragraph. Think about the tone in this paragraph. (Hint: The author uses fairly serious language.) In your opinion, what attitude does the author show toward her mother here?

_____

_____

_____

_____

_____

How does this photo from the 1950s help you imagine what the narrator's mother is like?

She respected the rare few who broke through to new ways. "Look," she'd say, "here's an intelligent apron." She called upon us to admire intelligent control knobs and intelligent pan handles, intelligent andirons and picture frames and knife sharpeners. She questioned everything, every pair of scissors, every knitting needle, gardening glove, tape dispenser. Hers was a restless mental vigor that just about ignited the dumb household objects with its force.

Torpid **conformity** was a kind of sin; it was stupidity itself, the mighty stream against which Mother would never cease to struggle. If you held no minority opinions, or if you failed to risk total **ostracism** for them daily, the world would be a better place without you. . . .

She simply tried to keep us all awake. And in fact it was always clear to Amy and me, and to Molly when she grew old enough to listen, that if our classmates came to cruelty, just as much as if the neighborhood or the nation came to madness, we were expected to take, and would be each separately capable of taking, a stand.

Word Power

conformity (kən fôr´ mə tē) *n.* behavior that matches everyone else's
ostracism (os´ trə siz´ əm) *n.* exclusion from a group or society

Respond to Literature

An American Childhood

A Comprehension Check

Answer the following questions in the spaces provided.

1. The narrator's mother finds humor in situations that ordinarily would not be funny. Give an example from the story. _____

_____

_____

2. According to the author, what does the narrator's mother expect of her daughters? _____

_____

B Reading Skills

Complete the following activities in the spaces provided.

1. **Problem and Solution** The narrator's mother invents a product called the Lendalarm. What common problem does this invention attempt to solve? What is the solution? _____

_____

_____

2. **Respond** The narrator's mother constantly "tests" the people around her with her sense of humor. Choose an episode from the story and tell how you would react in that situation. _____

_____

_____

C Word Power

Complete each sentence below, using one of the words in the box.

improvised   scenario   galled   tedious
conformity   ostracism

1. It _____ me that I got a B on my paper when I really deserved an A.

2. It's worth it to risk _____ by going against others if you really believe you are right.

3. I hadn't memorized my dialogue, so I just performed a quick and _____ skit for the audition.

4. Some people say our school's dress code is unfair because it enforces _____ for everyone to dress the same way.

5. We thought up an elaborate _____ to make sure my father's birthday party would be a surprise.

6. I think cleaning my room is a dull, _____ job that takes too much time!

D Literary Element: Tone

Read the passage below from *An American Childhood*. As you read, think about the author's use of tone. Then answer the questions that follow.

Mother's energy and intelligence suited her for a greater role in a larger arena—mayor of New York, say—than the one she had.[1] She followed American politics closely; she had been known to vote for Democrats.[2] She saw how things should be run, but she had nothing to run but our household.[3] Even there, small minds bugged her; she was smarter than the people who designed the things she had to use all day for the length of her life.[4]

1. In sentences 1–2, what details does the author use to show an attitude of respect and admiration toward her mother? _____

_____

_____

_____

_____

2. In sentences 3–4, how does the author show sympathy toward her mother? What does she say that indicates she might feel sorry about her mother's situation? Explain. _____

_____

_____

_____

_____

E A Letter from the Author

Imagine that you are the author of *An American Childhood*. Some friends of yours are coming over to your house and will meet Mother for the first time. Write to your friends telling them what to expect when they arrive.

Dear Friends,

Before you arrive on Saturday, there are a few things I should probably warn you about.

If you want to play checkers, make sure the game doesn't get boring.

My mother will probably _____

_____

If you catch her at it, she'll just _____

_____

When my mother plays bridge with my father, she often _____

_____

And if she asks you to play a card game called Michigan, beware! She is testing you to see if _____

_____

And last but certainly not least, be prepared for a lot of practical jokes and craziness!

I know I'm making her sound a little strange, but I really think my

mother is _____

I'm sure you will too!

Annie

Assessment

Fill in the circle next to each correct answer.

1. What phrase does the narrator's mother like to use over and over again?
   - ○ A. "Death to Privilege"
   - ○ B. "Terwilliger bunts one"
   - ○ C. "Tele pole"
   - ○ D. "Alligator Alley"

2. What problem did the narrator's mother solve by gluing sandpaper under the cabinets?
   - ○ A. The cabinets stuck when she tried to open them.
   - ○ B. She needed a convenient place to light a match.
   - ○ C. She didn't like the way the kitchen was decorated.
   - ○ D. She wanted to make sure Molly couldn't find the matches.

3. Which of the sentences below **best** describes the narrator's mother's solution to the problem of getting bored at bridge games?
   - ○ A. She writes the score down incorrectly.
   - ○ B. She tries to make her daughter furious.
   - ○ C. She does outrageous things to surprise the other players.
   - ○ D. She asks the guests to stop playing cards.

4. Which of the following sentences **best** illustrates the author's humorous tone?
   - ○ A. During a family trip to the Highland Park Zoo, Mother and I were alone for a minute.
   - ○ B. One Sunday afternoon Mother wandered through our kitchen, where father was making a sandwich and listening to the ball game.
   - ○ C. She followed American politics closely; she had been known to vote for Democrats.
   - ○ D. If the poor man could stay a round without breaking down or running out, he got to marry one of us, if he still wanted to.

5. Which of the following words means the same thing as "irritated"?
   - ○ A. ostracism
   - ○ B. galled
   - ○ C. tedious
   - ○ D. improvised

Get Ready to Read!

By Any Other Name

Meet Santha Rama Rau

Santha Rama Rau
(sän′ thä rä′ mä rou) was born
in Madras, India, in 1923 and was
raised in a traditional Indian
family. She has always been close
to her family and retained her
sense of cultural identity. Her
novels and nonfiction reflect
her love for her native land.
"By Any Other Name" first
appeared in *The New Yorker*
magazine and is part of the
author's autobiography,
published in 1961.

What You Know

Think about your name. How important is your name to you?
Is it just a name, or does it mean more? How would you feel
if someone changed it?

Reason to Read

Read this autobiographical story to find out what the author's
name means to her.

Background Info

This selection takes place in Zorinabad, India, in the late 1920s.
Between 1858 and 1947, India was a colony of Great Britain. During
this time, British culture had a strong influence on Indian life.
Some Indians took on British traditions, while others struggled
to keep their own customs and culture. In 1920 Mohandas
Gandhi, a leader of the Indian people, organized a movement
to get independence for India. As a result, tensions between
Great Britain and India were very high throughout the 1920s.
Great Britain finally granted India independence in 1947.

Word Power

precarious (pri kār ́ ē əs) *adj.* not safe or sure; uncertain; risky; p. 252
The pitcher of milk wobbled on the edge of the table in a *precarious* way.

valid (val ́ id) *adj.* based on facts or good evidence; p. 253
Pedro's doctor appointment was a *valid* reason for missing class.

detached (di tacht ́) *adj.* not taking sides or involved emotionally; neutral; p. 254
When my friends and I argue, we ask a *detached* observer to decide who is right.

incomprehensible (in ́ kom pri hen ́ sə bəl) *adj.* not understandable; p. 255
The directions were so *incomprehensible* that the students could not follow them.

eternity (i tur ́ nə tē) *n.* a seemingly endless length of time; p. 257
I waited for the bus for what seemed like an *eternity*.

sedately (si dāt ́ lē) *adv.* in a quiet, steady manner; p. 257
Mia walked *sedately* down the aisle to receive her college diploma.

rigid (rij ́ id) *adj.* stiff; firm and inflexible; p. 260
The clay dried out and became so *rigid* that I could not bend it.

Answer the following questions, using one of the new words above.
Write your answers in the spaces provided.

1. Which word goes with "not getting involved in an argument"? _____

2. Which word goes with "something that seems to last forever"? _____

3. Which word goes with "unstable or unsteady"? _____

4. Which word goes with "calmly, with a steady pace"? _____

5. Which word goes with "beyond one's understanding"? _____

6. Which word goes with "unbending"? _____

7. Which word goes with "factual and supported by truth"? _____

By Any Other Name

Santha Rama Rau

Literary Element

Autobiography Reread the highlighted passage. Underline the words that help you understand that the writer is telling her own story. (Hint: What words do you use when you talk about yourself or when you include yourself in a group?)

Comprehension Check

Reread the boxed text. Why does the headmistress change the girls' names?

_____

_____

_____

At the Anglo-Indian day school in Zorinabad to which my sister and I were sent when she was eight and I was five and a half, they changed our names. On the first day of school, a hot, windless morning of a north Indian September, we stood in the headmistress's study and she said, "Now you're the new girls. What are your names?"

My sister answered for us. "I am Premila, and she"—nodding in my direction—"is Santha."

The headmistress had been in India, I suppose, fifteen years or so, but she still smiled at her helpless inability to cope with Indian names. Her rimless half-glasses glittered, and the **precarious** bun on the top of her head trembled as she shook her head. "Oh, my dears, those are much too hard for me. Suppose we give you pretty English names. Wouldn't that be more jolly? Let's see, now—Pamela for you, I think." She shrugged in a baffled way at my sister. "That's as close as I can get. And for you," she said to me, "how about Cynthia? Isn't that nice?"

Word Power

precarious (pri kār′ ē əs) *adj.* not safe or sure; uncertain; risky

My sister was always less easily intimidated than I was, and while she kept a stubborn silence, I said, "Thank you," in a very tiny voice.

We had been sent to that school because my father, among his responsibilities as an officer of the civil service, had a tour of duty to perform in the villages around that steamy little provincial town, where he had his headquarters at that time. He used to make his shorter inspection tours on horseback, and a week before, in the stale heat of a typically postmonsoon day, we had waved good-bye to him and a little procession—an assistant, a secretary, two bearers, and the man to look after the bedding rolls and luggage. They rode away through our large garden, still bright green from the rains, and we turned back into the twilight of the house and the sound of fans whispering in every room.

Up to then, my mother had refused to send Premila to school in the British-run establishments of that time, because, she used to say, "you can bury a dog's tail for seven years and it still comes out curly, and you can take a Britisher away from his home for a lifetime and he still remains insular." The examinations and degrees from entirely Indian schools were not, in those days, considered **valid.** In my case, the question had never come up, and probably never would have come up if Mother's extraordinary good health had not broken down. For the first time in my life, she was not able to continue the lessons she had been giving us every morning. So our Hindi books were put away, the stories of the Lord Krishna as a little boy were left in midair, and we were sent to the Anglo-Indian school.

Word Power

valid (val´ id) *adj*. based on facts or good evidence

English Coach

In India, the monsoon is a seasonal wind that brings heavy rains. The prefix *post-* means "after." What then does *postmonsoon* mean?

_____

_____

Comprehension Check

Reread the boxed sentence. What does the author's mother mean when she talks about the British people this way? Check the correct response below.

☐ Some people will have dogs with curly tails for seven years.

☐ Some people never change and will always be prejudiced.

☐ Some people will stay away from home for a lifetime.

Background Info

India's official language is Hindustani, also called Hindi. Most Indians practice Hinduism, a religion in which Lord Krishna is one of the most important gods.

Reading Skill

Respond Reread the sentences highlighted in green. Santha's new, foreign name makes her feel like two people: "Cynthia" is someone else. How would you feel in this situation?

_____

_____

_____

Connect to the Text

Reread the boxed sentences. Think about a time when you were the "new kid" entering a new class or meeting a group of people for the first time. How did you feel? What did you do?

_____

_____

_____

Literary Element

Autobiography Reread the text highlighted in blue. How do you know the author is telling about a personal past event? Underline the words that help you know the story is an autobiography.

That first day at school is still, when I think of it, a remarkable one. At that age, if one's name is changed, one develops a curious form of dual personality. I remember having a certain **detached** and disbelieving concern in the actions of "Cynthia," but certainly no responsibility. Accordingly, I followed the thin, erect back of the headmistress down the veranda to my classroom feeling, at most, a passing interest in what was going to happen to me in this strange, new atmosphere of School.

The building was Indian in design, with wide verandas opening onto a central courtyard, but Indian verandas are usually white-washed, with stone floors. These, in the tradition of British schools, were painted dark brown and had matting on the floors. It gave a feeling of extra intensity to the heat.

I suppose there were about a dozen Indian children in the school—which contained perhaps forty children in all—and four of them were in my class. They were all sitting at the back of the room, and I went to join them. I sat next to a small, solemn girl who didn't smile at me. She had long, glossy-black braids and wore a cotton dress, but she still kept on her Indian jewelry—a gold chain around her neck, thin gold bracelets, and tiny ruby studs in her ears. Like most Indian children, she had a rim of black kohl around her eyes. The cotton dress should have looked strange, but all I could think of was that I should ask my mother if I couldn't wear a dress to school, too, instead of my Indian clothes.

I can't remember too much about the proceedings in class that day, except for the beginning. The teacher pointed to me and asked me to stand up. "Now, dear, tell the class your name."

I said nothing.

Did You Know?

Kohl is a powder used to darken the eyelids and eyelashes.

· · · · · · · · · · · · · · · · · ·

Word Power

detached (di tacht´) _adj._ not taking sides or involved emotionally; neutral

How does this image show how the author might have felt? In what ways do you think the author lost her identity? In what ways did she "lose her voice?"

"Come along," she said, frowning slightly. "What's your name, dear?"

"I don't know," I said, finally.

The English children in the front of the class—there were about eight or ten of them—giggled and twisted around in their chairs to look at me. I sat down quickly and opened my eyes very wide, hoping in that way to dry them off. The little girl with the braids put out her hand and very lightly touched my arm. She still didn't smile.

Most of that morning I was rather bored. I looked briefly at the children's drawings pinned to the wall, and then concentrated on a lizard clinging to the ledge of the high, barred window behind the teacher's head. Occasionally it would shoot out its long yellow tongue for a fly, and then it would rest, with its eyes closed and its belly palpitating, as though it were swallowing several times quickly. The lessons were mostly concerned with reading and writing and simple numbers—things that my mother had already taught me—and I paid very little attention. The teacher wrote on the easel blackboard words like "bat" and "cat," which seemed babyish to me; only "apple" was new and **incomprehensible.**

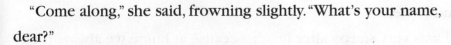

Word Power

incomprehensible (in´ kom pri hen´ sə bəl) *adj.* not understandable

Connect to the Text

Reread the boxed sentences. Think of the last time you were bored somewhere. What did you do to help overcome the boredom?

_____

_____

_____

_____

_____

When it was time for the lunch recess, I followed the girl with braids out onto the veranda. There the children from the other classes were assembled. I saw Premila at once and ran over to her, as she had charge of our lunchbox. The children were all opening packages and sitting down to eat sandwiches. Premila and I were the only ones who had Indian food—thin wheat chapatties, some vegetable curry, and a bottle of buttermilk. Premila thrust half of it into my hand and whispered fiercely that I should go and sit with my class, because that was what the others seemed to be doing.

The enormous black eyes of the little Indian girl from my class looked at my food longingly, so I offered her some. But she only shook her head and plowed her way solemnly through her sandwiches.

I was very sleepy after lunch, because at home we always took a siesta. It was usually a pleasant time of day, with the bedroom darkened against the harsh afternoon sun, the drifting off into sleep with the sound of Mother's voice reading a story in one's mind, and, finally, the shrill, fussy voice of the ayah waking one for tea.

At school, we rested for a short time on low, folding cots on the veranda, and then we were expected to play games. During the hot part of the afternoon we played indoors, and after the shadows had begun to lengthen and the slight breeze of the evening had come up we moved outside to the wide courtyard.

I had never really grasped the system of competitive games. At home, whenever we played tag or guessing games, I was always allowed to "win"—"because," Mother used to tell Premila, "she is the youngest, and we have to allow for that." I had often heard her say it, and it seemed quite reasonable to me, but the result was that I had no clear idea of what "winning" meant.

When we played twos-and-threes that afternoon at school, in accordance with my training, I let one of the small English boys catch me, but was naturally rather puzzled when the other children did not return the courtesy. I ran about for what seemed like hours without ever catching anyone, until it was time for school to close. Much later I learned that my attitude was called "not being a good sport," and I stopped allowing myself to be caught, but it was not for years that I really learned the spirit of the thing.

When I saw our car come up to the school gate, I broke away from my classmates and rushed toward it yelling, "Ayah! Ayah!" It seemed like an **eternity** since I had seen her that morning—a wizened, affectionate figure in her white cotton sari, giving me dozens of urgent and useless instructions on how to be a good girl at school. Premila followed more **sedately,** and she told me on the way home never to do that again in front of the other children.

Did You Know?
The sari (sär ʹ ē) is an outer garment worn mostly by women of India and Pakistan.
. . . .

Reading Skill

Respond Reread the highlighted paragraph. At school Santha is told that she isn't a "good sport." Do you agree that she's not a "good sport"? Why or why not?

_____

_____

_____

_____

_____

STOP Stop here for **Break Time** on the next page.

Word Power

eternity (i tur ʹ nə tē) *n.* a seemingly endless length of time
sedately (si dāt ʹ lē) *adv.* in a quiet, steady manner

Break Time

In "By Any Other Name," important events in the author's life take place both in school and at home. Think about the things that are the same in both places. Then think about how the two places are different for the author. In the middle of the diagram below, list three things that are alike. Then, in each circle on the left and right, list three ways things in each place are different.

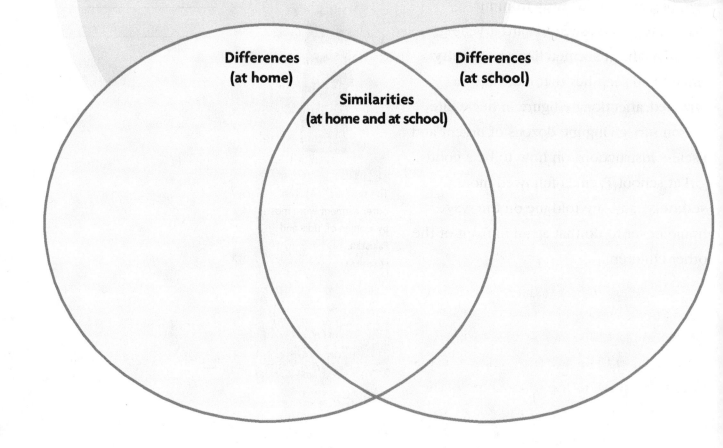

Differences (at home)

Similarities (at home and at school)

Differences (at school)

GO Continue reading on the next page.

When we got home we went straight to Mother's high, white room to have tea with her, and I immediately climbed onto the bed and bounced gently up and down on the springs. Mother asked how we had liked our first day in school. I was so pleased to be home and to have left that peculiar Cynthia behind that I had nothing whatever to say about school, except to ask what "apple" meant. But Premila told Mother about the classes, and added that in her class they had weekly tests to see if they had learned their lessons well.

I asked, "What's a test?"

Premila said, "You're too small to have them. You won't have them in your class for donkey's years." She had learned the expression that day and was using it for the first time. We all laughed enormously at her wit. She also told Mother, in an aside, that we should take sandwiches to school the next day. Not, she said, that she minded. But they would be simpler for me to handle.

That whole lovely evening I didn't think about school at all. I sprinted barefoot across the lawns with my favorite playmate, the cook's son, to the stream at the end of the garden. We quarreled in our usual way, waded in the tepid water under the lime trees, and waited for the night to bring out the smell of the jasmine. I listened with fascination to his stories of ghosts and demons, until I was too frightened to cross the garden alone in the semidarkness. The ayah found me, shouted at the cook's son, scolded me, hurried me in to supper—it was an entirely usual, wonderful evening.

Did You Know?
Jasmine (jaz′ min) is a sweet-smelling flower of a plant in the olive family.
. . . .

Comprehension Check

Reread the boxed sentences. Why does Santha tell Mother so little about her first day of school? Check the **best** response.

- [ ] She is happy to be home and would rather leave school behind.
- [ ] She doesn't think Mother knows what "apple" means.
- [ ] She wants to let Premila talk first.

Reading Skill
Problem and Solution Reread the highlighted sentence. What problem is Premila trying to solve by bringing sandwiches to school rather than Indian food? Check the **best** response.

- [ ] She is tired of eating Indian food.
- [ ] She doesn't want to look different from the others.
- [ ] She is afraid of spilling Indian food on her clothes.

English Coach

Here, *fast* means "close and loyal." Which is **not** another meaning of *fast*? Check the correct response below.

☐ brief and sluggish
☐ swift and quick
☐ speedy and rapid

Comprehension Check

Reread the boxed sentences. On the day of Premila's first test, what does she tell Santha to do?

_____

_____

_____

_____

_____

It was a week later, the day of Premila's first test, that our lives changed rather abruptly. I was sitting at the back of my class, in my usual inattentive way, only half listening to the teacher. I had started a rather guarded friendship with the girl with the braids, whose name turned out to be Nalini (Nancy, in school). The three other Indian children were already fast friends. Even at that age it was apparent to all of us that friendship with the English or Anglo-Indian children was out of the question. Occasionally, during the class, my new friend and I would draw pictures and show them to each other secretly.

The door opened sharply and Premila marched in. At first, the teacher smiled at her in a kindly and encouraging way and said, "Now, you're little Cynthia's sister?"

Premila didn't even look at her. She stood with her feet planted firmly apart and her shoulders **rigid,** and addressed herself directly to me. "Get up," she said. "We're going home."

I didn't know what had happened, but I was aware that it was a crisis of some sort. I rose obediently and started to walk toward my sister.

"Bring your pencils and your notebook," she said.

I went back for them, and together we left the room. The teacher started to say something just as Premila closed the door, but we didn't wait to hear what it was.

In complete silence we left the school grounds and started to walk home. Then I asked Premila what the matter was. All she would say was "We're going home for good."

Word Power

rigid (rij´ id) *adj.* stiff; firm and inflexible

It was a very tiring walk for a child of five and a half, and I dragged along behind Premila with my pencils growing sticky in my hand. I can still remember looking at the dusty hedges, and the tangles of thorns in the ditches by the side of the road, smelling the faint fragrance from the eucalyptus trees and wondering whether we would ever reach home. Occasionally a horse-drawn tonga passed us, and the women, in their pink or green silks, stared at Premila and me trudging along on the side of the road. A few coolies and a line of women carrying baskets of vegetables on their heads smiled at us. But it was nearing the hottest time of day, and the road was almost deserted. I walked more and more slowly, and shouted to Premila, from time to time, "Wait for me!" with increasing peevishness. She spoke to me only once, and that was to tell me to carry my notebook on my head, because of the sun.

Did You Know?

In India, a tonga is a small, two-wheeled carriage.
....

When we got to our house the ayah was just taking a tray of lunch into Mother's room. She immediately started a long, worried questioning about what are you children doing back here at this hour of the day.

Mother looked very startled and very concerned, and asked Premila what had happened.

Premila said, "We had our test today, and she made me and the other Indians sit at the back of the room, with a desk between each one."

Mother said, "Why was that, darling?"

"She said it was because Indians cheat," Premila added. "So I don't think we should go back to that school."

Literary Element

Autobiography Reread the sentence highlighted in blue. Underline the words that tell you that the author is writing about an experience from her childhood.

Background Info

Coolies are unskilled, poorly paid laborers who often do hard work that no one else is willing to do.

Reading Skill

Respond Reread the sentences highlighted in green. How do you feel about the way Premila and the other Indian children are treated at school?

_____

_____

_____

_____

Reading Skill

Problem and Solution Reread the highlighted sentences. What problem is Mother thinking about as she sits quietly? How does she decide to solve the problem?

_____

_____

_____

_____

_____

_____

_____

Mother looked very distant, and was silent a long time. At last she said, "Of course not, darling." She sounded displeased.

We all shared the curry she was having for lunch, and afterward I was sent off to the beautifully familiar bedroom for my siesta. I could hear Mother and Premila talking through the open door.

Mother said, "Do you suppose she understood all that?"

Premila said, "I shouldn't think so. She's a baby."

Mother said, "Well, I hope it won't bother her."

Of course, they were both wrong. I understood it perfectly, and I remember it all very clearly. But I put it happily away, because it had all happened to a girl called Cynthia, and I never was really particularly interested in her.

Compare the feeling that the room in this photograph expresses with Santha's thoughts and feelings after she comes home with Premila.

Respond to Literature

By Any Other Name

A Comprehension Check

Answer the following questions in the spaces provided.

1. What happens when Santha and Premila go to the headmistress's study?

_____

_____

2. What happens on the day of Premila's test? _____

_____

_____

B Reading Skills

Answer the following questions in the spaces provided.

1. **Problem and Solution** During her first week at the Anglo-Indian school, Santha has problems making friends. How does she solve this problem?

_____

_____

2. **Respond** On the day of Premila's test, she marches into Santha's classroom, ignores the teacher, and takes Santha straight home. How do you feel about Premila's actions? Do you think she was right? Why or why not?

_____

_____

_____

C Word Power

Complete each sentence below, using one of the words in the box.

precarious	valid	detached
incomprehensible	eternity	sedately	rigid

1. Camilla did not have a _____ reason for her angry comments.

2. I used to know how to play, but it seems like an _____ since I last sat down at the piano.

3. As the coach gave the orders, the players stood at attention with their backs _____.

4. Kamil did not like soccer, and felt bored and _____ as he watched the game.

5. The librarian carried a large stack of books in a _____ tower that looked like it would topple any second.

6. As the young child skipped down the street, his grandmother walked _____ after him.

7. French was _____ to me until I started my language lessons.

D Literary Element: Autobiography

Read the passage below from "By Any Other Name." As you read, think about the events that led up to the ending as well as about the characteristics of an autobiography. Then answer the questions that follow.

I could hear Mother and Premila talking through the open door.[1]

Mother said, "Do you suppose she understood all that?"[2]

Premila said, "I shouldn't think so.[3] She's a baby."[4]

Mother said, "Well, I hope it won't bother her."[5]

Of course, they were both wrong.[6] I understood it perfectly, and I remember it all very clearly.[7] But I put it happily away, because it had all happened to a girl called Cynthia, and I never was really particularly interested in her.[8]

1. In sentences 1–4, what details show that the author is writing about an event from a much earlier time in her life? _____

_____

_____

_____

2. In sentences 5–8, how does the author show that the event is important to her? _____

_____

_____

_____

E Santha's Diary

Imagine that you are Santha, and you have just come home from your first day at the new school. Write a diary entry to tell about your experience.

Dear Diary,

Today was my first day at the Anglo-Indian school. The first thing Premila and I did was meet the headmistress. When we told her our names, she _____

_____

I could tell Premila didn't like this, but I just felt _____

_____

Next I went to my classroom. When the teacher asked me to introduce myself, _____

_____

The English children laughed, and I _____

_____

I feel happier at home than at school because _____

_____

Assessment

Fill in the circle next to each correct answer.

1. Why does the headmistress change Santha's name to Cynthia?
   - ○ A. *Santha* means "Cynthia" in English.
   - ○ B. Santha doesn't like her Indian name.
   - ○ C. She thinks that Cynthia is easier to pronounce.
   - ○ D. Cynthia is the name of an English flower.

2. What problem does Mother have with British-run schools that at first makes her refuse to send Premila?
   - ○ A. She doesn't want to send Premila until Santha is old enough to go too.
   - ○ B. She feels that the British are not always accepting of Indian ways.
   - ○ C. She doesn't like the headmistress.
   - ○ D. She wants the girls to stay home while their father is away.

3. Which of the choices below **best** describes Premila's solution to the problem of being called a "cheater"?
   - ○ A. She leaves school with Santha and tells Mother they should never go back.
   - ○ B. She ignores the teacher when she marches into the room.
   - ○ C. She closes the door so she can't hear what the teacher is saying.
   - ○ D. She asks to speak directly to the headmistress.

4. In an autobiography, the author describes important personal events. Which of the following events is **most** important to the author?
   - ○ A. Santha doesn't pay attention in school.
   - ○ B. Santha doesn't know how to play a game at recess.
   - ○ C. Santha doesn't have to take any tests at school until she gets older.
   - ○ D. Santha has her name changed to Cynthia by the headmistress.

5. Which of the following words means the same thing as "forever"?
   - ○ A. detached
   - ○ B. sedately
   - ○ C. eternity
   - ○ D. valid

Get Ready to Read!

Farewell to Manzanar

Meet Jeanne Wakatsuki Houston and James D. Houston

James D. Houston was born in 1933. Houston's wife, Jeanne Wakatsuki Houston, was born in 1934. She spent more than three years of her childhood at the Manzanar Relocation Center in California, where Japanese Americans were imprisoned during World War II. The Houstons wrote about that experience in a book titled *Farewell to Manzanar*, which was first published in 1973.

What You Know

How might you react if you and your family were forced to pack up and move on very short notice?

Reason to Read

Read this autobiography to find out what life was like for many Japanese Americans who were forced to leave their homes during World War II.

Background Info

The events described in this selection take place in California in 1941 and 1942, after Japan's surprise attack on the U.S. Pacific Fleet in Pearl Harbor, Hawaii, on December 7, 1941. After this attack, the United States entered World War II, declaring war on Japan on December 8, 1941.

After the Japanese attack on Pearl Harbor, many Americans were distrustful of people who were born in Japan and now living in the United States. In February 1942, President Franklin D. Roosevelt issued Executive Order 9066. This gave the U.S. War Department the authority to remove Japanese Americans from their homes on the West Coast and confine them to special camps for the duration of the war. Some 110,000 Japanese Americans, two-thirds of them American citizens, were relocated by the military to ten remotely situated, prisonlike camps.

Word Power

heirlooms (ār′ lōōmz) *n.* valued things passed down from one generation to the next; p. 272
Anni received many *heirlooms* from her grandmother, such as a pearl necklace.

irrational (i rash′ ən əl) *adj.* illogical; absurd; lacking reason or understanding; p. 273
Judith's remarks were totally *irrational,* and nobody could understand her.

barracks (bar′ əks) *n.* buildings that are used as temporary housing, usually by the military; p. 275
The soldiers got up early every morning to clean their *barracks* before inspection.

grueling (grōō′ ling) *adj.* extremely difficult and very tiring; p. 278
Jonathan and the other scouts were exhausted after their *grueling* ten-mile hike.

alleviate (ə lē′ vē āt′) *v.* to relieve; to make a hardship easier to bear; p. 278
Our government programs tried to *alleviate* the problem of unemployment.

scrounged (skrounjd) *v.* managed to get something by hunting around or by begging; p. 279
The stray cat *scrounged* for food in the alley.

grimacing (grim′ is ing) *v.* showing pain or disgust with a facial expression; p. 282
Alberto was *grimacing* at the thought of eating liver and onions for dinner.

**Answer the following questions that contain the new words above.
Write your answers in the spaces provided.**

1. If you do a *grueling* exercise routine, is it easy or hard to do? _____

2. If a babysitter is *grimacing* as she changes a baby's diaper, is she enjoying the experience or disliking the experience? _____

3. Would family *heirlooms* be items the family recently bought or items they have had for a very long time? _____

4. If you *alleviate* pain, is the pain going away or getting worse? _____

5. Would the rooms in *barracks* be simple or very fancy? _____

6. If Apu is being *irrational,* is he making sense or not making sense? _____

7. If a camper *scrounged* around to find wood for a campfire, was there a lot of wood or little wood in the campground? _____

Adapted from
Farewell to Manzanar

Jeanne Wakatsuki Houston
and James D. Houston

In December of 1941 Papa's disappearance didn't bother me nearly so much as the world I soon found myself in.

When he started fishing, we moved to Ocean Park, near Santa Monica. Until they picked him up, that's where we lived, in a big frame house with a brick fireplace, a block back from the beach. We were the only Japanese family in the neighborhood. Papa didn't want to be labeled or grouped by anyone. But with him gone and no way of knowing what to expect, my mother moved all of us down to Terminal Island.

Woody already lived there, and one of my older sisters had married a Terminal Island boy. Mama's first concern now was to keep the family together. Once the war began, she felt safer there than isolated racially in Ocean Park. At age seven, it was the first time I had lived among other Japanese, and I was terrified all the time.

In those days it was a ghetto owned and controlled by the canneries. The men went after fish, and whenever the boats came back—day or night—the women would be called to process the catch. My mother had to go to work right after we moved there.

The house we lived in was nothing more than a shack with single, plank walls and rough wooden floors. The people around us were hardworking, boisterous, a little proud of their nickname, *yo-go-re,* which meant literally *uncouth one,* or roughneck. They not only spoke Japanese exclusively, they spoke a dialect peculiar to Kyushu, where their families had come from in Japan. It was a rough, fisherman's language, full of oaths and insults. They would pick on anyone who didn't speak as they did. I had never spoken anything but English, and the other kids in the second grade despised me for it. Each day after school my brother Kiyo, three years older, would wait for me at the door. We would decide whether to run straight home together, or split up, or try a new and unexpected route.

None of these kids ever actually attacked. It was the threat that frightened us, their fearful looks, and the noises they would make in a language we couldn't understand.

We lived there about two months. Late in February the navy decided to clear Terminal Island completely. Even though most of us were American-born, it was dangerous having that many Orientals so close to the Long Beach Naval Station. There were four of us kids, Mama, and Granny, sixty-five then, speaking no English, and nearly blind. On February 25 we were given forty-eight hours to clear out.

The secondhand dealers had been prowling around like wolves, offering humiliating prices for goods and furniture they knew many of us would have to sell. Mama had left all but her most valuable possessions in Ocean Park.

My Workspace

Comprehension Check

Reread the boxed sentences. Why does Mama have to sell the china? Check the **best** response below.

- [ ] The car is too crowded to hold it.
- [ ] It is the least important of the heirlooms.
- [ ] She doesn't like the blue and white pattern.

Reading Skill

Respond Reread the highlighted paragraph. Rather than sell the dishes for a cheap price, Mama smashes them all on the ground. How does this make you feel about her?

_____

_____

_____

She had brought along her pottery, her silver, **heirlooms** like the kimonos Granny had brought from Japan, tea sets, lacquered tables, and one fine old set of china, blue and white porcelain. On the day we were leaving, Woody's car was so crammed with boxes and luggage and kids we had just run out of room. Mama had to sell this china.

One of the dealers offered her fifteen dollars for it. She said it was a full setting for twelve and worth at least two hundred. He said fifteen was his top price. Mama started to quiver. She had been packing all night. Mama's nerves were shot, and now navy jeeps were patrolling the streets. She just glared at this man, all the rage and frustration channeled at him through her eyes.

He watched her for a moment and said he couldn't pay more than seventeen fifty. She reached into the red velvet case, took out a dinner plate and hurled it at the floor right in front of his feet.

The man leaped back shouting, "Hey! Hey, don't do that! Those are valuable dishes!"

Mama took out another dinner plate and hurled it at the floor, then another and another, just quivering and glaring at the retreating dealer, with tears streaming down her cheeks. When he was gone she stood there smashing cups and bowls and platters until the whole set lay in scattered blue and white fragments.

Word Power

heirlooms (âr′ loomz) *n.* valued things passed down from one generation to the next

The American Friends Service helped us find a small house in Boyle Heights, another minority ghetto, in downtown Los Angeles. Executive Order 9066 had been signed by President Roosevelt, giving the War Department authority to define military areas in the western states and to exclude from them anyone who might threaten the war effort. There was a lot of talk about internment in store for all Japanese Americans. I remember my brothers talking very intently about how we would keep the family together. They had seen how quickly Papa was removed. Just before leaving Terminal Island Mama had received her first letter, from Bismarck, North Dakota. He had been imprisoned at Fort Lincoln, in an all-male camp for enemy aliens.

These were mainly days of quiet, desperate waiting. There is a phrase the Japanese use in such situations, when something difficult must be endured. You would hear the older heads, the Issei, telling others very quietly, *"Shikata ga nai"* (It cannot be helped). *"Shikata ga nai"* (It must be done).

Mama and Woody went to work packing celery for a Japanese produce dealer. Kiyo and my sister May and I enrolled in the local school. In Ocean Park my teacher had been a kind, grandmotherly woman who used to sail with us in Papa's boat and who wept the day we had to leave. In Boyle Heights the teacher felt cold and distant. I was having trouble with the classwork, but she would have nothing to do with me.

Looking back, it is easy enough to explain. In the first few months of the Pacific war, America was on the run. Tolerance had turned to distrust and **irrational** fear. The hundred-year-old tradition of anti-Orientalism on the west coast resurfaced, more vicious than ever. About a month later, we were told to make our third and final move.

Word Power

irrational (i rash′ ən əl) *adj.* illogical; absurd; lacking reason or understanding

My Workspace

Literary Element

Autobiography Reread the highlighted sentences. When the author was a child, the name Manzanar meant nothing to her. Do you think she feels differently as an adult looking back at the experience? How do you know?

_____

_____

_____

_____

_____

_____

_____

_____

Connect to the Text

Reread the boxed sentences. Think about a time when you tried to be friendly to someone who was not friendly in return. How did it make you feel? What did you do?

_____

_____

_____

How would you feel if your family were asked to immediately move into buildings like the ones shown in the photo?

The name Manzanar meant nothing to us when we left Boyle Heights. We didn't know where it was or what it was. We went because the government ordered us to. My older brothers and sisters went with a certain amount of relief. They had all heard stories of Japanese homes being attacked, of beatings in the streets of California towns. They were as frightened of the Caucasians as Caucasians were of us. Moving, under what appeared to be government protection, to an area less directly threatened by the war seemed not such a bad idea at all.

Our pickup point was a Buddhist church in Los Angeles. Mama had bought heavy coats for all of us. She grew up in eastern Washington and knew that anywhere inland in early April would be cold. I remember sitting on a duffel bag trying to be friendly with the Greyhound driver. I smiled at him. He didn't smile back. Someone tied a numbered tag to my collar and to the duffel bag (each family was given a number), someone else passed out box lunches for the trip, and we climbed aboard.

I had never traveled more than ten miles from the coast, had never even ridden on a bus. I wanted to look out the window. But for the first few hours the shades were drawn. The bus felt very secure to me. Almost half its passengers were close relatives. Mama and my older brothers had succeeded in keeping most of us together. The strategy had been, first, to have everyone living in the same district when the evacuation began, and then to get all of us included under the same family number, even though names had been changed by marriage.

We rode all day. By the time we reached our destination, the shades were up. The first thing I saw was a yellow swirl across a blurred, reddish setting sun. The bus was being pelted by what sounded like splattering rain. This was my first look at a billowing flurry of dust and sand churned up by the wind through Owens Valley.

We drove past a barbed-wire fence and into an open space where trunks and sacks and packages had been dumped from the baggage trucks. I could see a few tents set up and beyond them rows of **barracks** that seemed to spread for miles across this plain. People were sitting on cartons or walking around, waiting to see which friends or relatives might be on this bus. As we approached, they turned or stood up. But inside the bus no one stirred. They just stared out the windows. Hadn't we finally arrived, our whole family intact? I opened a window, leaned out, and yelled happily. "Hey! This whole bus is full of Wakatsukis!"

Outside, the greeters smiled. Inside there was an explosion of hysterical, tension-breaking laughter that left my brothers choking and whacking each other across the shoulders.

 Stop here for **Break Time** on the next page.

Word Power

barracks (bar′ əks) *n.* buildings that are used as temporary housing, usually by the military

Reading Skill
Problem and Solution Reread the highlighted sentences. How does the family solve the problem of staying together?

_____

_____

_____

_____

_____

Background Info

Manzanar was built in Owens Valley, which is near Death Valley. This area is about two hundred miles north of Los Angeles.

Comprehension Check

Reread the boxed sentences. What does the narrator do when the bus arrives? What effect does she have on the others?

_____

_____

_____

_____

Break Time

When you read an autobiography, keep track of not only *what* happens, but also *why* it happens. Recognizing causes and effects can help you understand how events shaped the author as a person. To find the cause in a passage, ask *Why?* To find the effect, ask *What is the result?* Use the cause-and-effect graphic organizer below to write about what has happened so far. Some of the information has been provided for you.

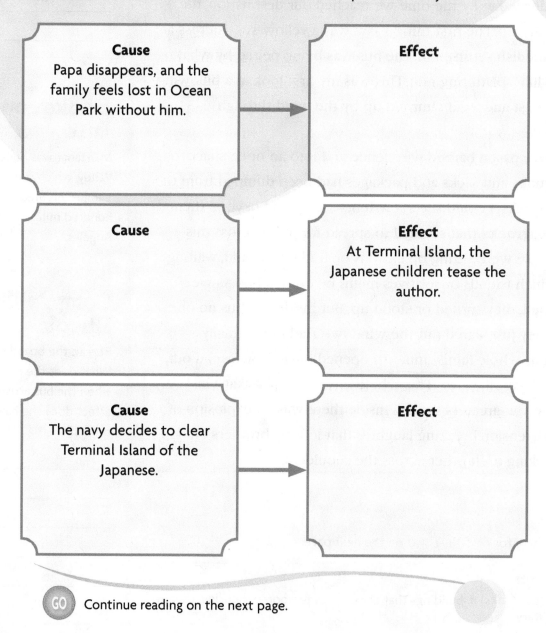

Cause
Papa disappears, and the family feels lost in Ocean Park without him.

Effect

Cause

Effect
At Terminal Island, the Japanese children tease the author.

Cause
The navy decides to clear Terminal Island of the Japanese.

Effect

GO   Continue reading on the next page.

We had pulled up just in time for dinner. A chow line snaked around a half-finished building that broke a good part of the wind. They issued us army mess kits and plopped in scoops of canned sausage, canned string beans, steamed rice that had been cooked too long, and on top of the rice a serving of canned apricots. Among the Japanese, rice is never eaten with sweet foods, only with salty or savory foods. I was horrified when I saw the apricot syrup seeping through my little mound of rice. I opened my mouth to complain. My mother jabbed me in the back to keep quiet. We joined the others squatting out of the wind behind half-raised walls, dabbing courteously at what was, for almost everyone there, inedible.

After dinner we were taken to Block 16, fifteen barracks that had just been finished a day or so earlier. The shacks were built of one thickness of pine planking covered with tar paper. They sat on concrete blocks, with about two feet of open space between the floorboards and the ground. Gaps showed between the planks. Knotholes gaped in the uncovered floor.

Each of the barracks was divided into six units, sixteen by twenty feet, with one bare bulb hanging from the ceiling and an oil stove for heat. We were assigned two of these for the twelve people in our family group. We were issued steel army cots, two brown army blankets each, and some mattress covers, which my brothers stuffed with straw.

The first task was to divide up what space we had for sleeping. Bill and Woody contributed a blanket each and partitioned off the first room: one side for Bill and Tomi, one side for Woody and Chizu and their baby girl. Woody also got the stove, for heating formulas.

Did You Know?
A soldier in the field eats from a mess kit, which is a metal container that holds eating utensils and opens into a plate with two compartments.
....

Connect to the Text
Reread the boxed text. Think about a time when you had to be polite and eat something you didn't like. What did you have to eat? How did you feel about it?

_____

_____

_____

_____

Literary Element

Autobiography Reread the highlighted paragraph. How would the description of the barracks be different if it had been written for an encyclopedia article instead of an autobiography?

_____

_____

_____

_____

_____

_____

Comprehension Check

Reread the boxed sentences. Why do the author's sister and her husband go to Idaho? Check the **best** response below.

- ☐ They want to have their own room.
- ☐ They don't mind grueling work.
- ☐ They like sugar beets.

Reading Skill

Problem and Solution Reread the highlighted sentences. What problem does Mama solve by unpacking all the clothes and putting them on the beds at night?

_____

_____

_____

_____

Our two rooms were crowded, but at least it was all in the family. My oldest sister and her husband were with six people they had never seen before. All they had to use for room dividers were those army blankets, two of which were barely enough to keep one person warm. They argued over whose blanket should be sacrificed and later about noise at night. They continued arguing for six months, until my sister and her husband left to harvest sugar beets in Idaho. It was **grueling** work, but when the call came for workers to **alleviate** the wartime labor shortage, it sounded better than their life at Manzanar. They knew they'd have a room of their own.

That first night in Block 16, the rest of us squeezed into the second room—Granny, Lillian, age fourteen, Ray, thirteen, May, eleven, Kiyo, ten, Mama, and me. Being youngest meant I got to sleep with Mama. Before we went to bed I had a great time jumping up and down on the mattress. The boys had stuffed so much straw into hers, we had to flatten it some so we wouldn't slide off.

We woke early, shivering and coated with dust that had blown up through the knotholes and in through the slits around the doorway. During the night Mama had unpacked all our clothes and heaped them on our beds for warmth. I looked over Mama's shoulder at Kiyo, buried under jeans and overcoats and sweaters. His eyebrows were gray. He was looking at me, at my gray eyebrows and coated hair, and pretty soon we were both giggling. I looked at Mama's face to see if she thought Kiyo was funny. She lay very still next to me on our mattress, her eyes scanning everything slowly. Woody's voice just then came at us through the wall.

Word Power

grueling (grōō′ ling) *adj.* extremely difficult and very tiring
alleviate (ə lē′ vē āt′) *v.* to relieve; to make a hardship easier to bear

"Hey!" he yelled. "You guys fall into the same flour barrel as us?"

"No," Kiyo yelled back. "Ours is full of Japs."

All of us laughed at this.

"Well, tell 'em it's time to get up," Woody said. "If we're gonna live in this place, we better get to work."

Then he came in carrying a broom, a hammer, and a sack full of tin can lids he had **scrounged** somewhere. Woody would be our leader for a while now, grinning behind his mustache. He had just turned twenty-four.

"Hey, brother Ray, Kiyo," he said. "You see these tin can lids?"

"Yeah, yeah," the boys said drowsily.

"You see all them knotholes in the floor and in the walls?"

They looked around. You could see about a dozen.

Woody said, "You get those covered up before breakfast time. Any more sand comes in here through one of them knotholes, you have to eat it off the floor with ketchup."

"What about sand that comes in through the cracks?" Kiyo said.

"Don't worry about the cracks. Different kind of sand comes in through the cracks."

He put his hands on his hips and gave Kiyo a sternly comic look, squinting at him through one eye the way Papa would when he was asserting his authority. "And I can tell the difference. So be careful."

The boys laughed and went to work. I was helping Mama fold the clothes, when Woody came over and put his arm around her shoulder. He was short; she was even shorter, under five feet.

He said softly, "You okay, Mama?"

She just kept folding clothes and said, "Can we get the cracks covered too, Woody?"

"We'll get this whole place as tight as a barrel, Mama. I already met a guy who told me where they pile all the scrap lumber."

Word Power

scrounged (skrounjd) *v.* managed to get something by hunting around or by begging

What does this photo tell you about life in the internment camp?

Reading Skill

Respond Reread the highlighted sentences. Based on what you have read up to now, how would you feel if you were asked to live at Manzanar? Explain.

_____

_____

_____

_____

Background Info

Hotcakes is another word for *pancakes* or *griddle cakes.*

"Scrap?"

"They're still building the camp, you know. Sixteen blocks left to go. After that, they say maybe we'll get some stuff to fix the insides a little bit."

Her eyes blazed then, her voice quietly furious. "Woody, we can't live like this. Animals live like this."

Grief flickered in his eyes. He blinked it away and hugged her tighter. "We'll make it better, Mama. You watch."

Beyond the wall Woody's baby girl started to cry.

"I have to go over to the kitchen," he said, "see if those guys got a pot for heating bottles. I'll find out what they're giving us for breakfast."

"Probably hotcakes with soy sauce," Kiyo said.

"No." Woody grinned. "Rice. With Log Cabin Syrup and melted butter."

That first morning we stood for half an hour in cutting wind waiting to get our food. Then we took it back and ate huddled around the stove. Inside, it was warmer than when we left, because Woody was already tacking up some thin strips of wood he'd found, stuffing rolled paper around the door frame.

The camp was no more ready for us when we got there than we were ready for it. Most of the families, like us, had moved out from southern California with as much luggage as each person could carry. Some old men left Los Angeles wearing Hawaiian shirts and Panama hats and stepped off the bus at an altitude of 4000 feet, with nothing available but sagebrush and tarpaper to stop the April winds pouring down off the back side of the Sierras.

The War Department began to issue military surplus from the First World War—olive-drab knit caps, earmuffs, peacoats, canvas leggings. Later on, sewing machines were shipped in, and one of the barracks was turned into a clothing factory. By fall dozens of seamstresses were working full-time transforming thousands of these old army clothes into capes, slacks and stylish coats. But until that factory got going, warmth was more important than style. I couldn't help laughing at Mama walking around in army earmuffs and a pair of wide-cuffed, khaki-colored wool trousers several sizes too big for her.

I was sick continually, with stomach cramps and diarrhea. At first it was from the shots they gave us for typhoid, in very heavy doses and in assembly-line fashion: swab, jab, swab. *Move along now.* That knocked all of us younger kids down at once, with fevers and vomiting. Later, it was the food that made us sick, young and old alike. Food would spoil from being left out too long. The refrigeration kept breaking down. The cooks, in many cases, had never cooked before. Each block had to provide its own volunteers. The first chef in our block had been a gardener all his life and suddenly found himself preparing three meals a day for 250 people.

"The Manzanar runs" became a condition of life, and you only hoped that when you rushed to the latrine, one would be in working order.

That first morning, on our way to the chow line, Mama and I tried to use the women's latrine in our block. Outside, men were working in an open trench, up to their knees in muck. Inside, the floor was covered with excrement, and all twelve bowls were erupting like a row of tiny volcanoes.

Mama stopped a kimono-wrapped woman stepping past us with her sleeve pushed up against her nose and asked, "What do you do?"

"Try Block Twelve," the woman said, **grimacing.** "They have just finished repairing the pipes."

It was about two city blocks away. Inside it was like all the other latrines. Each block was built to the same design as each of the ten camps from California to Arkansas. It was an open room, over a concrete slab. The sink was a long metal trough against one wall, with a row of spigots for hot and cold water. Down the center of the room twelve toilet bowls were arranged in six pairs, back to back, with no partitions.

One old woman had already solved the problem by dragging in a large cardboard carton. She set it up around one of the bowls, like a three-sided screen. The upended carton was about four feet high. The old woman behind it wasn't much taller.

With great effort she was trying to fold the sides of the screen together. Mama happened to be at the head of the line now. As she approached the vacant bowl, she and the old woman bowed to each other. Mama then moved to help her with the carton, and the old woman said very graciously, in Japanese, "Would you like to use it?"

Comprehension Check

Reread the boxed sentences. Why does the woman tell Mama to go to Block Twelve?

_____

_____

_____

_____

Reading Skill
Problem and Solution

Reread the highlighted paragraph. What problem does the old woman solve with the cardboard carton?

_____

_____

_____

_____

Word Power

grimacing (grim´ is ing) *v.* showing pain or disgust with a facial expression

Mama bowed again and said, *"Arigato gozaimas"* (Thank you very much). "I will return it to your barracks."

"Oh, no. It is not necessary. I will be glad to wait."

Those big cartons were a common sight in the spring of 1942. Eventually sturdier partitions were built of scrap lumber. Word would get around that Block such and such had partitions now, and Mama and my older sisters would walk halfway across the camp to use them.

Like so many of the women there, Mama never did get used to the latrines. It was a humiliation she just learned to endure: *shikata ga nai,* this cannot be helped. She knew cooperation was the only way to survive. At the same time she placed a great deal of importance on personal privacy. Almost everyone at Manzanar had inherited this pair of traits from the generations before them who had learned to live in a small, crowded country like Japan. Because of the first they were able to take a desolate stretch of wasteland and gradually make it livable. But the entire situation there was an open insult to that other, private self, a slap in the face you were powerless to challenge.

Reading Skill

Problem and Solution Reread the highlighted sentences. What problem do the Japanese people try to solve at the camp?

_____

_____

_____

_____

_____

Farewell to Manzanar

A Comprehension Check

Answer the following questions in the spaces provided.

1. Why does the Wakatsuki family have to go to Manzanar? _____

    _____

    _____

2. What are the barracks like at Manzanar? _____

    _____

    _____

B Reading Skills

Answer the following questions in the spaces provided.

1. **Problem and Solution** How does the Wakatsuki family manage to stay

    together during the move to Manzanar? _____

    _____

    _____

    _____

2. **Respond** When the bus arrives at Manzanar, the narrator breaks the
    tension by calling out that the bus is full of members of her family. How
    would you feel if a family member paid too much attention to you in
    public? Would you feel ashamed? Why or why not?

    _____

    _____

C Word Power

Complete each sentence below, using one of the words in the box.

heirlooms	irrational	barracks
grueling	alleviate	scrounged	grimacing

1. Sabrina _____ around in the refrigerator, but found nothing good to eat for lunch.

2. Some people have an _____ fear of small insects.

3. The Johnsons still have many family _____, including a cedar chest built by Edgar Johnson in 1899.

4. The soldiers returned to their _____ to rest after another hard day of training.

5. Our mayor hoped that the new highway would _____ the problem of too much traffic downtown.

6. Many children were _____ at the thought of swallowing the medicine.

7. It was hard for Miguel to enjoy the beautiful view from the mountain's summit after the _____ five-hour climb.

D Literary Element: Autobiography

Read the passage below from *Farewell to Manzanar*. As you read, think about how the passage helps you recognize that the story is an autobiography. Then answer the questions that follow.

We had pulled up just in time for dinner.[1] A chow line snaked around a half-finished building that broke a good part of the wind.[2] They issued us army mess kits and plopped in scoops of canned sausage, canned string beans, steamed rice that had been cooked too long, and on top of the rice a serving of canned apricots.[3] Among the Japanese, rice is never eaten with sweet foods, only with salty or savory foods.[4] I was horrified when I saw the apricot syrup seeping through my little mound of rice.[5] I opened my mouth to complain.[6] My mother jabbed me in the back to keep quiet.[7] We joined the others squatting out of the wind behind half-raised walls, dabbing courteously at what was, for almost everyone there, inedible.[8]

1. What clue words in the passage tell you that the author is writing about a personal experience from her past? _____

_____

_____

2. Reread sentences 3–7. How might the description of the food served be told differently if this were written by a reporter for a newspaper article?

_____

_____

_____

_____

E A Diary Entry

Imagine that you are the narrator. You are keeping a diary about your experiences at Manzanar. Write a journal entry. Tell how you and your family felt when you arrived at Manzanar, and how you and your family got used to the camp.

Dear Diary,

After a long bus ride, we arrived at Manzanar. The camp was not at all what we expected. It was _____

_____

_____

_____

When we woke up the next morning, we were _____

_____

Woody found some _____,

and then he and my brothers _____

We are getting used to camp now. The food is _____

_____

The bathrooms are even worse. They are _____

_____

Mother hates it here. So do I. I hope _____

_____

Assessment

Fill in the circle next to each correct answer.

1. What does the narrator's mother do when the dealer offers her fifteen dollars for her set of dishes?
   - ○ A. She takes the money gratefully.
   - ○ B. She smashes the dishes angrily.
   - ○ C. She bargains with him successfully.
   - ○ D. She breaks a dinner plate accidentally.

2. How do the people at Manzanar make living conditions more livable?
   - ○ A. They ask for the bathrooms to be relocated closer to the barracks.
   - ○ B. They build a cafeteria where only Japanese food is served.
   - ○ C. They partition parts of rooms and seal up holes in the walls.
   - ○ D. They tear up cardboard boxes to make furniture.

3. How do the older Japanese people deal with life at Manzanar?
   - ○ A. by staying in close contact with each other
   - ○ B. by complaining to the authorities
   - ○ C. by trying to escape from the camp
   - ○ D. by accepting the situation and cooperating with each other

4. Which sentence **best** shows that the author is writing about an event from her past?
   - ○ A. It was an open room over a concrete slab.
   - ○ B. In December of 1941 Papa's disappearance didn't bother me nearly as much as the world I soon found myself in.
   - ○ C. Executive Order 9066 had been signed by President Roosevelt.
   - ○ D. The men went after fish, and whenever the boats came back—day or night—the women would be called to process the catch.

5. Which of the following words means "extremely difficult and physically exhausting"?
   - ○ A. grueling
   - ○ B. alleviate
   - ○ C. scrounged
   - ○ D. grimacing

5 Wrap-up

Compare and Contrast

The literary element of **autobiography** is very important in "By Any Other Name" and *Farewell to Manzanar*. Both stories are autobiographical, and the authors share important personal experiences about past events that have deep meaning for them. Think about the reason that each author wrote her story.

Complete the chart below. In the left column, describe the experiences of the author of "By Any Other Name." In the right column, describe the author's personal experiences in *Farewell to Manzanar*. In the center column, list similarities between the two autobiographies.

"By Any Other Name"	Similarities	*Farewell to Manzanar*

Glossary

A

accessible (ak ses´ ə bəl) *adj.* capable of being reached easily; p. 59

acre (ā´ kər) *n.* an area of land equal to 43,560 square feet; p. 72

affront (ə frunt´) *n.* an insult; something that causes a person to feel offended; p. 57

agile (aj´ əl) *adj.* able to move quickly and with great control; p. 26

alleviate (ə lē´ vē āt´) *v.* to relieve; to make a hardship easier to bear; p. 278

allies (al´ īz) *n.* persons, groups, or nations joined together to help and support each other; p. 195

anguish (ang´ gwish) *n.* great suffering or pain; agony; p. 171

annihilate (ə nī´ ə lāt´) *v.* to destroy completely; p. 94

anxiety (ang zī´ ə tē) *n.* a feeling of worry or nervousness; p. 28

appraise (ə prāz´) *v.* to estimate someone's ability or the value of something; p. 224

aristocratic (ə ris´ tə krat´ ik) *adj.* belonging to upper-class society; p. 14

B

barracks (bar´ əks) *n.* buildings that are used as temporary housing, usually by the military; p. 275

beseeching (bi sēch´ ing) *adj.* pleading; begging; p. 121

botched (bocht) *adj.* failed; poorly done; p. 73

C

censorship (sen´ sər ship´) *n.* the practice of removing anything thought unfit for people to see or read; p. 38

confidences (kon´ fə dəns iz) *n.* secrets; p. 211

confidential (kon´ fə den´ shəl) *adj.* told in secret; meant to be kept private; p. 38

conformity (kən fôr´ mə tē) *n.* behavior that matches everyone else's; p. 244

confronted (kən frun´ tid) *v.* faced someone or something in a challenge; p. 196

contrition (kən trish´ ən) *n.* a feeling of sorrow for having done something wrong; p. 116

convulsive (kən vul´ siv) *adj.* sudden and violent; p. 127

correspondence (kōr´ ə spon´ dəns) *n.* a communication exchange through the mail; p. 74

D

decapitate (di kap´ ə tāt´) *v.* to cut off the head of someone or something; p. 77

detached (di tacht´) *adj.* not taking sides or involved emotionally; neutral; p. 254

dictatorship (dik´ tā´ tər ship´) *n.* a government in which one person has complete power; p. 91

diminished (di min´ isht) *v.* became less or smaller; p. 227

disdain (dis dān´) *n.* a feeling of disrespect for something thought to be inferior or unworthy; p. 13

dissected (di sekt´ id) *v.* took or cut apart to examine; p. 174

distraction (dis trak´ shən) *n.* something that takes one's attention away from something else; p. 41

diverted (di vur´ tid) *v.* drew away someone's attention; changed the direction of something; p. 224

Glossary

E

eternity (i tur´ nə tē) *n.* a seemingly endless length of time; p. 257

exasperated (ig zas´ pə rāt´ id) *adj.* extremely annoyed and irritated; p. 165

excessively (ik ses´ iv lē) *adv.* more than what is needed or wanted; p. 5

expendable (iks pen´ də bəl) *adj.* not necessary; able to be sacrificed without being missed; p. 95

exquisite (iks kwiz´ it) *adj.* beautiful and delicate; p. 108

F

ferocity (fə ros´ ə tē) *n.* fierceness; intensity; p. 198

fitful (fit´ fəl) *adj.* not regular or steady; p. 143

futile (fū´ til) *adj.* hopeless; useless; not likely to have results; p. 138

G

galled (gôld) *v.* irritated; annoyed; got on one's nerves; p. 239

gleam (glēm) *n.* reflected brightness; p. 210

grimacing (grim´ is ing) *v.* showing pain or disgust with a facial expression; p. 282

grueling (grōō´ ling) *adj.* extremely difficult and very tiring; p. 278

H

hastily (hās´ ti lē) *adv.* doing or acting very quickly; p. 11

heirlooms (ār´ lōōmz) *n.* valued things passed down from one generation to the next; p. 272

hesitation (hez´ ə tā´ shən) *n.* the act of holding back because of feeling unsure; p. 211

I

idly (īd´ lē) *adv.* without doing any purposeful activity; p. 119

implore (im plôr´) *v.* to ask urgently; p. 52

improvised (im´ prə vīzd´) *adj.* made up or invented on the spot; p. 236

incomprehensible (in´ kom pri hen´ sə bəl) *adj.* not understandable; p. 255

incredulous (in krej´ ə ləs) *adj.* unwilling to believe something; p. 126

indifference (in dif´ ər əns) *n.* complete lack of concern or interest; p. 164

inevitably (i nev´ ə tə blē) *adv.* certain to happen; p. 54

innocence (in´ ə səns) *n.* the condition of being simple; free from guilt or evil; p. 139

inquisitive (in kwiz´ ə tiv) *adj.* curious; p. 121

intercept (in´ tər sept´) *v.* to stop or delay on the way; p. 39

intimidated (in tim´ ə dāt´ id) *adj.* feeling frightened by something more powerful or superior; p. 50

irrational (i rash´ ən əl) *adj.* illogical; absurd; lacking reason or understanding; p. 273

Glossary

L

lapses (laps´ iz) *n.* temporary interruptions; p. 128

ledger (ləj´ ər) *v.* a book in which records are kept, usually of income and expenses; p. 181

M

malfunctioning (mal´ fungk´ shən ing) *adj.* not working properly; p. 103

mutual (mū´ choo əl) *adj.* expressing the same feelings toward each other; p. 168

N

nimbleness (nim´ bəl nes) *n.* the ability to move quickly and with controlled movements; p. 51

O

ostracism (os´ trə siz´ əm) *n.* exclusion from a group or society; p. 244

P

patriotic (pā´ trē ot´ ik) *adj.* showing great love for and support of ones own country; p. 41

persistence (pər sis´ təns) *n.* the continued action of something in spite of problems or setbacks; p. 26

precarious (pri kār´ ē əs) *adj.* not safe or sure; uncertain; risky; p. 252

preoccupied (prē ok´ yə pīd´) *adj.* absorbed in doing something and not noticing other things; p. 142

primeval (pri mē´ vəl) *adj.* having to do with the first or earliest age of the world; primitive; p. 105

promoted (prə mōt´ id) *v.* raised to a higher position or rank; p. 40

proximity (prok sim´ ə tē) *n.* the closeness of one thing to another; p. 26

R

reared up (rērd up) *v.* rose up on hind legs; p. 198

receded (ri sēd´ id) *v.* moved back or away; p. 227

reinforce (rē´ in fôrs´) *v.* to strengthen by repairing or adding something; p. 141

rejuvenate (ri joo´ və nāt´) *v.* to make fresh or young again; p. 23

relics (rel´ iks) *n.* objects used a long time ago that still survive today; p. 79

repentance (ri pent´ əns) *n.* a feeling of regret for doing something wrong; p. 29

resilient (ri zil´ yənt) *adj.* capable of springing back to shape after being bent, stretched, or smashed; p. 100

rigid (rij´ id) *adj.* stiff; firm and inflexible; p. 260

S

sarcastic (sär kas´ tik) *adj.* a way of saying the opposite of what one means to make fun of someone or something; p. 78

scenario (si när´ ē ō´) *n.* a sequence of events that might happen in a particular situation; p. 239

Glossary

scrounged (skrounjd) *v.* managed to get something by hunting around or by begging; p. 279

sedately (si dāt′ lē) *adv.* in a quiet, steady manner; p. 257

senseless (sens′ lis) *adj.* not being able to think or feel; unconscious; p. 210

smoldering (smōl′ dər ing) *adj.* feeling anger or hate but keeping it under control; p. 147

sophisticated (sə fis′ tə kā′ tid) *adj.* having worldly knowledge and experience; p. 141

squalor (skwol′ ər) *n.* filth; misery from a state of poverty; p. 148

strategic (strə tē′ jik) *adj.* highly important to an intended goal; p. 200

stupor (stoo′ pər) *n.* a dazed condition in which a person can barely think, feel, or act; p. 162

subversive (səb vur′ siv) *adj.* seeking to weaken, destroy, or overthrow; p. 41

superfluous (soo pur′ floo əs) *adj.* beyond what is necessary; p. 58

T

tedious (tē′ dē əs) *adj.* tiring and boring; p. 241

torment (tôr′ ment) *n.* extreme pain or suffering; p. 125

trespasser (tres′ pəs ər) *n.* something or someone who goes somewhere he or she is not allowed to go; p. 57

U

unconventional (un′ kən ven′ shən əl) *adj.* unusual, out of the ordinary; p. 6

utter (ut′ ər) *v.* to speak or make a sound with the voice; p. 209

utterance (ut′ ər əns) *n.* words that are said or sounds that are made; p. 225

V

valid (val′ id) *adj.* based on facts or good evidence; p. 253

vaulted (vôl′ tid) *v.* leaped or jumped quickly over or onto something; p. 198

vengeance (ven′ jəns) *n.* the act of getting even with someone; revenge; p. 174

vile (vīl) *adj.* very evil or disgusting; p. 30

vintage (vin′ tij) *adj.* old, but highly valued because of quality or importance; p. 74

virtuous (vur′ choo əs) *adj.* having high morals; p. 4

W

widower (wid′ ō ər) *n.* a man whose wife has died; p. 8

My Personal Dictionary

My Personal Dictionary

My Personal Dictionary

ACKNOWLEDGMENTS

LITERATURE

UNIT 1

"The Boar Hunt" by José Vasconcelos, translated by Paul Waldorf, adapted from *The Muse in Mexico: A Mid-Century Miscellany,* edited by Thomas Mabry Cranfill. Copyright © 1959. By permission of the University of Texas Press.

Anderson Literary Management, LLC: An adapted excerpt from "The Censors" copyright © 1988 by Luisa Valenzuela, from *Open Door: Stories* (North Point Press), copyright © 1988 by Luisa Valenzuela. Adapted and reprinted by permission.

"Appetizer" from *Ghost Traps.* Copyright © 1991 by Robert H. Abel. Adapted and reprinted by permission of the University of Georgia Press.

UNIT 2

Adaptation of "Catch the Moon" from *An Island Like You: Stories of the Barrio* by Judith Ortiz Cofer. Published by Orchard Books/Scholastic Inc. Copyright © 1995 by Judith Ortiz Cofer. Reprinted by permission.

"A Sound of Thunder" reprinted by permission of Don Congdon Associates, Inc. Copyright © 1952 by Crowell Collier Publishing Company, renewed 1980 by Ray Bradbury.

"Through the Tunnel" from *The Habit of Loving* by Doris Lessing. Copyright © 1955 by Doris Lessing. Originally appeared in *The New Yorker.* Reprinted by permission of HarperCollins Publishers.

Adapted from "Marigolds" by Eugenia Collier. Adapted and reprinted by permission of the author.

UNIT 3

Act I, Scene 1 from *A Raisin in the Sun* by Lorraine Hansberry, copyright © 1958 by Robert Nemiroff, as an unpublished work. Copyright © 1959, 1966, 1984 by Robert Nemiroff. Used by permission of Random House, Inc.

UNIT 4

"Where the Girl Rescued Her Brother" from *The Girl Who Married the Moon,* by Joseph Bruchac and Gayle Ross. Copyright © 1994 by Joseph Bruchac and Gayle Ross. Reprinted by permission of Barbara S. Kouts.

UNIT 5

Excerpt from "The Angry Winter" in *The Unexpected Universe,* copyright © 1968 by Loren Eiseley and renewed 1996 by John A. Eichmann, III, reprinted by permission of Harcourt Inc.

Excerpt from *An American Childhood,* by Annie Dillard. Copyright © 1987 by Annie Dillard. Reprinted by permission of HarperCollins Publishers.

"By Any Other Name" from *Gifts of Passage* by Santha Rama Rau. Copyright © 1951 by Santha Rama Rau. Copyright renewed © 1979 by Santha Rama Rau. Reprinted by permission of HarperCollins Publishers. "By Any Other Name" originally appeared in *The New Yorker.*

Adapted from *Farewell to Manzanar* by James D. Houston and Jeanne Wakatsuki Houston. Copyright © 1973 by James D. Houston. Reprinted by permission of Houghton Mifflin Company. All rights reserved.